My
iPad®
for Seniors
THIRD EDITION

Gary Rosenzweig
Gary Jones

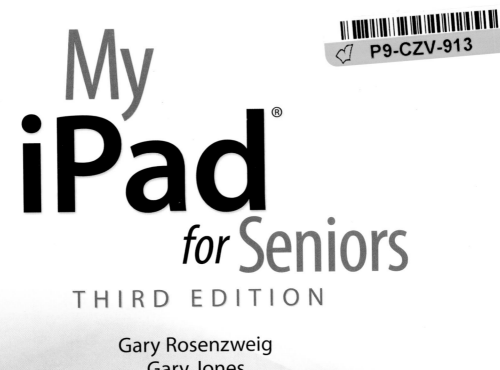

800 East 96th Street,
Indianapolis, Indiana 46240 USA

Real Possibilities

My iPad® for Seniors, Third Edition

Copyright © 2016 by Pearson Education, Inc. All rights reserved.

ISBN-13: 978-0-7897-5533-9
ISBN-10: 0-7897-5533-5

Library of Congress Control Number: 2015952359

Printed in the United States of America

Second Printing: January 2016

Trademarks

All terms mentioned in this book that are known to be trademarks or service marks have been appropriately capitalized. Que Publishing cannot attest to the accuracy of this information. Use of a term in this book should not be regarded as affecting the validity of any trademark or service mark.

Warning and Disclaimer

Every effort has been made to make this book as complete and as accurate as possible, but no warranty or fitness is implied. The information provided is on an "as is" basis. The author(s), AARP, and and the publisher shall have neither liability nor responsibility to any person or entity with respect to any loss or damages arising from the information contained in this book.

Special Sales

For information about buying this title in bulk quantities, or for special sales opportunities (which may include electronic versions; custom cover designs; and content particular to your business, training goals, marketing focus, or branding interests), please contact our corporate sales department at corpsales@pearsoned.com or (800) 382-3419.

For government sales inquiries, please contact governmentsales@pearsoned.com.

For questions about sales outside the U.S., please contact international@pearsoned.com.

Editor-in-chief
Greg Wiegand

Senior Acquisitions Editor and Development Editor
Laura Norman

Managing Editor
Kristy Hart

Marketing
Dan Powell

Director, AARP Books
Jodi Lipson

Project Editor
Lori Lyons

Proofreader
Kathy Ruiz

Indexer
Erika Millen

Cover Designer
Mark Shirar

Compositor
Bronkella Publishing

Graphics Technician
Tammy Graham

Contents at a Glance

Chapter 1   Getting Started 3

Chapter 2   Customizing Your iPad 39

Chapter 3   Networking and Syncing 63

Chapter 4   Playing Music and Video 89

Chapter 5   Reading Books 117

Chapter 6   Organizing Your Life 133

Chapter 7   Surfing the Web 159

Chapter 8   Communicating with Email and Messaging 185

Chapter 9   Taking and Editing Photos 209

Chapter 10 The World of Apps 239

Chapter 11 Exploring the World with Your iPad 271

Chapter 12 Enhancing Your Next Meal with Your iPad 315

Chapter 13 Communicating with Loved Ones Using Your iPad 339

Chapter 14 Finding and Using Apps for Entertainment 371

Chapter 15 Keeping Informed Using News and Weather Apps 409

Chapter 16 Using Apps That Help You Stay Healthy and Fit 435

Chapter 17 Using Apps to Enhance Your Daily Life and Save Money ... 467

Index 503

Bonus Chapter, "Writing with Pages," available online.

Register your book at quepublishing.com/register for access to the bonus chapter.

Find this bonus chapter and other helpful information on this book's website at quepublishing.com/title/9780789755339.

Table of Contents

1 **Getting Started** **3**

Generations of iPads..3
   Identifying Your iPad...4
   iOS 9..5
The iPad Buttons and Switches..6
   The Home Button..6
   The Wake/Sleep Button..7
   The Volume Control..8
   The Side Switch..9
   Orientation and Movement...9
Screen Gestures...10
   Tapping and Touching...10
   Pinching..10
   Dragging and Flicking...11
   Pull Down and Release to Update......................................11
   Four-Finger Gestures...12
Learning Your Way Around..13
   The Lock Screen..13
   The Home Screen..13
   An App Screen..14
   Home Screen Searching...15
Virtual Buttons and Switches...16
   Switches..17
   Toolbars..17
   Menus...18
   Tab Bars..18
Entering Text..18
   Using the On-Screen Keyboard..19
   Keyboard Modes...19
   Undocking and Splitting the Keyboard...............................21
   Using the Keyboard Shortcut Bar New!...............................22

Using Predictive Text 24

Dictating Text 25

Editing Text 27

Copy and Paste 28

Talking to Your iPad with Siri 29

Asking Siri Questions 30

Using Notifications and Control Center 32

Open Notifications Center 33

Open Control Center 36

2 Customizing Your iPad   **39**

Changing Your Wallpaper 40

Setting Alert Sounds 43

Password Protecting Your iPad 45

Make Access Easier with Touch ID 49

Setting Side Switch Functionality 50

Setting Your Date and Time 51

Modifying Keyboard Settings 52

Do Not Disturb Settings 54

Setting Parental Restrictions 56

Making Text Easier to Read 58

Controlling Automatic Downloads 59

Other Useful Settings 60

3 Networking and Syncing   **63**

Setting Up Your Wi-Fi Network Connection 63

Setting Up Your Cellular Data Connection 65

Syncing with iCloud 67

Connecting to iCloud 68

Syncing with iTunes 72

Syncing Options 73

Syncing Music 74

Syncing Photos 76

Syncing Everything Else 78

Sharing with AirDrop 80

    Using AirDrop 80

Viewing Your Mac's Files with iCloud Drive New! 83

    Accessing Your Files 83

4   Playing Music and Video   89

Playing a Song 89

Building a Playlist 92

    Creating Playlists 93

Making iTunes Purchases 94

    Buying on Your iPad 95

Sharing Purchases with Your Family 97

    Setting Up Family Sharing 97

Having It All with Apple Music New! 100

    Signing Up for Apple Music 101

    Using Apple Music 102

Listening to Podcasts 104

    Subscribing to Podcasts 104

Playing Video 106

Using AirPlay to Play Music and Video on Other Devices 109

    Accessing AirPlay 109

Home Sharing 110

Listening to iTunes Radio 111

    Selecting a Station 112

5   Reading Books   117

Buying a Book from Apple 117

Reading a Book 120

Using Reading Aids 121

Adding Notes and Highlights 123

Adding Bookmarks 125

Organizing Your Books 125

Using iBooks Alternatives 129

6	**Organizing Your Life**	**133**
	Using the Contacts App	133
	Adding a Contact	134
	Searching for a Contact	136
	Working with Contacts	137
	Using the Calendar App	138
	Creating a Calendar Event	139
	Using Calendar Views	141
	Exploring Day View	141
	Exploring Week View	143
	Exploring Month View	144
	Creating a Calendar	145
	Using the Notes App	147
	Creating a Note	148
	Creating Checklists in Notes New!	150
	Adding Photos and Sketches to Notes New!	151
	Using the Reminders App	152
	Setting a Reminder	153
	Using the Clocks App	155
	Setting Clock Alarms	155

7	**Surfing the Web**	**159**
	Getting Started with Safari	159
	Browsing to a URL and Searching	160
	Viewing Web Pages	163
	Opening Multiple Web Pages with Tabs	165
	Viewing Articles with Safari Reader	167
	Bookmarks, History, and Reading List	168
	Using Bookmarks and Favorites	168
	Using History	170
	Deleting Your Bookmarks	172
	Creating Home Screen Bookmarks	173
	Building a Reading List	174

Working with Web Forms 176

   Filling in Web Forms 177

   Saving Time with AutoFill 178

   Setting Up AutoFill 179

   Using AutoFill 181

8   Communicating with Email and Messaging   185

Configuring Your iPad for Email 186

   Set Up Your Email Account 186

Reading Your Email 189

Composing a New Message 192

Deleting and Moving Messages 194

Searching Email 196

Customizing Your Email 197

   Configuring How You Receive Email 197

   Creating a Signature 199

   More Email Settings 200

Working with Messaging 202

   Setting up Messaging 202

   Conversing with Messages 204

9   Taking and Editing Photos   209

Working with Photos 209

   Taking Photos 210

   Editing and Adjusting Photos 212

   Taking Panoramic Photos 216

   Using Photo Booth 218

Photo Sources 220

   Browsing Your Photos 221

   Viewing Your Photos 225

   Sharing Your Photos 226

Working with Albums 230

   Viewing Albums 230

   Creating Albums 232

Creating a Slideshow 233

Capturing the Screen 235

10 **The World of Apps** **239**

Purchasing an App 239

Organizing Apps on Your iPad 244

Arranging Apps on the Home Screen 244

Creating App Folders 245

Working with Apps 247

Viewing Currently Running Apps 248

Quitting Apps 249

Viewing a Second App with Slide Over New! 250

Interacting with Two Apps at Once with Split View New! 252

Viewing Video with Picture-In-Picture New! 254

Finding Good Apps 255

Using iPhone/iPod touch Apps 256

Getting Help with Apps 257

Monitoring and Managing Your Apps 259

Viewing App Storage Information 260

Viewing Battery Usage 262

Viewing Location Usage 263

Viewing Information Sharing Permissions 265

Modifying Notifications Settings 266

11 **Exploring the World with Your iPad** **271**

Using the AARP App 272

Finding Interesting Accommodations with the Airbnb App 275

Using Foursquare to Enhance Your Travel Choices 282

Exchanging Homes Is a Great Way to See the World 285

Using Intervac Home Exchange 286

Arranging Travel Using the Kayak App 289

Finding Your Way Using the iPad Maps App 292

SeatGuru by TripAdvisor 295

Communicating in a Foreign Country Is Easy When You Use
  Talking Translator 298

Getting Travel Advice from Others Using TripAdvisor 302

Getting a Ride Using the Uber App 306

12 Enhancing Your Next Meal with Your iPad   **315**

Finding Recipes 316

Helpful Tools for Cooking 321

Using the Internet to Search for Recipes 326

Using Open Table for iPad to Make Dining Reservations 328

Choosing a Restaurant Using Yelp 332

13 Communicating with Your Loved Ones Using Your iPad   **339**

Using Email to Stay in Touch 339

Sharing Photos, Videos, and Other Information 340

  Facebook 340

  Instagram 344

Communicating (Almost) Face to Face with FaceTime and Skype 347

  FaceTime 348

  Skype for iPad 352

Using Photo Sharing, Storage, and Management Apps 354

  Sharing with Shutterfly for iPad 355

  Flickr by Yahoo 359

YouTube 363

14 Finding and Using Apps for Entertainment   **371**

Getting Times and Tickets Using the Fandango Movies App 372

Playing Games on the iPad 375

  Playing Solitaire 376

  Words with Friends 379

Finding and Reading Books in iBooks 381

iTunes Movies..381
Accessing Music Through iTunes...384
National Public Radio (NPR) for iPad..384
Watching Movies and TV Shows Using Netflix...................................386
Listening to Music Through Pandora Radio..390
Finding and Listening to Podcasts...394
  Viewing TED Talks...398
Finding and Purchasing Event Tickets...401

15 Keeping Informed Using News and Weather Apps   409

Getting Local and Global News...409
Getting Financial News...414
Staying Informed...417
Staying Current on Your iPad with Drippler..419
Following Your Favorite Team...423
Staying Alert with Weather Radar...425
Using the Weather Channel App for iPad...428
Using the Yahoo! Tech Website..431

16 Using Apps That Help You Stay Healthy and Fit   435

Exercising Your Brain...435
Staying in Shape..439
Using Fooducate - Healthy Weight Loss, Food Scanner & Diet Tracker....445
Walking or Jogging with Pedometers..449
Staying on Track with Medication Reminder Apps...............................452
Using a Pharmacy App to Refill Prescriptions.....................................458
Getting Medical Information from WebMD for iPad.............................461

17 Using Apps to Enhance Your Daily Life and Save Money   467

Finding Your Roots with Ancestry..468
Shopping on the iPad Using Amazon...474
Finding Deals Using the Craigslist App..479
Bidding on eBay for iPad..483

Paying Less at the Pump 486
Using Gadgets with iPad 488
Using Pinterest to Save and Organize Website Links 493
Avoiding Traffic Jams 497

Index   **503**

About the Authors

Gary Rosenzweig is an Internet entrepreneur, software developer, and technology writer. He runs CleverMedia, Inc., which produces websites, computer games, apps, and podcasts. CleverMedia's largest site, MacMost.com, features video tutorials for Apple enthusiasts. It includes many videos on using Macs, iPhones, and iPads.

Gary has written numerous computer books, including *ActionScript 3.0 Game Programming University*, *MacMost.com Guide to Switching to the Mac*, and *Special Edition Using Director MX*.

Gary lives in Denver, Colorado, with his wife, Debby, and daughter, Luna. He has a computer science degree from Drexel University and a master's degree in journalism from the University of North Carolina at Chapel Hill.

Website: http://garyrosenzweig.com

Twitter: http://twitter.com/rosenz

More iPad Tutorials and Book Updates: http://macmost.com/ipadguide/

Gary Jones is a retired school administrator. In retirement he has become an avid traveler, foodie, rare book seller, and an individual who uses his iPad in most of his ventures. He runs Juniper Point Books, an online rare and used book business, travels the world attempting to live, shop, and eat like a local, occasionally provides educational consulting services, and works hard at retirement. Gary has degrees in English, philosophy, and a master's degree in school administration.

He lives in Round Lake, NY, with his wife, Susan, and has two children, Karianne and Katelyn, and a dog, Bubba.

Note: Most of the individuals pictured throughout this book are the authors themselves, as well as friends and relatives (and sometimes pets) of the authors. Some names and personal information are fictitious.

About AARP and AARP TEK

AARP is a nonprofit, nonpartisan organization, with a membership of nearly 38 million, that helps people turn their goals and dreams into *real possibilities*™, strengthens communities, and fights for the issues that matter most to families such as healthcare, employment and income security, retirement planning, affordable utilities, and protection from financial abuse. Learn more at aarp.org.

The AARP TEK (Technology Education & Knowledge) program aims to accelerate AARP's mission of turning dreams into *real possibilities*™ by providing step-by-step lessons in a variety of formats to accommodate different learning styles, levels of experience, and interests. Expertly guided hands-on workshops delivered in communities nationwide help instill confidence and enrich lives of the 50+ by equipping them with skills for staying connected to the people and passions in their lives. Lessons are taught on touchscreen tablets and smartphones—common tools for connection, education, entertainment, and productivity. For self-paced lessons, videos, articles, and other resources, visit aarptek.org.

Acknowledgments

Thanks, as always, to my wife, Debby, and my daughter, Luna. Also thanks to the rest of my family: Jacqueline Rosenzweig, Jerry Rosenzweig, Larry Rosenzweig, Tara Rosenzweig, Rebecca Jacob, Barbara Shifrin, Richard Shifrin, Barbara H. Shifrin, Tage Thomsen, Anne Thomsen, Andrea Thomsen, and Sami Balestri.

Thanks to all the people who watch the show and participate at the MacMost website.

—Gary Rosenzweig

Thanks to my wife, Susan, for being on my team with all that we do.

—Gary Jones

Thanks to everyone at Pearson Education who worked on this book: Laura Norman, Lori Lyons, Tricia Bronkella, Kathy Ruiz, Kristy Hart, Kristen Watterson, Mark Shirar, and Greg Wiegand.

We Want to Hear from You!

As the reader of this book, *you* are our most important critic and commentator. We value your opinion and want to know what we're doing right, what we could do better, what areas you'd like to see us publish in, and any other words of wisdom you're willing to pass our way.

We welcome your comments. You can email or write to let us know what you did or didn't like about this book—as well as what we can do to make our books better.

Please note that we cannot help you with technical problems related to the topic of this book.

When you write, please be sure to include this book's title and author as well as your name, email address, and phone number. We will carefully review your comments and share them with the author and editors who worked on the book.

Email: feedback@quepublishing.com

Mail: Que Publishing
ATTN: Reader Feedback
800 East 96th Street
Indianapolis, IN 46240 USA

Reader Services

Visit our website and register this book at quepublishing.com/register for convenient access to any updates, downloads, or errata that might be available for this book.

Learn to tap, swipe, flick, and
pinch to use your iPad.

Learn to use the iPad's
physical switches.

In this chapter, you learn how to perform specific tasks on your iPad to become familiar with the interface.

→ Generations of iPads

→ The iPad Buttons and Switches

→ Screen Gestures

→ Learning Your Way Around

→ Virtual Buttons and Switches

→ Entering Text

→ Using the On-Screen Keyboard

→ Selecting and Copying Text

→ Talking to Your iPad with Siri

→ Using Notifications and Control Center

Getting Started

Before you learn how to perform specific tasks on your iPad, you should become familiar with some basic concepts. If you have used an iPhone or iPod touch before, you already know how to use a touch screen device. But if the iPad is your first such device, you need to take time to become accustomed to interacting with it.

Generations of iPads

The first thing you may want to do is identify which iPad you have and what features are available to you. There have been many versions of the iPad since the original appeared in 2010.

Identifying Your iPad

The following table shows the major differences between these iPads:

iPad Comparison Chart

Model	Released	Display (inches)	Retina Display	Processor	Connector
iPad	4/2010	9.7		A4	30-pin
iPad 2	3/2011	9.7		A5	30-pin
3rd Gen	3/2012	9.7	✔	A5X	30-pin
4th Gen	11/2012	9.7	✔	A6X	Lightning
iPad mini 1st Gen	11/2012	7.9		A5	Lightning
iPad Air	11/2013	9.7	✔	A7	Lightning
iPad mini 2	11/2013	7.9	✔	A7	Lightning
iPad Air 2	10/2014	9.7	✔	A8X	Lightning
iPad mini 3	10/2014	9.7	✔	A7	Lightning
iPad mini 4	9/2015	7.9	✔	A8	Lightning
iPad Pro	11/2015	12.9	✔	A9X	Lightning

iPad displays vary not only in size, with the iPad mini models being smaller than the other iPads, but also in pixel density. The retina display has four pixels for every one of a regular display. While a regular display is 768x1024 pixels, a retina display is 1536x2048 pixels. This means photographs and text are crisper and clearer. In fact, you can't even distinguish the individual pixels with your eye unless you hold the iPad very close. The iPad Pro has even more pixels at 2048x2732.

Another difference between iPad models is the camera. The original iPad had no camera at all. The 2nd and 3rd generations had cameras, but the more recent iPads also have a rear-facing camera that is capable of much higher resolution for both still photos and video.

Each iPad has also become a little more powerful with a faster processor at its heart. Other parts have picked up speed and power as well, processing graphics and accessing memory faster. Early models aren't powerful enough to use features like voice dictation and advanced 3D game graphics.

>>>Go Further

THE NEED FOR SPEED

With each generation of iPad, the processor changes. Each iPad is faster and more powerful than its predecessor. It is hard to quantify, but by some metrics the iPad Pro has more processing power than many desktop computers. This also helps apps to run smoother, games to display faster with more detailed graphics, and helps taxing tasks like editing video or flipping through hundreds of high-resolution photos work faster.

iOS 9

The primary piece of software on the iPad is the operating system, known as iOS. This is what you see when you flip through the screens of icons on your iPad and access default apps such as Mail, Safari, Photos, and iTunes.

This book covers iOS 9, the version released in September 2015. There have been eight generations of the software that runs iPhones and iPads. The original iPhone OS was developed for the first iPhone. The third version, iOS 3, worked on iPhones and the iPad. This latest version, iOS 9, works on the iPad 2 and newer. If you have an original iPad, you can only use up to iOS 5.

Many features and tasks in this book work the same in iOS 5, 6, 7, and 8, but you will not be able to use the latest features such as the new News app or Split View. To find out which version you are using and to learn how to update, you use the Settings app. In the Settings app, under the General settings, tap the About item. The About screen shows you information about your iPad, including its model number, serial number, version of iOS currently running, and available memory. You learn how to use the Settings app when you get to Chapter 2, "Customizing Your iPad."

Also keep in mind that the iPad 2, although it supports iOS 9, cannot use some of the features of iOS 9—most notably Siri. Some features, like Split View, only work on an iPad Air 2 or newer.

New to iOS 9

There are some changes in iOS 9 you will notice. For features that have changed significantly, or are completely new, we have added an indicator to the text and table of contents to help you easily locate them. When you see **New!**, be sure to check out those tasks to quickly get up to speed on what's new in iOS 9.

The iPad Buttons and Switches

The iPad features a Home button, a Wake/Sleep button, a volume control, and side switch.

The Home Button

The Home button is probably the most important physical control on the iPad and the one that you will use the most often. Pressing the Home button returns you to the Home screen of the iPad when you are inside an application, such as Safari or Mail, and you want to get back to your Home screen to launch another app. You can also double press the Home button to switch between apps. We'll look at this in the section titled "Viewing Currently Running Apps" in Chapter 10, "The World of Apps."

Wake/sleep button

Side switch (older models)

Volume control

Home button

Where's the Quit Button?

Few, if any, apps on the iPad have a way to quit. Instead, think of the Home button as the Quit button. It hides the current app and returns you to your Home screen. The app is actually still running, but hidden, in the background. It is usually unnecessary to truly "quit" an app. But if you really want to completely quit an app, see "Quitting Apps" in Chapter 10.

The Wake/Sleep Button

The primary function of the Wake/Sleep button (sometimes called the On/Off or Power button) at the top of your iPad is to quickly put it to sleep. Sleeping is different than shutting down. When your iPad is in sleep mode, you can instantly wake it to use it. You can wake up from sleep by pressing the Wake/Sleep button again or pressing the Home button.

Peek a Boo!

If you are using the Apple iPad Smart Cover, Smart Case, or the iPad Pro Smart Keyboard, your iPad will go to sleep when you close it and wake up when you open it, as long as you use the default settings. Many third-party cases and covers also do this.

The Wake/Sleep button can also be used to shut down your iPad, which you might want to do if you leave your iPad for a long time and want to preserve the battery life. Press and hold the Wake/Sleep button for a few seconds, and the iPad begins to shut down and turn off. Confirm your decision to shut down your iPad using the Slide to Power Off button on the screen.

To start up your iPad, press and hold the Wake/Sleep button for a few seconds until you see the Apple logo appear on the screen.

When Should I Turn Off My iPad?

It is normal to never turn off your iPad. In sleep mode, with the screen off, it uses little power. If you plug it in to power at night or during longer periods when you aren't carrying it with you, you don't need to ever shut it down.

The Volume Control

The volume control on the side of your iPad is actually two buttons: one to turn the volume up, and the other to turn it down.

Your iPad keeps two separate volume settings in memory: one for headphones and one for the internal speakers. If you turn down the volume when using headphones and then unplug the headphones, the volume changes to reflect the last settings used when the headphones were not plugged in, and vice versa. A bell icon and a series of rectangles appear on the screen to indicate the current level of volume.

The Side Switch

The side switch is a feature on older iPads. The switch can do one of two things: It can be set as a mute switch or an orientation lock. You can decide which function this button performs in your iPad's settings. See "Setting Side Switch Functionality" in Chapter 2.

If you choose to use this switch as a mute switch, it will mute all sound if switched to the off position. You will see a speaker icon appear briefly in the middle of the screen when you do this. A line through the icon means you just muted the sound; otherwise, you just unmuted your iPad. By default, the iPad comes with the switch configured to mute.

If you choose to use this switch as an orientation lock, it will do something else entirely. Your iPad has two primary screen modes: vertical and horizontal. You can use almost every default app in either orientation. For example, if you find that a web page is too wide to fit on the screen in vertical orientation, you can turn the iPad sideways and the view changes to a horizontal orientation.

When you don't want your iPad to react to its orientation, slide the iPad side switch so that you can see the orange dot, which prevents the orientation from changing. When you need to unlock it, just slide the lock off.

This comes in handy in many situations. For instance, if you are reading an eBook in bed or on a sofa while lying on your side, then you may want vertical orientation even though the iPad is lying sideways.

Newer model iPads don't have a side switch. The controls for orientation lock and mute appear in the Control Center, which we look at in the later task "Open Control Center."

Orientation and Movement

In addition to the physical switches you see on your iPad, the entire iPad is a physical control.

Your iPad knows which way it is oriented, and it knows if it is being moved. The simplest indication of this is that it knows whether you hold it vertically with the Home button at the bottom or horizontally with the Home button to one of the sides. Some apps, especially games, use the screen orientation of the iPad to guide screen elements and views.

Shake It Up!

One interesting physical gesture you might perform is the "shake." Because your iPad can sense movement, it can sense when you shake it. Many apps take advantage of this feature and use it to set off an action, such as shuffling songs in the Music app, erasing a drawing canvas, or as an "undo" function.

Screen Gestures

Who knew just a few years ago that we'd be controlling computing devices with taps, pinches, and flicks rather than drags, key presses, and clicks? Multitouch devices such as the iPhone, iPod Touch, and the iPad have added a new vocabulary to human-computer interaction.

Tapping and Touching

Since there is no mouse, a touch screen has no cursor. When your finger is not on the screen, there is no arrow pointing to anything.

A single, quick touch on the screen is usually called a "tap" or a "touch." You usually tap an object on the screen to perform an action.

Occasionally you need to double-tap—two quick taps in the same location. For instance, double-tapping an image on a web page zooms in to the image. Another double-tap zooms back out.

Pinching

The screen on the iPad is a multitouch screen, which means it can detect more than one touch at the same time. This capability is used with the pinch gesture.

A pinch (or a pinch in) is when you touch the screen with both your thumb and index finger and move them toward each other in a pinching motion. You can also pinch in reverse, which is sometimes called an "unpinch" or "pinch out."

An example of when you would use a pinch/unpinch gesture would be to zoom in and out on a web page or photograph.

Dragging and Flicking

If you touch the screen and hold your finger down, you can drag it in any direction along the screen. This action often has the effect of moving the content on the screen.

For instance, if you are viewing a long web page and drag up or down, the page will scroll. Sometimes an app will let you drag content left and right as well.

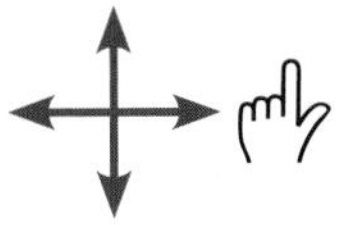

What if you have a long web page or a list of items inside an app? Instead of dragging the length of the screen, lifting your finger up, and moving it to the bottom to drag again, you can "flick." Flicking is like dragging, but you move quickly and lift your finger off the screen at the last moment so that the content continues to scroll after you have lifted your finger. You can wait for it to stop scrolling or touch the screen to make it stop.

Jump Up

In certain apps, such as Settings, Mail, and Safari, you can quickly jump back to the top of a screen by tapping near where the time is shown at the top-middle of the screen.

Pull Down and Release to Update

A common gesture is to tap in a list of items, drag down, and release. For instance, you would do this in Mail to get new messages. With your email inbox on the left, tap and drag down in the list. A blank space appears above the first message, and a circle of lines appears to let you know more mail is being downloaded.

Many Apple and third-party apps use this gesture to let you signal that you want to update the list of items. So if you don't see an obvious "update now" button, try this gesture.

Four-Finger Gestures

You can perform one of three special functions by using four or five fingers at a time on the screen. If you put four or five fingers on the screen and pinch them all together, you will be taken out of your current app and back to the Home screen, similar to just pressing the Home button.

You can swipe left or right using four or more fingers to quickly page between running apps without going to the Home screen first. Swiping up with four fingers will bring you to the multitask switcher. See "Viewing Currently Running Apps" in Chapter 10.

Learning Your Way Around

When you pick up your iPad and touch either the Wake/Sleep button or the Home button to activate the screen, you see what is called the Lock Screen. From there, you would unlock your iPad and return to the last screen you were using—either the Home screen or an app's screen.

Let's look at the different types of screens you see every day on your iPad, and how to navigate between them,

The Lock Screen

The default state of your iPad when you are not using it is the lock screen. This is just your background wallpaper with the time at the top and the words Slide to Unlock at the bottom.

You can see the date under the time. The battery status is at the top right, and you can also see it under the time, alternating with the date, if the iPad is currently charging. There is also a small button at the bottom right for quick access to the camera app. The top and bottom of the screen show short bars to allow you to access the Notifications Center at the top and the Control Center at the bottom.

We look at customizing the lock screen in Chapter 2, as well as the Control Center and the Notifications Center later in this chapter.

By default, you see the lock screen when you wake up your iPad. Sliding your finger from left to right near the words Slide to Unlock takes you to the Home screen or to whichever app you were using when you put the iPad to sleep.

The Home Screen

Think of the Home screen as a single screen but with multiple pages that each features different app icons. At the bottom of the Home screen are app icons that do not change from page to page.

The number of pages on your Home screen depends on how many apps you have. The number of pages you have is indicated by the white dots near the bottom of the screen, just above the bottom icons. The brightest dot represents the page you are currently viewing. You can move between pages on your Home screen by dragging or flicking left or right.

We'll look at adding more apps to your iPad in the tasks found in Chapter 10.

An App Screen

When you tap on an app icon on the Home screen, you run that app just like you would run an application on your computer. The app takes over the entire screen.

At this point, your screen can look like anything. If you run Safari, for instance, a web page displays. If you run Mail, you see a list of your new email or a single incoming email message.

If you are on your Home screen looking at page one of your app icons, you can drag from the center of the screen downward to bring up a Spotlight Search field at the top and a keyboard at the bottom. This allows you to search your iPad for apps, contacts, events, and other information.

Home Screen Searching

You can type in anything to search for a contact, app, email message, photo, and so on. You don't have to define what type of thing you want to search for.

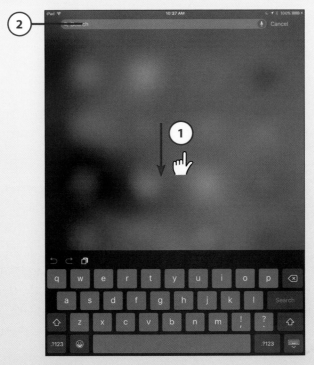

1 From the Home screen, tap in the center of the screen and drag down. Don't start at the very top of the screen, as that will bring up Notifications Center instead. This can be a bit tricky; so if you do accidentally open Notification Center, just swipe it back up out of the way and try again.

If you've been using your iPad for a while and have Siri enabled, you will see suggestions for apps, contacts, and other content on this screen even before you type a search term.

2 Type a search term using the on-screen keyboard.

(3) You see a list of items on your iPad that match the search term. The search results show apps, calendar events, email messages, reminders, or even web search results.

(4) Tap the Search button on the keyboard to dismiss the keyboard and complete the search.

(5) Tap the X in the search field to clear the search and start again.

(6) Tap any of the items to go to the appropriate app and view the content.

Virtual Buttons and Switches

Several interface elements are more complex than a simple button. In typical Apple style, these elements are often self-explanatory, but if you have never used an iPad before, you might find some that give you pause.

Switches

A switch is a simple button that allows you to turn something on or off. You need to only tap the switch to change it—no need to slide it. The background of a switch turns green when it is "on."

For example, two switches indicate whether the iCloud Music Library and Sound Check features of the Music app are on or off. Tapping on either switch changes the position of the switch.

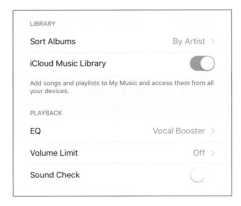

Toolbars

Some apps have a set of controls in a toolbar at the top of the screen. Buttons shown there are sometimes nothing more than a word or two that you can tap on to trigger an action. The toolbar might disappear or the buttons might vary depending on the mode of the app. If a toolbar disappears, a tap on the screen brings it up again.

An example of a toolbar is in the iTunes app. When you are viewing the music section of the iTunes store, it has a button to access Genres, a title in the middle, a button that brings up more controls, and a search field. But, this toolbar can change. For instance, if you switch from viewing the Music screen to viewing Top Charts, you get a set of buttons that let you switch between Music, Movies, TV, or Audiobook charts.

Menus

Often tapping a single button in a toolbar brings up more buttons or a list of choices, which are like menus on your computer. The choices in the list are usually related. For example, a button in Safari gives you many different ways to share a web page.

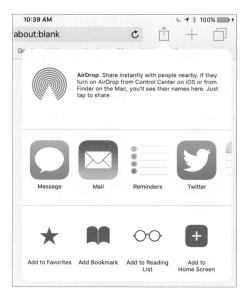

Tab Bars

Sometimes you see a row of buttons at the bottom of the screen that function similarly to toolbars, but each button represents a different mode for the app. For instance, at the bottom of the iTunes app, you see a Tab bar that you use to switch between various screens: Music, Movies, TV Shows, Audiobooks, Top Charts, Genius, and Purchased.

Entering Text

Entering text on your iPad means interacting with an on-screen keyboard or speaking to your iPad. Even if you are not a writer, you'll need to do this quite often to enter addresses in the web browser, or to compose messages and emails.

Using the On-Screen Keyboard

The on-screen element you might interact with the most is the keyboard. It pops up from the bottom of the screen automatically whenever you are doing something that requires entering some text.

Keyboard Modes

An on-screen keyboard can have many different modes. With the default keyboard, the first mode shows you letters and a few punctuation marks. There are two shift keys that enable you to enter uppercase letters. You also have a Backspace key and a Return key.

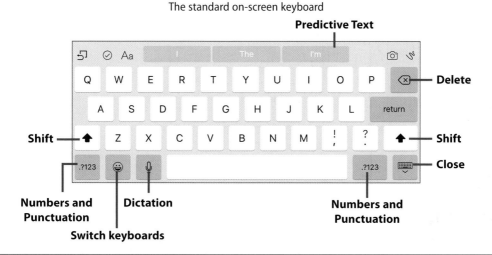

The standard on-screen keyboard

Is There a Quicker Way to Capitalize?

To capitalize a word, you tap the Shift key, and then type the letter, right? You can. But a faster way is to tap the Shift key; then, without letting your finger off the screen, drag it to the letter and release in a single tap, slide, release action.

You can do the same with numbers and punctuation by tapping the .?123 key and sliding and releasing over the key you want.

To enter numbers and some other punctuation, tap the .?123 key to switch your keyboard into a second mode for numbers and punctuation. In addition, this mode includes an Undo key for undoing your recent typing. To return to the letters, just tap the ABC key.

Numbers and punctuation mode

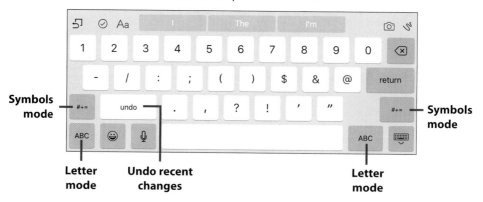

Symbols
mode

Letter
mode

Undo recent
changes

Letter
mode

Symbols
mode

From the numbers and punctuation mode, you can tap the #+= key to go to a third keyboard mode that includes less frequently used punctuation and symbols. On this screen, the Undo button is now a Redo button that you can use in case you hit Undo by mistake.

Punctuation and symbols mode

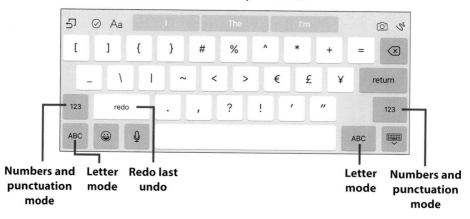

Numbers and
punctuation
mode

Letter
mode

Redo last
undo

Letter
mode

Numbers and
punctuation
mode

There are other keyboard variations. For instance, in some cases if you type in a location that needs a web address, a keyboard that doesn't have a spacebar appears that instead has commonly used symbols such as colons, slashes, underscores, and even a .com button.

Not only are there other keyboard variations, there are completely different keyboards you can use. The iPad has many non-English language keyboards, and even a keyboard composed of little images (smiley faces and other pictures) called Emoji. Plus, you can add third-party keyboards from developers. We look at adding new keyboards in the task "Modifying Keyboard Settings" in Chapter 2.

Undocking and Splitting the Keyboard

You can also split the keyboard and/or move it up away from the bottom of the screen. This can make it easier for you to type if you are holding your iPad. Grasp it with your hands on either side of the iPad, and type with your thumbs.

1. To undock or split your keyboard, just tap and hold the keyboard button at the bottom-right corner.

2. Select Undock to simply move the keyboard up from the bottom of the screen and give you control of its vertical position.

3. Select Split to undock the keyboard, but also split it in half so you can reach all the keys from either side using your thumbs. You can also do this by tapping the keyboard button and dragging up.

Unpinch
Another way to activate the split keyboard, if it's undocked already, is to tap in the middle of the keyboard with two fingers and unpinch.

4. When the keyboard is undocked or split, you can tap and hold the keyboard button to drag it vertically to find the best position for you. If you tap and hold but do not drag, then you get the option to Merge, or Dock and Merge.

5. Tap Merge to merge the two halves of the keyboard back into one. You can also do this by tapping in the middle of the keyboard and pinching inward.

6 Tap Dock and Merge to merge the halves, and also lock the keyboard to the bottom of the screen. You can also do this by dragging the keyboard all the way back down to the bottom of the screen.

Using the Keyboard Shortcut Bar New!

Above the letter and number keys on the on-screen keyboard is the shortcut bar. This narrow horizontal strip can contain a variety of buttons and some predictive text shortcuts. We look at predictive text in the next section.

The buttons in the shortcut bar vary depending on which app you are using and even what type of text you are typing within the app.

If you don't see the shortcuts bar, but instead see a narrow line with a smaller white line in the center, then tap and drag that small white line up to reveal the shortcut bar.

So far, we've been looking at the keyboard as it appears in the Notes app. Let's take a tour of the shortcut bar as it appears when typing in Notes.

1 Tapping this button brings up undo and paste from the clipboard buttons. If you have text selected, it instead brings up cut, copy, and paste buttons.

2 This undoes the last insertion or edit.

3 This redoes the last undo.

4 You can paste text you may have previously copied into the clipboard. This is similar to using Command or Control+v on a desktop computer.

5 In Notes, you get a button to begin writing a checklist.

6 You can also choose from a variety of other text styles such as Title, Heading, Body, and so on.

7 You can tap this button to take a picture with your iPad's camera or insert a photo from your library.

8 Notes includes a special sketch function that lets you add a drawing to your note. We take a closer look at that in Chapter 6, "Organizing Your Life."

>>>Go Further
MORE KEYBOARD VARIATIONS

If you bring up the on-screen keyboard in the Mail app while composing a message, you get a slightly different set of buttons. Instead of the Undo, Redo, and Paste buttons being combined into one button on the left, you get each as its own button. In addition, you get a style button on the right that lets you choose bold, italic, or underline and an attach button that lets you choose a file to attach to your message.

Another example of a shortcut bar is the one you get when typing a URL or search term in the address field in the Safari web browser. Here, you only get Cut, Copy, and Paste buttons.

Using Predictive Text

You may have noticed that while you are typing, three buttons with words in them appear on top of the keyboard in the shortcut bar. This is the predictive text feature of the keyboard, also sometimes referred to by Apple as QuickType.

While typing, these three buttons enable you to complete a word with just one tap. For instance, you may be typing the word "Clever." As you type, the three buttons change to represent what comes closest to the letters you have typed so far. When you have typed "Cle," you might get "Clearer" and "Clear" as suggestions. But when you get to "Cleve," you will probably see "Clever" as one of the buttons. Simply tap that button and the word is completed without you needing to type "r." Notice that a space is automatically inserted as well. If the word you inserted was the end of your sentence, simply tap the space bar two times and a period is inserted and the app is ready to start a new sentence.

Predictive text is not just looking at the letters in the word you are typing, but also in the context of the whole sentence. For instance, if you type "pur," you might get "put" and "pure" as suggestions. But if you type "color pur," you will get "purple" as a suggestion.

Also note that the leftmost button of the three usually displays the text exactly as you have typed, but with quotes around it. This allows you to type a name or unusual word without having autocorrect get in the way.

Predictive text also looks at which app you are using and what the situation involves. For instance, it might suggest different words based on the person whom you are emailing, whether it is a work colleague or friend. When you respond to text messages in the Messages app, you might see "Yes" and "No" appear automatically when you are responding to a question. If someone messages you asking whether you want to meet at 6:00, 7:00, or 8:00, you will see those three options appear before you even type the first letter of your response.

Dictating Text

If you have a 3rd generation iPad or newer, any model of iPad mini, or iPad Pro, you can also dictate text using your voice rather than typing on the keyboard. Almost any time you see a keyboard, you should also see a small microphone button to the left of the spacebar. Tap that and you will be prompted to speak to your iPad. You will need to be connected to the Internet through a Wi-Fi or cellular connection for this to work.

1   Any time you see the default keyboard, there is a microphone button to the left of the spacebar. Tap it to begin dictating.

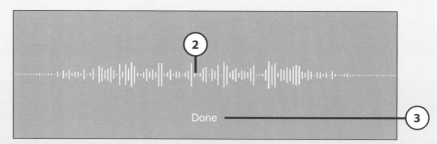

(2) The keyboard is replaced with a waveform line that vibrates as you speak. Speak a few words or a sentence or two. As you speak, the text appears in your document or text field, though it may lag behind by a few seconds.

(3) Tap Done when you are finished speaking. You can now edit the dictated text as needed before sending it.

Speak Clearly

Speak somewhat slowly and clearly, and in segments about the length of a sentence for best results. Of course, this feature isn't perfect. Pay careful attention to what is transcribed and correct any mistakes using the keyboard. Over time you will get better at speaking in a way that minimizes mistakes.

>>>Go Further
DICTATION TIPS

The dictation button appears any time a standard keyboard is present in any app. You can use it in Notes, Pages, or any writing app. You can use it in search fields and text entry fields on the web. You cannot use it when there are specialty keyboards, like the ones used to enter in email addresses, web URLs, and telephone numbers. So, for instance, you can use it in the Contacts app to speak a name or address, but not to enter an email address.

You need to be connected to the Internet for dictation to work. Your iPad sends the audio to Apple's servers, which handle the transcription and send the text back to your iPad. If you are not connected, it does not work.

Dictation works according to your language set in Settings, General, Language & Region. Not all languages are supported, but Apple is adding more all the time.

You can indicate the end of a sentence by saying "period" or "question mark." You can also speak other punctuation like "comma" or "quote."

You can speak commands like "new line," or "cap" to capitalize the next word. There is no official list of what the dictation feature supports, and since the transcription takes place on Apple's servers, they can change how it handles commands at any time.

Editing Text

Editing text has its challenges on a touch-screen device. Even though you can just touch any portion of your text on screen, your fingertip is too large for the level of precision you usually get with a computer mouse and cursor. To compensate, Apple developed an editing technique using a magnifying glass area of the screen that you get when you touch and hold over a piece of text.

For example, if you want to enter some text into a field in Safari, touch and hold on the field. A circle of magnification appears with a cursor placed at the exact location you selected.

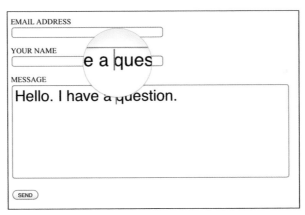

When you find the exact location that you want to indicate, release your finger from the screen. A variety of options then display, depending on what kind of text you selected, such as Select, Select All, and Paste. You can ignore the options presented and start typing again to insert text at this location.

Copy and Paste

You can copy and paste text inside an app, and between apps, on your iPad. Here's how you might copy a piece of text from one place in a document to another in the Notes app.

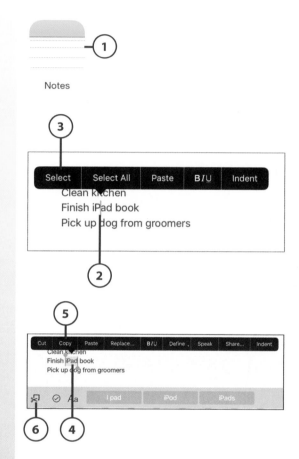

Notes

1. Launch Notes. If you don't have any notes yet, create one by typing some sample text.

2. Touch and hold over a word in your note. The Select/Select All pop-up menu appears.

3. Choose Select.

4. Some text appears highlighted surrounded by dots connected to lines. Tap and drag the dots so the highlighted area is exactly what you want.

5. Tap Copy.

6. Alternatively, you can tap this icon on the keyboard shortcut bar to bring up Cut, Copy, and Paste icons, and then choose the Copy icon.

Variations

In other apps, you may find the Cut, Copy, and Paste icons already visible on the keyboard shortcut bar; and in still other apps, you may not find this alternative at all.

(7) Tap at the bottom of the document once to bring up a pop-up
menu with the Paste command.

(8) Tap Paste to insert the copied text.
Alternatively, you can use the same
method as in step 6 to paste.

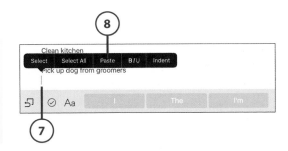

>>>Go Further

YOUR KEYBOARD AS A TRACKPAD New!

A new feature in iOS 9 is the ability to more precisely position the text cursor in apps where
you work with text such as Notes, Pages, Mail, and so on. With the on-screen keyboard visible,
tap on it with two fingers and keep your fingers pressed to your iPad. Then drag your fingers
around, and you can move the cursor as if you were using a trackpad or mouse on a computer.
Notice that the keyboard letters disappear when you are doing this to indicate that you are in
trackpad mode.

You can also tap quickly with two fingers to simply select the word that currently contains the
text cursor. Two taps with two fingers selects the whole paragraph. Then you can tap and drag
with two fingers to expand the selection.

This takes some getting used to. If you plan to use this feature, you may want to practice with a
sample document first.

Talking to Your iPad with Siri

Siri is another way to communicate with your iPad. You can use your voice and
speak commands to your iPad, and Siri will respond. It will either give you information or take action using one of the apps on the iPad.

To use Siri, you need to make sure you have Siri turned on in the Settings app
under General settings. Then, you use the Home button to activate Siri. We look
at how to work with the Settings app in Chapter 2.

Asking Siri Questions

(1) Press and hold the Home button for about a second. The Siri interface pops up, showing a waveform line at the bottom of the screen that reacts to the sound of your voice.

If you hesitate for a few seconds, you are shown a list of examples of things you can ask Siri.

(2) Speak clearly at a normal pace and say, "What's the weather like today?" As you speak, the words appear near the top of the screen. When you stop speaking, Siri attempts to perform an action based on those words.

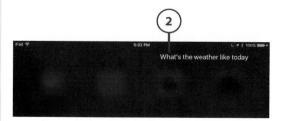

(**3**) In this case, a short weather forecast appears.

(**4**) Siri also responds with a state-
ment and speaks it audibly.
The text of the response typically appears above the screen
content.

(**5**) You can ask Siri another question
by tapping the microphone but-
ton at the bottom of the screen.

(**6**) If you wait for the list of suggestions to appear, you also see a
question mark appear at the bottom left. Tap it to get a detailed
list of apps that Siri can interact
with, and things you can say for
each app.

Siri Tips

To use Siri, you must have a connection to the Internet. It can be a Wi-Fi connection or
a mobile connection. When you speak text, the audio is transmitted to Apple's servers
to convert it to text and interpret the command. The results are sent back to your iPad.

It is best to speak clearly and to limit background noise. Using Siri in a quiet room works
better than in a crowded outdoor space or in a car with the radio on, for instance.

Because Apple's servers control Siri, they can update Siri's capabilities at any time. For
example, originally Siri did not understand a request for local sports scores, but after an
update this functionality was added. Siri includes greatly expanded functionality in iOS 9.

You can use Siri to perform many tasks on your iPad without typing. For example, you
can search the Web, set reminders, send messages, and play music. Throughout the rest
of this book, look for the Siri icon for tips on how to use Siri to perform a task related to
that section of the book.

>>>*Go Further*

HEY SIRI!

You can activate Siri without pressing the home button. In the Settings app, just under the setting to turn on Siri, is a switch labeled Allow "Hey Siri." Turn that on and anytime you utter the words "Hey Siri" followed by a question, Siri will respond.

There's an initial setup sequence when you first turn it on. You need to speak a few phrases so Siri can distinguish your voice from other people and react only to you. Since this means your iPad needs to leave your microphone on and constantly monitor input, it only works when your iPad is plugged into AC power. Otherwise, it would drain your battery very quickly.

Using Notifications and Control Center

To move between pages on your Home screen, you swipe left and right. But you can also pull down and pull up two special screens from any Home screen, or just about any screen at all, even if you are in an app.

Open Notifications Center

Swiping from the very top of your screen downward pulls down the Notifications Center.

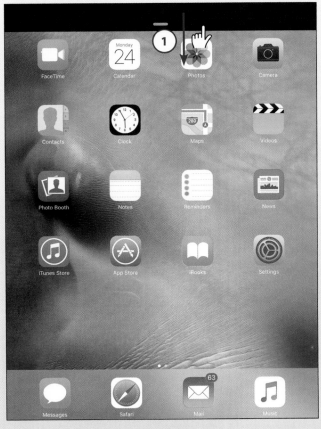

(1) Swipe down from the top of the screen to pull down the Notifications Center. If you are having trouble, try placing your finger above the screen, outside of the actual screen area, and moving your finger down onto the screen, continuing all the way down.

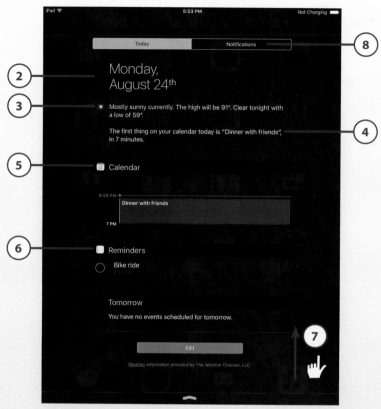

(2) In large type at the top of the screen, you will see today's date.

(3) Under that, you may see a summary of today's weather, depending on your settings for the Notifications Center.

(4) Under the weather, you usually find information about your next calendar event.

(5) A preview of more calendar events for the day are shown. You can tap on an event to open the Calendar app and go right to it.

(6) If you have any items set for today in the Reminders app, you will see them here. You can tap them to open the Reminders app. Or, tap on the circle to the left of the item to mark it as completed without going to the Reminders app at all.

(7) If you have more information than can fit on the screen, you can swipe up to see it. This screen shows information about tomorrow as well as today.

(8) Tap Notifications to see other notifications, such as incoming email, messages, and App Store updates. You can also swipe right to left to get to this screen.

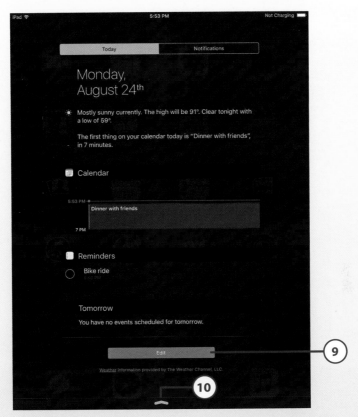

(9) Tap Edit to decide which items appear in the Today list. For instance, you could turn off Reminders but leave Calendar events.

(10) Tap the flat arrow at the bottom of the screen and drag up to the top of the screen to close the Notifications Center. You can also just press the Home button at the bottom of your iPad.

Quickly Dismiss Notifications

While looking at Notifications in the Notifications Center, you can quickly dismiss items by swiping right to left to reveal a small X button. Tap that button to clear the item from the screen. In addition, each app heading in the notifications list has a small X button that you can tap twice to clear all the items for that app. The first time you tap, it turns into a "Clear" button; and then the second time you tap, it clears that section.

You can customize the Notifications Center in the Settings app, deciding exactly what appears in it. See "Modifying Notifications Settings" in Chapter 10.

Open Control Center

The Notifications Center comes down from the top of your iPad's screen, but the Control Center comes up from the bottom.

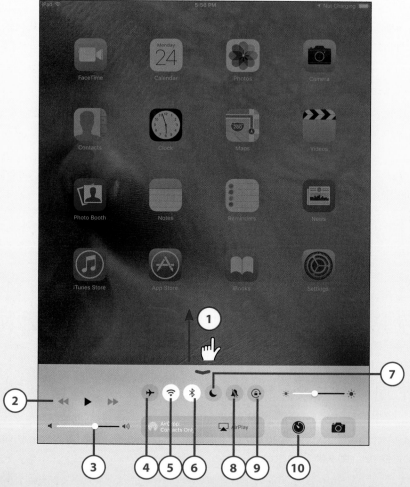

1. To bring up the Control Center, swipe up from the very bottom of the screen. If you are having trouble, try starting below the screen and swiping up onto the screen area all the way to the top.

2. The upper-left corner of the Control Center is a complete set of music playback controls. You see the name of the song playing and can pause or resume the song, and move the white line to jump around inside the song. You can also skip to the next or go back to the previous song.

3. Below the playback controls is a volume slider.

(4) The first in a set of buttons in the middle of the Control Center is a switch that lets you quickly turn on Airplane mode. This shuts off all Wi-Fi, Bluetooth, and cellular data connections.

(5) The next button lets you toggle on and off the Wi-Fi connection.

(6) Likewise, you can toggle on and off the Bluetooth connection that you may be using with wireless headphones, a keyboard, or to connect to a wireless audio speaker.

(7) You can quickly switch to Do Not Disturb mode, which silences all notifications such as incoming messages.

(8) This button mutes your iPad. If you have an older iPad with a side switch, and you have set that side switch to act as a mute switch, then this button may not appear here.

(9) This button locks your iPad's orientation. If you have an older iPad with a side switch, and you have set that side switch to act as an orientation lock, then this button may not appear here.

(10) This is a shortcut to take you to the Clock app.

(11) This is a shortcut to take you to the Camera app.

(12) If you have an iPad that supports AirDrop, this button lets you turn AirDrop on or off. We'll look at AirDrop in Chapter 3.

(13) The AirPlay button lets you choose a device to stream audio or video to, assuming you have such a device connected to your network. We look at AirPlay in Chapter 4.

(14) The bottom-right corner of Control Center lets you adjust the brightness of the iPad's screen.

(15) To dismiss Control Center, you can tap the flat arrow at the top and drag down. You can also tap the screen above Control Center or simply press the Home button.

There's not much that Control Center does that cannot be done in the Settings app or the Home screen. Control Center simply provides quick access to a variety of functions.

Customize how your iPad
looks and works through
the Settings app.

In this chapter, you learn how to change some of the settings on your iPad such as your background images, sounds, passcode, and how some apps behave.

→ Changing Your Wallpaper
→ Setting Alert Sounds
→ Password Protecting Your iPad
→ Make Access Easier with Touch ID
→ Setting Side Switch Functionality
→ Setting Your Date and Time
→ Modifying Keyboard Settings
→ Do Not Disturb Settings
→ Setting Parental Restrictions
→ Making Text Easier to Read
→ Controlling Automatic Downloads
→ Other Useful Settings

2

Customizing Your iPad

Like with any relationship, you fall in love with your iPad for what it is. And then, almost immediately, you try to change it.

It's easier, though, to customize your iPad than it is your significant other because you can modify various settings and controls in the Settings app. You can also move icons around on the Home screen and even change how the Home button works.

Changing Your Wallpaper

The wallpaper is the image behind the icons on the Home screen and on the lock screen. You'll see it often, so make sure it's something you like.

Settings

(1) Tap the Settings icon on your Home screen.

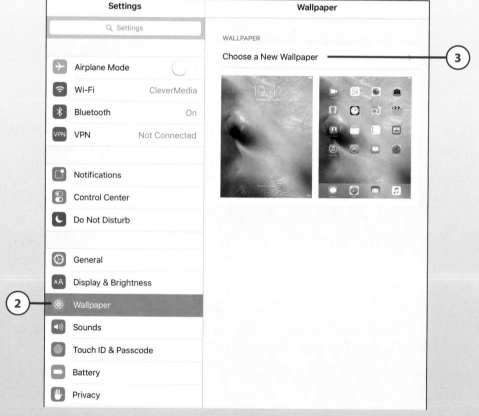

(2) Choose Wallpaper from the Settings app on the left side of the screen.

(3) Tap Choose a New Wallpaper.

4 Now you have three choices. The first, Dynamic, is if you want to use one of Apple's dynamic wallpapers. Dynamic wallpapers have patterns that slowly animate.

5 A second choice is to use a photo from your photo library—either of a photo you took with your iPad or one you synced from your computer. Tap one of the groups of photos listed.

6 A third choice is Stills, which is a collection of Apple's default wallpaper images.

7 Choose an image from the category you selected in step 4, 5, or 6.

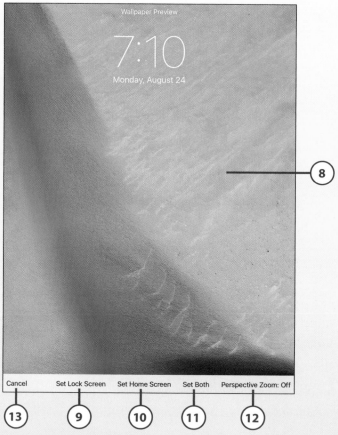

8 You'll see the full image in a preview covering the entire screen.

9 Choose Set Lock Screen to set this image as the background of your lock screen.

10 Choose Set Home Screen to set this image as the background for your Home screen.

11 Choose Set Both to make the image the background for both screens.

12 Perspective Zoom is an option that appears when you choose one of Apple's stills or your own photo. When it is on, the image is slightly enlarged and seems to sit in a 3D space below your lock screen text or home screen icons. As you move your iPad, you see the image move slightly behind the other elements. You can turn this off by tapping the Perspective Zoom: On button.

13 Tap Cancel at the bottom-left corner of the screen to go back to the wallpaper icons.

Adjusting the Wallpaper Image

You can touch and drag in a photo to move to other areas of the image so you can choose the part of the image you want as your wallpaper. You can also pinch to zoom in and out on your photographs.

If Lost, Call…

In later chapters, you find out about apps that allow you to create and edit images. Some apps make it easy to create an image that includes information like an emergency contact phone number on your iPad's lock screen. Then if you lose your iPad, someone could see the number on the lock screen and be able to contact you to return it. You can check out Sticky Notes by TapFactory in the App Store as one option for creating this type of image.

Setting Alert Sounds

Your iPad can be a noisy device with various events that trigger alert sounds. Just typing on the on-screen keyboard can produce a series of clicks. Here's how to adjust your iPad's sound settings.

1 Just as we did in the "Changing Your Wallpaper" task, tap the Settings icon on your Home screen to launch the Settings app. Then, tap Sounds from the list of settings on the left.

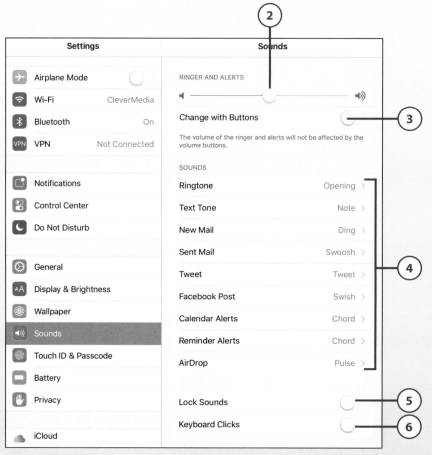

(2) Adjust the volume of system sounds, like FaceTime ringtones and notification alerts. This does not affect the volume of music or video.

(3) When this is turned on, the volume in step 2 can change by using the buttons on the side of the iPad. If you turn this off, you can still use the buttons to adjust the volume of music and video when those are playing; but otherwise, the side volume controls won't affect the system sound volume.

(4) Tap any of these settings to set the sound that plays when an event occurs. You can choose ringtones, alert tones, or custom tones for any of the events. Ringtone refers to FaceTime calls and Text Tone refers to the Messages app.

(5) Switch the Lock Sounds on or off. When this setting is on, a sound plays when you unlock the Lock screen.

(6) Switch Keyboard Clicks on or off.

How About Custom Sounds?

Any sound event can play a ringtone rather than a plain alert sound. You will see a list of "Alert Tones" that are built into iOS, as well as a list of ringtones, which include the built-in ringtones and any custom ringtones. You can add your own custom ringtones in iTunes on your Mac or PC and then sync them with your iPad. After the sync, you will see them listed when selecting an alert sound. See "Syncing with iTunes" in Chapter 3. By obtaining or creating your own custom ringtones, you can set your alert sounds to anything you want.

Password Protecting Your iPad

Password protecting your iPad is very important. By using a passcode, you can make sure that someone else can't access your information or use your iPad. It is so important, in fact, that Apple includes setting up a passcode as part of the welcome screens you go through when you first use your new iPad. If you skipped that, you'll want to set it up now.

1. Open the Settings app and tap Touch ID & Passcode from the list of settings on the left. If you have previously set a passcode, you are required to enter it before moving into the Passcode settings. If you have an older iPad without Touch ID, the button on the left will read simply Passcode instead of Touch ID & Passcode. See the "Make Access Easier with Touch ID" section later in this chapter to learn more about Touch ID.

Even More Security

To lock your iPad automatically when you aren't using it, choose Auto-Lock from the General Settings and set your iPad to automatically lock at 2, 5, 10, or 15 minutes. You can also choose to never have it auto-lock. Of course, you can manually lock your iPad at any time by pressing the Wake/Sleep button at the top.

2 Tap Turn Passcode On to activate this feature. You then are prompted to enter a passcode. If you already had a passcode set and you want to change it now, tap Change Passcode.

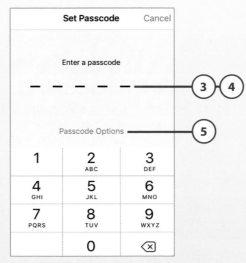

③ Type in a six-digit passcode that you can easily remember. Write it down and store it in a safe place—you can run into a lot of trouble if you forget it, most likely needing to erase your iPad and restore it from your last backup.

④ You are asked to re-enter your passcode.

⑤ Tap Passcode Options to switch from the default six digits to something else, like four digits or a longer alphanumeric passcode.

⑥ Tap the Require Passcode button and choose the delay before a passcode is required. If you choose anything other than Immediately, someone else using your iPad can work on it for that period of time before needing to enter the code.

⑦ Some features of your iPad's lock screen can be accessed even without a passcode. You can allow viewing of today's calendar events and reminders, notifications, and ask Siri questions without your passcode.

⑧ Turn on Erase Data if you want to erase the iPad data after 10 failed passcode attempts. This is a good idea from a security standpoint, but not so good if you think a mischievous child might grab your iPad and try guessing the passcode. If you use the Erase Data feature, be very sure you back up your iPad very often.

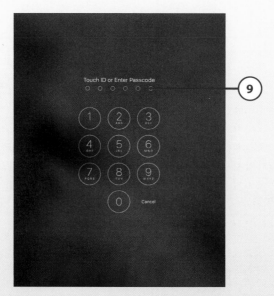

9) Press the Wake/Sleep button to confirm your new settings work. Then press the Home button and Slide to Unlock. The Enter Passcode screen displays.

Use a Real Password

Would you rather use a real password with letters and numbers instead of just a set of digits? If so, good for you! That's much more secure. And you can set one easily. Just follow steps 1 and 2 in the preceding task, and then in step 3 tap the Passcode Options button. You can set an alphanumeric code, a custom numeric code that can be as many digits as you like, or a four-digit numeric code that was the default option in iOS 8 and earlier.

It's Not All Good

You Forgot Your Passcode?

Well, it wouldn't be secure if there were a way to get around the passcode. So, you're out of luck until you can connect your iPad to your Mac or PC and use iTunes to restore it or erase the iPad using your Apple ID. Hopefully, this never happens to you. For the gory details on what to do in this dire situation, see http://support.apple.com/kb/ht1212. The one ray of hope is that if you have backed up your iPad recently, you'll be able to restore your data from that backup after you reset the iPad.

Make Access Easier with Touch ID

After you set a passcode for your iPad, you can make it easier to get access to your iPad by using Touch ID on newer iPads. Touch ID allows you to touch your fingertips to your Home button instead of typing the passcode.

1. Tap Touch ID & Passcode on the left side of the Settings app. If you only see Passcode instead of Touch ID & Passcode, then your iPad does not have a Touch ID sensor.

2. Tap Add a Fingerprint.

3. You are instructed by your iPad to repeatedly place and lift a finger on the Home button. Follow the instructions carefully as your iPad will continue to ask until it has enough information from your fingerprint. Remember to only use one finger while doing this. You will have the opportunity to add more fingers later.

4. When you are done, you will see your first fingerprint listed as Finger 1. You can tap here to change the name of this fingerprint or delete it.

5. You can now add more fingerprints. You may want to add both thumbs and both index fingers so you can use Touch ID while holding your iPad in different ways.

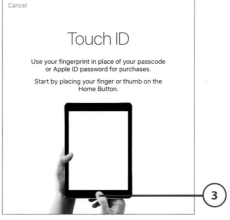

Buy with Touch ID

Touch ID not only makes it quicker and easier to unlock your iPad, but it also can be used by some third-party apps and in the iTunes store. Instead of needing to confirm your identity in those places, you may be asked to place your finger on the Home button to get access to data or purchase an item.

>>>Go Further
MAKING TOUCH ID WORK FOR YOU

If your iPad supports Touch ID, you are prompted to set it up while going through the welcome screens. You can always add more fingerprints, or redo the one you entered, in the Settings app. It can be useful to have both your thumbs and perhaps your index fingers recorded in the Touch ID settings. This makes it easier to unlock your iPad in different situations, depending on how you are holding it at the moment. Also, if it seems that Touch ID is often having trouble with one finger or another, you can erase that finger and re-record it.

Setting Side Switch Functionality

Most iPads, except the latest models, have a side switch. The switch on the side of your iPad can be used for one of two things: muting the sound or locking the screen orientation. Whichever one you choose for the switch, the other will then appear in the Control Center as a button. See "Using Notifications and Control Center" in Chapter 1. So either way, you have fairly quick access to both functions.

① Open the Settings app and tap General.

② Tap Lock Rotation if you want your side switch to be an orientation lock switch.

③ Tap Mute if you want the side switch to mute the volume on the speakers and earphones.

Setting Your Date and Time

You can set the date, time, and time zone for your iPad and even choose whether to display the time in 12- or 24-hour mode.

1 Launch the Settings app and tap General.

2 Scroll down to the bottom of the General Settings list and tap Date & Time.

3 Turn the 24-Hour Time switch on to show the time in 24-hour format (military time). Turn it off to revert to 12-hour format.

4 Turning on Set Automatically syncs the date and time with the Wi-Fi network or cellular network that the iPad is connected to. In most cases, you can just stick with this. But if you find this isn't working for you, make sure Set Automatically is turned off and continue to step 5 to set it up manually.

5 Tap the Time Zone button and then enter the name of your city, or a nearby city, to set the zone.

6 To manually set the time, tap the date and time shown to bring up a set of controls underneath.

7 The controls are four "wheels" that you can spin by dragging up and down. You can set the day, hour, minute, and AM or PM.

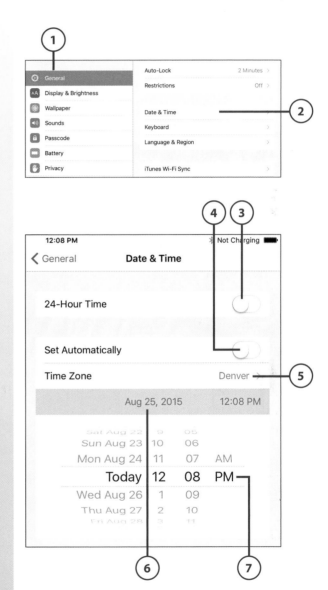

Modifying Keyboard Settings

If you use your iPad for email or word processing, you will use the on-screen keyboard a lot. The keyboard does several things to make it easier for you to type, but some of these might get in the way of your typing style. Use the following steps to modify the keyboard settings to your preferences.

(1) Open the Settings app and tap General.

(2) Scroll down to the bottom of the General Settings list and tap Keyboard.

(3) Use the Keyboards button to choose a different keyboard layout. In addition to keyboards commonly used in other countries, you can switch to a Dvorak keyboard or one of several other alternatives to the traditional QWERTY keyboard. You can also select a keyboard installed by a third-party app.

(4) You can add your own shortcuts. For instance, you can set it so when you type "omw," it will instantly expand to "On my way!" Add your own shortcuts for things you commonly type.

(5) Turn Auto-Capitalization on to automatically make the first character of a name or a sentence a capital letter.

(6) Turn Auto-Correction on to have mistyped words automatically corrected.

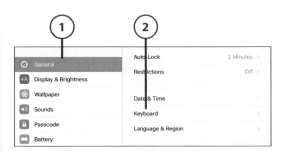

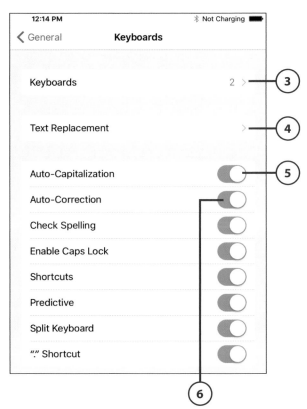

(7) Check Spelling underlines words in red that do not appear to be spelled correctly.

(8) Turn Enable Caps Lock on. When Caps Lock is turned on, you can double-tap the shift key to lock it.

(9) In Chapter 1, you learned about the shortcut bar. You can disable it with this switch if you prefer.

(10) Turn on or off Predictive Text. See "Using Predictive Text" in Chapter 1 for more about this time-saving feature.

(11) If you want to lock the keyboard so it can never be split and moved up vertically, then switch this to off. See "Using the On-Screen Keyboard" in Chapter 1 for more details on using a split keyboard.

(12) Turn on the "." shortcut if you want a double-tap of the spacebar to insert a period followed by a space.

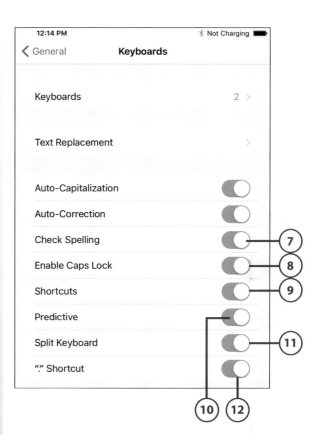

13 A shortcut to change keyboards is to use the key to the left of the spacebar that looks like a globe. Tap it to move to the next keyboard in your list, or tap and hold to get a list of keyboards to select one. You can also turn off Predictive Text and Shortcuts in this menu.

>>>Go Further
KEYBOARDS GALORE

You can add all sorts of keyboards created by third-party developers to your iPad. Doing this is just a matter of installing the developer's app on your iPad. Then you will see them appear in the list in step 3.

Some third-party keyboards allow you to type in different ways. For instance, the **Swype** and **TouchPal** apps give you keyboards that allow you to tap the first letter of a word, and then swipe with your finger across the keyboard to the other letters to form the word instead of tapping for each letter. The **TextExpander 3** app gives you advanced capabilities for creating shortcuts to type long pieces of text. See Chapter 10 to learn how to search for and install apps.

Do Not Disturb Settings

Your iPad is trying to get your attention. It beeps and rings with notifications, FaceTime calls, messages, and event alarms. In fact, it might be hard to have it nearby when you are trying to sleep or enjoying some time "offline."

Do Not Disturb is a mode where your iPad quiets down. Most audible alerts are silenced. You can set your iPad to enter this mode manually with the Do Not Disturb settings, or set a predefined block of time each day.

(1) Launch the Settings app and tap Do Not Disturb.

(2) You can turn on Do Not Disturb mode manually with this switch. (You can also turn Do Not Disturb on and off from the Control Center.)

(3) Tap Scheduled for Do Not Disturb mode to automatically start and end at a specific time. For instance, you can set it to start at 10 p.m. and end at 7 a.m. so you aren't disturbed while sleeping.

(4) Tap here to use time and date controls to set the start and end times.

(5) Tap Allow Calls From to allow FaceTime calls and messages from specific people by selecting a group in your contacts list.

(6) Turn on Repeated Calls so that someone can reach you in an emergency by calling twice within three minutes.

(7) Do Not Disturb can work at all times, or only when you have your iPad locked. Tap the desired setting so that a blue checkmark appears next to it.

Setting Parental Restrictions

If you plan to let your kids or grandkids play with your iPad, you might want to set some restrictions on what they can do.

(1) Open the Settings app and tap General.

(2) Tap Restrictions.

(3) Tap Enable Restrictions to turn restrictions on.

(4) Type in a four-digit code, and then re-enter the code when prompted. It is important to remember this code, or you can't turn off or change restrictions later!

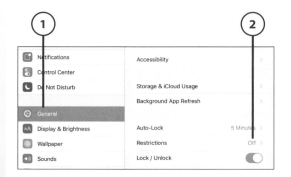

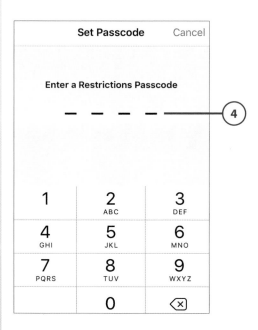

5 The Restrictions settings are a long list of apps and functions that you can allow or disallow. The switches you use depend on how much you want to restrict your iPad's use.

6 Continue to scroll down the list and review all the possible settings. Some settings, like the ones for movies, TV shows, books, and apps, allow you to set a maximum content rating. For instance, for apps you can set this to 4+, 9+, 12+, 17+, Allow All Apps, or Don't Allow Apps.

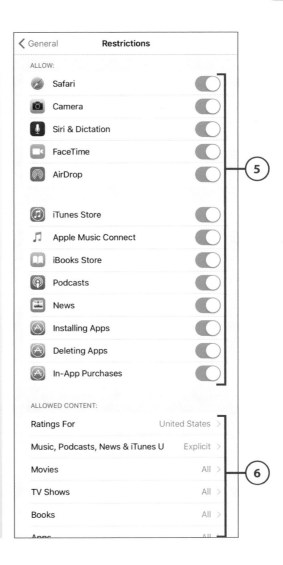

It's Not All Good

Settings Not Remembered

It would be nice if you could just switch Restrictions on and off so that you could hand your iPad to Junior after quickly turning them on. But the settings are reset each time you switch Restrictions off. So you need to set the switches again each time after turning Restrictions back on. Once they are on, however, you can go back any time and adjust the individual settings.

Making Text Easier to Read

If you find that text in standard apps like Calendar, Reminders, and Notes is difficult to read because it is too small or the letters are too thin, you can change that in the Display & Brightness settings.

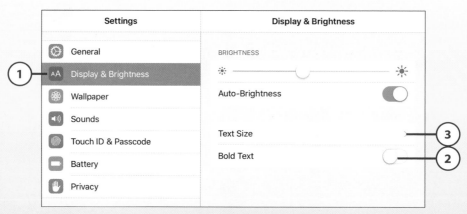

1. Open the Settings app and tap Display & Brightness.

2. You can make the letters of standard text thicker and easier to read. Changing this setting requires your iPad to restart.

3. Tap Text Size to make the default text larger or smaller.

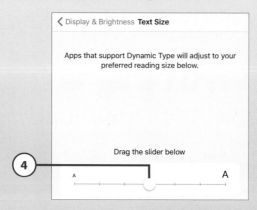

(**4**) Tap and drag the dot along the line to change the size of text. Because the Settings app is one of the apps affected by this, you'll see the changes in most of the text on the screen as you drag.

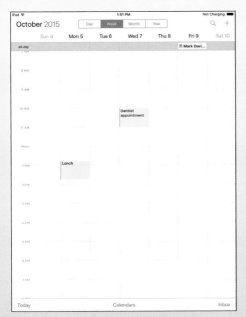

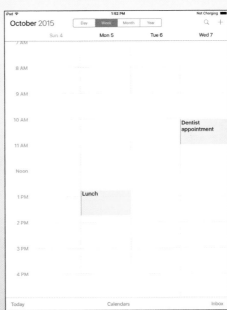

Here, you can see the Calendar app in Week view with text size set to the default.

Here, the text size is set to maximum.

Note that text size doesn't affect all apps. It works on some of the Apple preinstalled apps, but even in those, it only works in some places. With the Calendar app, you can see the change in Week and Day view but not Month view.

Controlling Automatic Downloads

You iPad can automatically download app updates when they become available. This saves you from missing an update to your favorite apps. You can also set your iPad to download new content that you purchase from iTunes on another device.

(1) Open the Settings app and tap App & iTunes Store on the left.

(2) There are three switches that control automatic content downloads. Turn these on if you want your iPad to automatically get music, apps, or books when you purchase them on another device such as your computer or an iPhone.

(3) Turn on Updates if you want updates to Apple and third-party apps to automatically download and install.

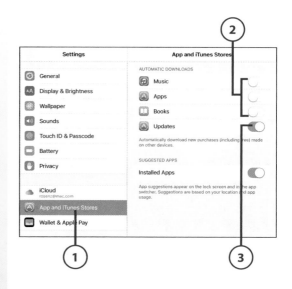

Cellular Data

Note that if you have an iPad with mobile wireless capability, you'll see another setting here for Use Cellular Data. Turn this off to prevent these automatic downloads from happening while you are away from a Wi-Fi connection.

Other Useful Settings

The Settings app contains too many controls to go into detail on each one. It is worth taking the time to explore each section of the Settings app to see what is possible. The item to tap on the left side of the Settings app screen is listed first in each of the following bullets, followed by the items you tap on the right side. For example, in the first bullet you open the Settings app, tap General on the left side, and then tap About on the right side. When the About settings appear, tap Available to see your available storage.

- **General, About, Available**: See the remaining amount of storage space you have on your iPad.

- **General, About, Version**: Quickly find out which version of iOS you are using.

- **General, About, Model**: Get the model number of your iPad. This could come in handy if you ever need to figure out if an accessory will work with your specific model.

- **Control Center, Access Within Apps**: If you find that you are accidentally bringing up the Control Center at the bottom of the screen while playing your favorite game, you can turn off Control Center inside apps. You can still access it by going to the Home screen first.

- **Wi-Fi, Ask to Join Networks**: Whether or not this switch is on, your iPad will look for and connect to any Wi-Fi network you have previously signed on to. If you switch this setting on, if it can't find any familiar network, it will pop up a dialog asking if you want to join the strongest network it can find. Since you don't want to join networks you don't know or trust, leave this off and simply go to the Wi-Fi settings to join a new network.

- **General, Spotlight Search**: Here you can turn on and off different types of content you see when you search the contents of your iPad. You can also set the order by dragging the items in the list up or down.

- **General, Lock/Unlock**: If you use an Apple Smart Cover, or some other case that can automatically put your iPad to sleep when it is closed, you can control whether or not this happens by changing this setting.

- **General, Reset**: Here is a set of potentially dangerous switches that allow you to erase your settings and content. If you ever decide that your iPad's home screens are too disorganized, you can use the Reset Home Screen Layout to move the Apple default apps back to their original positions and your other apps out of folders into alphabetical order starting on screen two. The other reset options should only be used if you understand their end result.

More Apps, More Settings

The Settings app adds new items as you add new apps to your iPad. Some apps have settings inside the app, while others have all their settings as an item along the left side of the Settings app. Still others put some settings in the app and some in Settings. It is a good idea to periodically check the Settings app to see what new items have appeared, and then look to see which settings are available for that app.

Put your favorite
photos on your iPad.

View your iCloud files.

Sync your music and other content with your Mac or PC.

In this chapter, you find out how to connect your iPad to your local Wi-Fi network. You also see how to sync your iPad with your Mac or Windows computer and with Apple's iCloud service.

→ Setting Up Your Wi-Fi Network Connection
→ Setting Up Your Cellular Data Connection
→ Syncing with iCloud
→ Syncing with iTunes
→ Syncing Photos with iTunes
→ Keeping Your iPad Up-To-Date
→ Sharing with AirDrop
→ Viewing Your Mac's Files with iCloud Drive

Networking and Syncing

Your iPad connects you to the world. You can surf the web, view all sorts of information, communicate with friends, and share photos. But first, you must connect your iPad to the Internet. You can do that using a Wi-Fi connection. Some iPads also have the capability to connect to a cellular network.

Setting Up Your Wi-Fi Network Connection

One of the first things you need to do with your iPad is to establish an Internet connection.

Chances are that you did this when you started your iPad for the first time. It should have prompted you to choose from a list of nearby Wi-Fi networks. You might need to do this again if you first used your iPad away from home, or if you need to switch to use another Wi-Fi network.

To connect your iPad to a wireless network, follow these steps.

(1) Tap the Settings icon on the Home
    screen.

(2) Choose Wi-Fi from the list of set-
    tings on the left.

(3) Make sure that Wi-Fi is turned on.

(4) Tap the item that represents your
    network. (Tap on the blue-circled
    i button next to each network to
    customize your network settings.)

I Don't Have a Wireless Network

If you don't have a Wi-Fi network but do
have high-speed Internet through a telephone or cable provider, you have several
options. The first is to call your provider and
ask for a new network modem that enables
wireless connections. Some providers might
upgrade your box for free or a small cost.

Another option is to keep your current box
and add a wireless base station of your
own, such as the Apple Airport Extreme
base station.

(5) If the network is protected by a
    password, you will be asked to
    enter the password.

(6) Tap Join. Once you enter the pass-
    word, your iPad will remember it.
    If you switch between two loca-
    tions, like work and home, you will
    be asked to enter the password
    the first time you use that connec-
    tion. From that point on, your iPad
    automatically logs on to each con-
    nection as you move around.

Settings

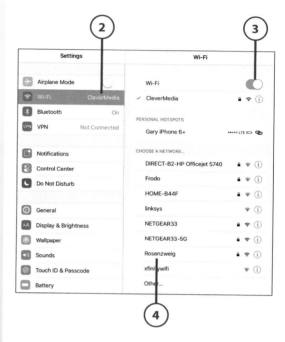

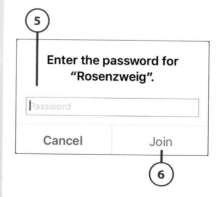

**Enter the password for
"Rosenzweig".**

>>>*Go Further*
SECURITY? YES!

Your wireless network at home should have security turned on. This means that you should see a padlock next to it in the list of Wi-Fi networks on your iPad. When you select it for the first time, you should be asked to supply a password.

If you don't require a password, seriously consider changing your Wi-Fi network box's settings to add security. The issue isn't simply about requiring a password to use your Internet connection. It is about the fact that a secure network will send encrypted data through the air. Otherwise, anyone can simply "sniff" your wireless connection and see what you are doing online—such as using credit cards and logging on to websites and services. See your network equipment's documentation to set up security.

Setting Up Your Cellular Data Connection

If you have an iPad with cellular data capabilities, you can set it up to use AT&T, Verizon, or any other compatible network. You can purchase a monthly data plan, or purchase service in shorter increments. If you have previously set up a plan, you cannot complete these steps again. You need to contact your service provider directly to change or cancel your plan.

(1) Open the Settings app and tap Cellular Data on the left.

(2) Turn on Cellular Data. In addition, turn on Enable LTE for a faster connection.

(3) Tap View Account.

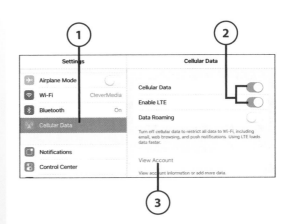

4 You have three options to set up an account with AT&T. (Other carriers may offer different options.) The first one is to set up a completely new account. If you choose this, skip to step 8.

5 Another option is to add your iPad's data plan as an additional service to your existing AT&T plan. Use this if you are already an AT&T customer. You will be prompted for your mobile phone number, zip code, passcode, and social security number to complete the setup.

6 The Transfer Service From Another iPad option is for those who already have an iPad data plan, and want to transfer it from an old iPad to a new one.

7 Choose a data plan that best fits your needs.

8 Tap and swipe up to scroll down. This screen consists of a long form that you need to fill out with your personal and payment information to complete the setup of your account. When you are done, you have to approve the service agreement and confirm your purchase. Still, it beats going to the mall and dealing with a salesperson at a mobile phone store, right?

It might take a few more minutes for your cellular data service to activate. After establishing service, you can return to this section of the Settings app to view your usage and modify your plan. Then you can see your pay details and status.

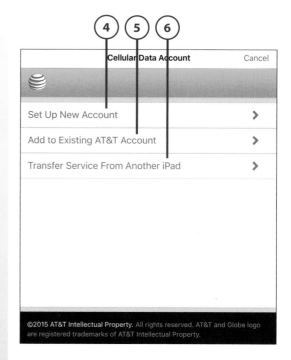

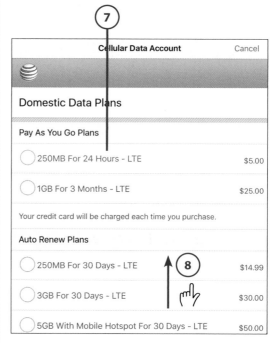

Working with Wi-Fi and Cellular Data

After you establish a cellular data plan, your iPad should still connect to your Wi-Fi networks when it is in range and use cellular data only when it cannot find a Wi-Fi network. You can also return to Settings and turn on or off Cellular Data to specifically prevent your iPad from using the cellular data network. This is handy when you are completely out of mobile data range but have local Wi-Fi; for instance, you might be on an airplane flight.

Looking at the top-left corner of your iPad's screen, you can tell which sort of connection you are currently using. You see the Wi-Fi symbol, a fan of four curves, when you are connected to Wi-Fi. If you have a cellular data plan, you see the name of your network next to it, such as "AT&T," plus a series of bars that show your connection strength. You are only using that connection if the characters "3G," "4G," or "LTE" are shown instead of the Wi-Fi symbol.

It's Not All Good

Watch for Data Roaming

In the Cellular Data settings, you can turn Data Roaming on or off. This is what enables your iPad to connect to wireless data networks that are outside of your data plan, such as networks in other countries. If you leave Data Roaming on and your iPad connects to such a network, you may find a surprise bill in the mail. You can avoid extra charges by leaving Data Roaming off or by purchasing a plan from AT&T for International data roaming.

Syncing with iCloud

When you think of your contacts, calendar events, and email messages, you might be tempted to think of that information as being "on your iPad" or "on your computer." But today this information is usually in both places, and more. This is referred to as "the cloud"—when the actual location of the information isn't important as long as it is where you need it, when you need it.

As an iPad user, you have access to several different cloud services, most notably Apple's system called iCloud. It is a free service that offers email, contacts, calendar, documents, and other types of data stored on Apple's servers and is automatically synced to your iPad and the other Apple devices you may own.

Or, you could choose to use other cloud services, such as Gmail or Yahoo!, for mail and calendar events. There's no reason to pick just one. For instance, you can use both iCloud and Gmail on your iPad.

When you use cloud services, you get automatic syncing as long as you have a connection to the Internet. For example, add a contact to your iPad and your iPhone automatically updates to show that new contact. Let's look at how to set up an iCloud account, or link to one you've already created.

Connecting to iCloud

① Open the Settings app and tap iCloud on the left.

② If you have never set up an account with Apple before, then tap Create a New Apple ID to set one up. Any account you have with Apple, such as an iTunes account, would be an Apple ID, and you should use that instead of starting a new account.

③ If you already have an Apple ID, even if you have never used iCloud before, enter your ID and password. Apple IDs can be any email address, not just an @iCloud.com email address.

④ Tap Sign In to access your account. If your account has only been used for things like iTunes in the past, you are prompted to set up the new iCloud part of your account.

⑤ If you think you have used an email address to log on to iTunes or some other Apple service before, but you can't remember the password, tap Forgot Apple ID or Password to reset your password.

It's Not All Good

Don't Confuse ID with Email

An Apple ID is a unique identifier that allows you to log in to your iCloud account. It can be an Apple email address, like myipadbook@icloud.com, but it can also be a non-Apple email address, like myipadbook@gmail.com. In the former case, the ID is the same as your iCloud email address. In the latter case, the ID is just an ID. Your email account would be a Gmail account and have nothing to do with your iCloud account.

(6) You can manage your iCloud Drive storage by tapping the iCloud Drive setting. iCloud Drive is the file and documents storage part of iCloud. For example, your Pages, Numbers, and Keynote documents can be stored on your iCloud Drive. You can then access them on other iOS or OS X devices. Also see the section about iCloud Drive later in the chapter.

(7) You can turn photo-related iCloud services such as Photo Stream and iCloud Photo Library on or off here. See Chapter 9 to learn about how photos are stored.

(8) You can use your iCloud email on your iPad. This would typically be an @icloud.com email address. These addresses are part of the free iCloud service. If you happen to be using a non-Apple email address as an Apple ID, note that this setting has nothing to do with that email account.

(9) If Contacts is on, iCloud stores all your contacts so they automatically sync with the iCloud servers and then to your other Apple devices.

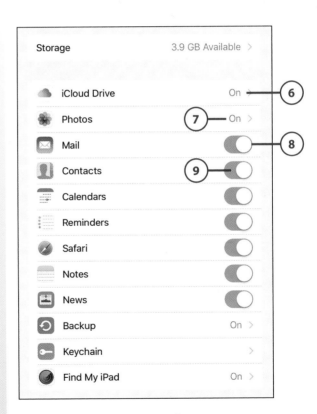

Storage	3.9 GB Available >
☁ iCloud Drive	On — (6)
✳ Photos	(7) — On >
✉ Mail	⬤ — (8)
👥 Contacts	(9) ⬤
📅 Calendars	⬤
☰ Reminders	⬤
🧭 Safari	⬤
▬ Notes	⬤
📰 News	⬤
↻ Backup	On >
🔑 Keychain	>
● Find My iPad	On >

(10) Likewise, iCloud can store your calendar events when the Calendars switch is on.

(11) Turn on Reminders to have the Reminders app use iCloud to store reminders and automatically sync them with your other devices.

(12) Safari can sync over iCloud as well. Things like your bookmarks, tabs, and reading list would sync across devices when the Safari switch is on.

(13) Turn the Notes switch on so that Notes can also sync over iCloud.

(14) You can have your News app preferences sync across your devices.

(15) iCloud Backup backs up your settings, documents, photos, and other data to iCloud wirelessly. If your iPad is lost or breaks, you are able to restore your data to a repaired or new iPad later. You should use iCloud Backup unless you prefer to back up to your computer via iTunes and do so on a regular basis.

(16) iOS allows you to store passwords while using Safari so you don't need to enter them each time. Syncing these over iCloud means that you can also access these passwords on other Apple devices. Tap Keychain to configure this setting. See "Saving Time with AutoFill" in Chapter 7 for more details on working with the Keychain.

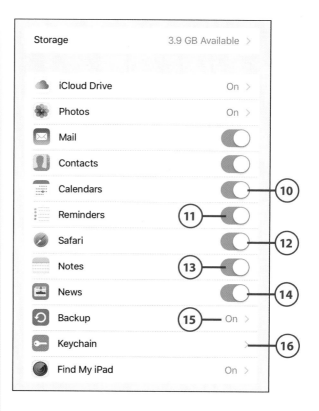

17 Find My iPad is an option that lets you locate your iPad on a map using another Apple device or the iCloud.com website. Be aware that if your Location Services are not on, this feature does not work.

18 You can check to see how much storage space you have remaining in your iCloud account. As of late 2014, Apple provides each iPad user with 5GB of free space. You can purchase more if you find that you have a lot of documents or other data, and 5GB isn't going to be enough.

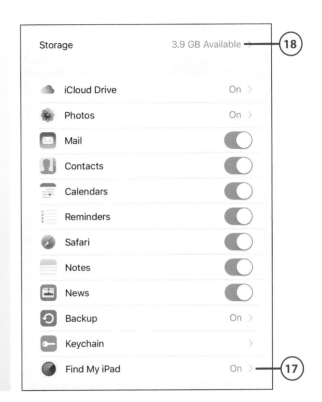

>>>Go Further
iCLOUD.COM

In addition to syncing between devices, much of your iCloud information is available if you go to iCloud.com and log in using your Apple ID. You can do this on any computer. So even if you are using your iPad as your only computing device, there still is another way to get to your data when you need it.

Syncing with iTunes

With iCloud, the iPad can be a truly stand-alone device, no desktop computer needed. iCloud is also great for keeping your iPad and your Mac in sync, sharing settings, music, photos, and so on. An alternative is to use iTunes to sync your iPad and your Mac or Windows computer. There are several advantages to doing so:

- Each day you sync your iPad, iTunes stores a backup of its content. You can restore all your data from these backups if you lose your iPad. You can do the same with iCloud backup, but it can take a lot longer to restore an iPad because it has to transfer the data across the Internet.

- Syncing with a computer is a good way to get a large number of photos from your collection on your iPad if you aren't using iCloud Photo Library.

- Syncing is how you get your music stored on your computer onto your iPad if you aren't using iTunes Match or Apple Music. If you have a large collection of music, you can opt to copy only a selection of it to your iPad at any one time.

You might get a message asking if it is okay to sync your iPad to this computer the first time you connect your iPad and open iTunes. The message won't reappear after you have connected the iPad to the computer.

After connecting the first time, iTunes should automatically open when you connect your iPad. While connected to your computer, you can always click the Sync button in iTunes to re-sync and apply any changes to the iPad.

You can also choose Sync over Wi-Fi connection in your iPad's options in iTunes. This allows you to sync when your iPad isn't connected to the computer by the USB cable. It only needs to be on the same network as your Mac or PC that is running iTunes.

As we look at some of the syncing options for the iPad, the Mac version of iTunes is used as an example. The Windows version of iTunes is similar but not exactly the same.

Syncing Options

After your device is in sync, you can change some general options for your iPad from the Summary screen in iTunes. Most of the options are self-explanatory, such as Open iTunes When This iPad Is Connected.

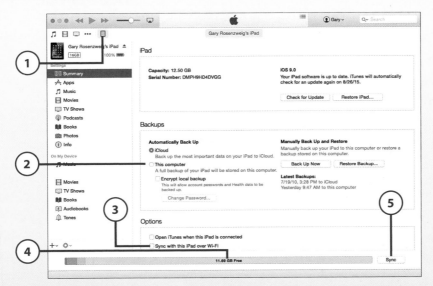

① Using iTunes 12.2 or newer, look for a button representing your iPad at the top of iTunes. After you select it, the items in the rest of the iTunes window will pertain to your iPad, with settings and content categories listed on the left.

② You can configure your backups. iCloud backups are convenient for those without regular access to a computer, but it uses Internet bandwidth and can be a problem if you have a slow connection. Backing up to your computer is a good option if you regularly sync to your computer anyway.

③ You can set your iPad to connect via Wi-Fi. From then on, you only need to be on the same network as your computer to sync with iTunes.

④ A handy chart of your iPad's storage is shown.

⑤ Any changes you make on this screen, or any other iTunes sync screen, requires that you click Sync to re-sync with the new settings.

One option that dramatically changes how your iPad syncs is Manually Manage Music and Videos. This option turns off automatic syncing of music and videos and enables you to simply drag and drop songs and movies from your iTunes library onto the iPad icon on the left. (You might need to scroll down the Summary page to locate this checkbox if your screen size is too small to show the entire page at once.)

>>>Go Further

BACK IT UP!

Perhaps the most important part of syncing with your computer is backing up your data. Everything you create with apps, every preference you carefully set, and every photo you take could be gone in a second if you drop your iPad or someone swipes it. Even a hardware failure is possible—the iPad isn't perfect.

Choosing This Computer saves all your data on your computer in a backup file. Try to do it once per day. With a good backup, you can replace a lost iPad and restore all your data from the backup. It works incredibly well.

You can always plug your iPad into your Mac or PC, launch iTunes, and click the Back Up Now button in the Backup section. Backup also happens automatically, once per day, if you connect your iPad to your computer and click Sync.

Your other option is iCloud. This backs up your data wirelessly to iCloud. It is your only option if you are not going to sync your iPad with a computer. It does use up your data storage allotment in your iCloud account, so you might need to upgrade your iCloud account to allow for more data.

Even so, backing up to iCloud is a great alternative, especially if you travel often and use your iPad for critical tasks. You can always do both types of backups by selecting iCloud in step 2, and connecting your iPad to your computer on a regular basis and clicking the Back Up Now button in iTunes.

Syncing Music

The simple way to sync music is to select Entire Music Library in iTunes on your computer. If you have more music than can fit on your iPad, though, you must make some choices. Syncing Movies, TV Shows, Podcasts, Tones (ringtones for messaging and FaceTime), iTunes U, and Books all work in a similar way to syncing music, so you can apply what you learn in these steps to those items as well.

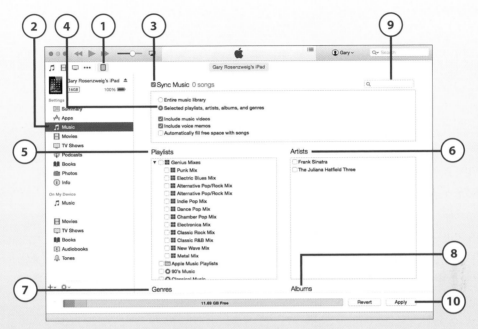

1. Select your iPad at the top of the iTunes window.

2. Click the Music button of your iPad's settings in iTunes.

3. Select Sync Music, if it isn't already turned on.

4. Click the Selected Playlists, Artists, Albums, and Genres button.

5. Check off any playlists in the Playlists section that you want to include.

6. Check off any artists for which you want to include every song by that artist.

7. Check off any genres to include in their entirety.

8. Check off any albums you want to include.

9. Use the search box to quickly find specific artists.

10. Click the Apply button if you want to apply the changes now.

One Copy Only

Note that songs are never duplicated on your iPad. For instance, if the same song appears in two playlists and is also by an artist that you have selected to sync, the song only has one copy on your iPad. But it appears in both playlists and under that artist, album, and alphabetical list of all songs.

>>>*Go Further*

MORE WAYS TO SYNC

iTunes Match is a service from Apple. For an annual fee, you can sync your music collection with Apple's servers. Then you can access all your music on your iPad by turning on iTunes Match in the Music settings in the Settings app. When you do this, you no longer need to sync your music. Instead, you see all your music on your iPad, and it will download from Apple's servers when you want to listen to a particular song.

Visit www.apple.com/itunes/itunes-match/ to find out more about Apple's iTunes Match service.

Apple Music is a service from Apple where you pay a monthly subscription fee in return for access to a huge library of music from iTunes. You can add any songs in the Apple Music catalog to your collection and they will appear on your iPad and other Apple devices for as long as you remain a subscriber. See "Having It All with Apple Music" in Chapter 4.

You can also sync your music and videos manually. This sounds like a lot of work, but it can be an easier way to sync your music for many people. If you check off Manually Manage Music and Videos on the iTunes Summary screen for your iPad, you can then drag and drop music from your iTunes music library on to your iPad. It requires a bit of knowledge about how the iTunes interface works, however. You'll need to choose View, Show Sidebar so you can see your iPad in the left sidebar. Then you can look at the Music item listed to see which songs are there. Switch to your iTunes Music library to see what songs you have on your computer and simply drag and drop songs, albums, or artists from the iTunes Music library to your iPad in the left sidebar.

Syncing Photos

The process for syncing photos from your computer to your iPad is very similar to how you move music, videos, and other data to your iPad. So let's use photos as an example. The steps here are very similar if you want to sync something else, like movies, to your iPad. You would just choose the Movies tab in iTunes instead of the Photos tab.

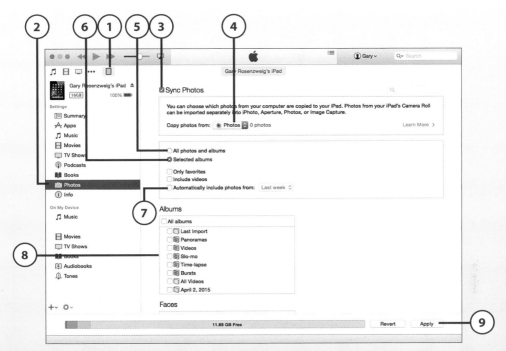

1. Select your iPad.

2. Choose Photos.

3. Click the checkbox to indicate that you want to sync photos.

4. You can choose from any applications that are compatible with iTunes and store photos. For instance, on Mac you can choose the new Photos app or the old iPhoto or Aperture apps, if you have them. You can also simply select a folder to use as the location for your photos. The rest of the steps here assume you are using iPhoto.

5. Click All photos and albums to sync all your photos. Only do this if you have a fairly small collection.

6. Choose Selected albums to select which albums to sync.

7. You can also have photos taken over a recent period of time automatically sync. For instance, you can have it sync all photos from the past 6 months.

8. Choose which albums you want to sync. Albums are collections of photos, like music playlists, that allow you to compile your favorite or related photos into a group.

9. When you are satisfied with your selections, click Apply to begin the transfer.

No Duplicates

Like with music, you get only one copy of each photo, no matter how many times the photo appears in albums, events, and faces. The photos appear in all the right places but take up only one spot in memory on your iPad.

It's Not All Good

One Direction

Syncing photos can be a confusing concept: You sync photos from your photo collection to your iPad using iTunes, but you sync photos from your iPad to your computer using iPhoto or a similar app.

Think of it this way. Syncing to your iPad works the same for music, videos, and photos. These are all media stored on your computer, and iTunes lets you copy them from your computer to your iPad. But when you take photos with your iPad, your iPad is acting just like a digital camera. You want to copy those to your photo-handling app on your computer as you would if you were using a digital camera.

When you sync photos from your computer to your iPad, the original is on your computer, and there is merely a copy on your iPad. Your iPad is just a viewing device for these photos. It is important that you maintain your real photo library on your computer and remember to back it up.

Syncing Everything Else

Music and photos are two out of many types of items you might want to sync between your computer and your iPad. In most cases, if you use iCloud for that type of item, there is no need to ever sync it via iTunes.

If you look in iTunes, you have the ability to sync Info, Apps, Tones, Music, Movies, TV Shows, Podcasts, Books, and Photos. Each has a similar screen to the Music and Photos syncing settings screens we have already examined. Let's take a look at each and see why you may or may not want to sync them using iTunes.

- **Info**: This means syncing Contacts and Calendars. If you use iCloud, this happens automatically as you make changes. There is no need to sync.

- **Apps**: Since your Mac or PC cannot run iOS apps, these settings in iTunes allow you to keep copies of your apps on your computer so you can restore them to your iPad in case of a problem. You can also use the iTunes interface to arrange the apps on your Home screens.

- **Tones**: This refers to ringtones and sounds used by Messages, FaceTime, and other things where your iPad sends you an audible alert. If you are creative and good with GarageBand on the Mac, you can create ringtones with it and use iTunes to sync these new ringtones to your iPad. You can also download iOS-compatible ringtones, which are .m4r files, and sync them this way.

- **Music**: If you are using Apple Music or iTunes Match, you don't need to use iTunes to sync your music. If you don't have much music, and want to save a few dollars, you can simply sync your music with iTunes on your computer.

- **Movies and TV Shows**: These two categories are used mainly to sync videos you have purchased in the iTunes Store. However, it also works for other videos you store in iTunes. Videos that are part of your photo collection are synced under Photos.

  One thing to keep in mind is that once you purchase a movie or TV show episode, you can always re-download it from Apple later. So if you buy 22 episodes of a TV season and watch them all, you don't need to keep them on either your iPad or your computer. You can remove those items from iTunes to save some storage space, and then download them again from Apple if you want to watch them again later.

- **Podcasts**: Thanks to the stand-alone Podcasts app that comes with your iPad, there's not much of a need to sync podcasts across from your computer to your iPad. You can simply download episodes directly to your iPad. See "Listening to Podcasts" in Chapter 4.

- **Books**: Books work in much the same way as Movies. When you buy a book from Apple, you can re-download it later. If a book is just text, it is a quick download. If you buy a book on your computer in iBooks, you can easily find it and download it in the iBooks app on your iPad, too. Syncing can also be useful for those who import other types of books into the iBooks library on a Mac, and then want to get it to their iPad later on.

- **Photos**: As noted earlier, the main reason to sync photos is if you aren't using iCloud Photo Library and you want to take some recent or favorite albums on your computer and put them on your iPad for viewing.

Sharing with AirDrop

A quick way to get files from your iPad to another iOS device or Mac is using AirDrop. This technique uses Wi-Fi, but instead of going through a Wi-Fi network, it uses your iPad's Wi-Fi hardware and goes directly from device to device. The devices don't need to be on the same network—they don't need to be on any Wi-Fi network at all. They just need to be nearby.

AirDrop requires the latest Wi-Fi hardware in your iPad, so it only works with the 4th generation iPad or newer, or an iPad mini. On a Mac, it requires a very recent model as well, running at least Mac OS X Yosemite. Using AirDrop is pretty straightforward.

Using AirDrop

To use AirDrop, follow these steps:

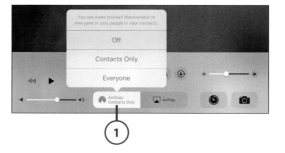

1. To use AirDrop, make sure you have turned it on. Do this by accessing Control Center. See "Using Notifications and Control Center" in Chapter 1. Make sure that it is set to Everyone. Another option is to set it to Contacts Only, which means you can only use AirDrop with devices that have Apple ID email addresses that are in your Contacts.

2 Let's use the Photos app as an example. You can use any app that can share items, such as the Notes app, Contacts app, and so on. Select a photo, and then tap the Share button. In Photos, the Share button is sometimes at the top, and sometimes at the bottom. It is always the same boxed arrow.

3 In addition to sharing options such as Message and Mail, you'll see a list of other AirDrop-compatible devices that are within range. You see whatever image the user has chosen as a user icon, plus their name. If you do not see your other device, it could be asleep, or have AirDrop disabled, or possibly is not a model that has AirDrop available.

4 After you tap the icon, you see a "Waiting" message below it. In the meantime, the recipient receives an alert asking them to accept the transfer. You can accept the cute picture of the puppy, or decline it. If the sender is in your contacts, however, you just get the photo without needing to confirm it.

Friends Share

The real power of AirDrop is sending between friends. For instance, if you are standing with your iPad next to a friend with an iPhone, you can send her a picture without both of you needing to share a common Wi-Fi network or exchanging email addresses. You just Share, select her for the AirDrop, and she accepts.

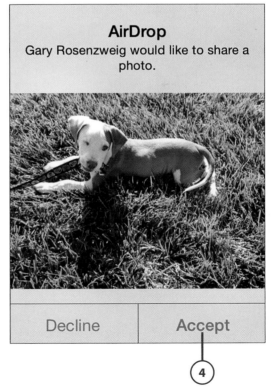

>>>*Go Further*

HANDOFF

Handoff is a feature of iOS and Mac OS X that allows you to put down one device and pick up another to continue what you are doing. There are no settings for this; it just works as long as both devices are signed into the same iCloud account, and they are nearby.

Suppose you start composing an email on an iPhone. Then you decide that it would be easier to type the message on your iPad. All you need to do is look at the Lock screen of your iPad. You'll see a little Mail app icon at the bottom left telling you that you can pick up your work on the iPad. Slide the icon up to unlock your iPad, instead of using the usual Slide to Unlock gesture. The result will be that the Mail app opens and your half-completed message appears, ready for you to finish. On your iPhone, the Mail app gracefully closes the composition screen.

There are a lot of things that need to be just right for Handoff to work. Both devices need to not only use the same iCloud account, but also need to see each other using Bluetooth and Wi-Fi systems. A little radio interference is all it takes for this to not work one time, but work other times.

Viewing Your Mac's Files with iCloud Drive New!

If you are a Mac user, you are probably already familiar with iCloud Drive. This special folder on your Mac enables you to store files in the cloud and access them on your other Macs. It is very useful if you have both a desktop and a laptop Mac.

You can also access your iCloud Drive files on your iPad in iOS 9. In iOS 8, you could access Pages, Numbers and Keynote files that were stored on your iCloud Drive in the appropriately named folders. You could only access these in the equivalent apps on your iPad.

With the new iCloud Drive app in iOS 9, you can see all your iCloud Drive files. In particular, it gives you access to text files, images, and PDFs, which can all be viewed inside the iCloud Drive app.

Accessing Your Files

Here is how to access your iCloud Drive files.

1. Open the Settings app and go to iCloud, iCloud Drive. You see a switch to turn on iCloud Drive access. It should be on by default.

2. Turn on Show on Home Screen. This shows the iCloud Drive app on your Home Screen. It may not be on the first page.

3 Find the iCloud Drive icon on your Home Screen and tap it.

iCloud Drive

4 The iCloud Drive app shows your iCloud Drive folders. This should match what you see on your Mac in iCloud Drive. You see some special default folders, like the one for Pages.

5 You also see folders created by third-party Mac apps you may have that use iCloud Drive, such as the image editing app Pixelmator.

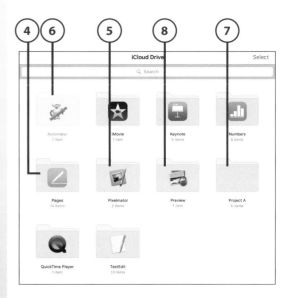

6 Some app-specific folders may be inactive and inaccessible. For instance, this folder is for Automator scripts, which can only be used on Macs.

7 If you have created any general use folders on your iCloud Drive, you see those, too. You can tap them to dig down to the folders and files inside.

8 You also see folders for Mac apps, such as Preview and TextEdit, that have no iPad equivalent. But you can still access the files inside with the iCloud Drive app. As an example, suppose you have a Preview document. You would tap this folder to view the file.

9 The next screen shows a list of files. In this case, there is only one: a PDF file. Tapping it opens the file, if it has a supported app for it.

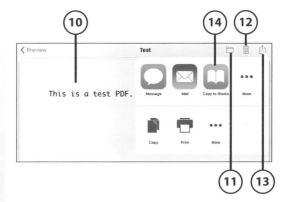

10 Although the iCloud Drive app does not allow you to edit or do much else with PDF files like this one, you can at least view it.

11 You can also move the file to a new location inside your iCloud Drive. This change is reflected on other iOS devices and your Mac.

12 You can also delete the file. This deletes it from iCloud Drive, so it also disappears from your Mac.

13 The action button allows you to take the file outside the iCloud Drive app.

14 In this case, the only app installed that handles PDF files is iBooks. You can use this button to copy the file to your iBooks library. If you have other apps installed, such as Adobe's PDF Reader app, you see it here and are able to copy the file to it.

Opening Files

The iCloud Drive app acts as a simple viewer for files like PDFs, text files, Word docs, images, and so on. You can use steps 13 and 14 to open those files in appropriate apps, if you have them installed.

>>>*Go Further*

YOU STILL MAY NEED AN APP

Just because you can see the file in iCloud Drive doesn't mean you can work with it on your iPad. The iCloud Drive app acts as a simple viewer for many file types. But, just like with desktop computers, you need the right app to work with the file.

For instance, if you get a Photoshop file on your desktop computer, you wouldn't expect to edit it unless you had Photoshop installed. The same is true on the iPad. You need the right app to work with the file. Sometimes, the app doesn't exist as an iPad app and there is nothing you can do to work with the file.

Creating documents and then saving them to iCloud Drive also requires the appropriate app. An app developer needs to build iCloud Drive compatibility into the app to allow you to save the file to iCloud Drive.

Purchase music and
buy or rent videos.

Listen to podcasts.

Play your music.

In this chapter, you learn how to use the Music and Video apps to play music and watch video. You also learn how to use Apple Music and iTunes Radio.

→ Playing a Song
→ Building a Playlist
→ Making iTunes Purchases
→ Sharing Purchases with Your Family
→ Having It All with Apple Music
→ Listening to Podcasts
→ Playing Video
→ Using AirPlay to Play Music and Video on Other Devices
→ Home Sharing
→ Listening to iTunes Radio

Playing Music and Video

The iPad handles playing music as well as any iPod or iPhone ever has, plus it has a large, beautiful screen for you to use to browse your collection. In Chapter 3, you learned how to sync music to your iPad from your computer. That's one way to get music onto your iPad. You can also use the iTunes app to purchase music, or the iTunes Match service to sync all your music from iCloud. Families can share purchases using the Family Sharing feature. A new option to subscribe to Apple Music gives you unlimited access to nearly all the songs on iTunes.

No matter how you put music on your iPad, you play your music using the Music app. You can also listen to iTunes Radio, free streaming music from Apple.

Playing a Song

So let's start by simply selecting and playing a song with the Music app.

(1) Tap the Music icon. It is located along the bottom of your Home screen, unless you've customized your toolbar and moved it elsewhere.

(2) Tap My Music on the bottom, if it isn't already selected.

(3) At the top of the screen, you see either Artists, Albums, Songs, Genres, or Composers. This indicates how your list is presented below. You can tap here to switch. Select Songs to see an alphabetical list of all your songs.

(4) Tap the name of a song to start it. You can also tap and drag up and down on the screen to scroll through the list. If you have a lot of songs, the letters of the alphabet will appear on the right side, and you can use these to jump to a position in the list of songs.

(5) At the bottom of the screen, the Play button changes to a Pause button. You can tap this button to pause the song.

(6) Tap the name of the song.

(7) Use the volume slider to adjust the volume, or use the physical volume controls on the side of your iPad.

(8) Tap the Repeat button to choose whether to repeat this song over and over again, or repeat the playlist or album you are currently listening to. After you have turned on Repeat, you can tap here again to change the repeat range, or turn it off.

9 Tap the Shuffle button to make your iPad play the songs in the album or playlist in a random order.

10 Tap the down-pointing arrow button at the top left to return to the main Music app interface.

11 Tap the list option at the top of the screen and change it to Artists.

12 A list of artists is shown on the left. Tap on an artist to view the songs by album for that artist.

13 The list of albums and songs appears on the right. You can scroll up and down and tap on any song to play it.

14 Tap the Search button at the top of the list to search your songs. When you use search in the Music app, you are given two options: My Music and Apple Music. If you are not a subscriber to Apple Music, be sure to choose My Music or you will not be able to use any of the results.

Playing iTunes Match Music

If you are using iTunes Match, you will see all your music in the list—even songs not currently on your iPad. You can still tap the name of a song to start it. The song downloads and plays, assuming you are connected to the Internet. You can also tap the iTunes Match (cloud) icon for each song to simply download each song so it is ready to listen to later, even if you are not connected. You would want to do this for some songs if you are going to be away from your Internet connection and plan to listen to music.

Visit www.apple.com/itunes/itunes-match/ to find out more about Apple's iTunes Match service.

How Else Can I Listen to Music?

You can also listen to music using third-party apps. Some apps access your music collection on your iPad, but the most interesting ones play streaming music from over the Internet. We look at apps, such as Pandora and Spotify, in Chapter 10. You can also use iTunes Radio to listen to streaming music. We look at that later in this chapter.

Siri: Playing Music

You can use Siri to play music. Here are some examples:

"Play The Beatles"
"Play Georgia On My Mind"
"Play some blues"
"Play my driving music" (plays the playlist named "driving music")
"Shuffle all songs"
"Skip"
"Pause"

Building a Playlist

Playlists are a way to take the songs you have on your iPad and arrange them in ordered groups. For instance, you can create one to listen to while working, while working out, while trying to go to sleep, or make a party mix for your next get-together.

Creating Playlists

You can create playlists on your Mac or PC in iTunes, but you can also build playlists on your iPad.

(1) Tap the Playlists button at the bottom of the main Music app screen.

(2) A list of current playlists appears. Tap the New button.

(3) Give the new playlist a name, such as *My Playlist*, by tapping here and typing a name.

(4) Tap the Add Songs button.

(5) A list of sorting options comes up. Tap Songs to see a list of all your songs to choose from. Otherwise, you can choose Artists, Albums, Genres, Composers, or Playlists to view all your music sorted differently.

(6) Tap any songs you want to add to the playlist.

(7) Use the Search field at the top to find songs faster. If you don't see the Search field, tap and drag your list of songs down so you reveal it at the top of the list.

(8) Tap the Done button when you have selected all the songs you want to add to the playlist.

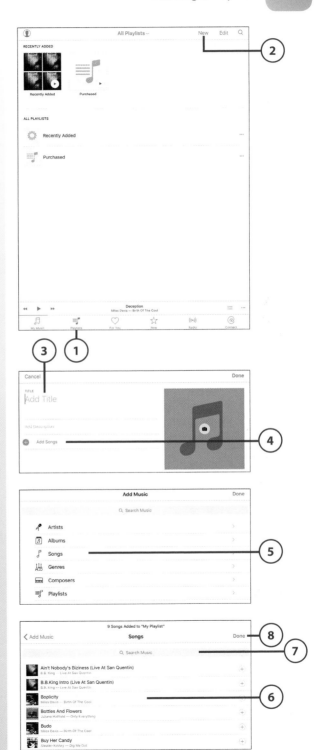

9 On the playlist screen, remove songs from the playlist by tapping on the red buttons. A Remove button appears to the right side of the listing. Tap the Remove button to confirm that you want to remove that song from the playlist.

10 Tap and drag on the three-line buttons to rearrange the songs.

11 Tap the + button to add more songs to the playlist.

12 Tap Done to exit editing the playlist.

13 You now see your playlist on the main Playlists screen. Tap it to start playing the songs.

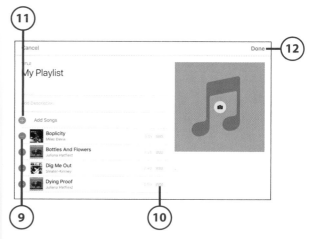

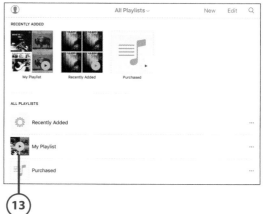

Making iTunes Purchases

You have lots of options when it comes to adding more music to your iPad. You can simply add more music to your iTunes collection on your computer and then sync those songs to your iPad. In that case, you can buy them from iTunes, from another online source, or import them from music CDs.

How Else Can I Get Music?

You can purchase music on your iPad only through the iTunes app. But you can sync music from your computer that you get from any source that doesn't use special copy protection, like CDs you import into iTunes. You can buy online from places such as Amazon.com, eMusic.com, cdbaby.com, or even directly from the websites of some artists.

Buying on Your iPad

In addition to syncing music to your iPad from your computer, you can purchase music, movies, TV shows, and audio books directly on your iPad using the iTunes app and using the same account that you use in iTunes on your computer.

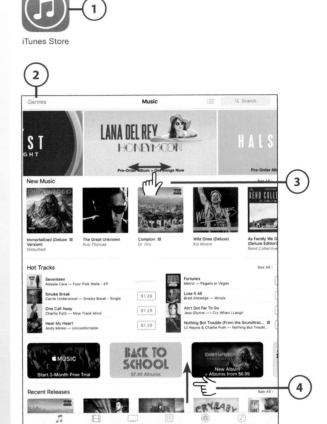

iTunes Store

1. Tap the iTunes Store app icon on your Home screen to go to the iTunes store. If this is the first time you have used the iTunes Store, you might be asked about setting up Family Sharing. See the next task for more information about this.

2. Initially, you'll be viewing a screen showing featured albums and songs from all genres. But you can select a specific genre of music instead.

3. Swipe left and right to browse more featured albums.

4. Drag the screen up to reveal more lists, such as top albums, top songs, and music videos.

5. Use the Search field at the top to search for an artist, album, or song by name.

6. Select a suggestion from the list, or tap the Search button on the keyboard to complete the search.

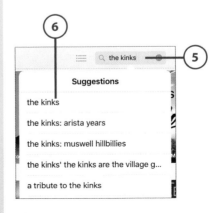

7 Find a song or album you want to buy, and tap its artwork to view more information.

8 If you move down the page by swiping upward, you'll also find ringtones, music videos, movies, and even books that match your search.

9 Tap a song name to listen to a sample of the song.

10 Tap outside the album window to close it and return to the previous view.

11 To buy a song, album, or any item in the iTunes music store, tap the price of that item, and then tap again on the Buy button.

Syncing Devices

After you make an iTunes purchase, the music, TV show, or movie you downloaded should transfer to your computer the next time you sync your iPad. From your computer, you can sync your new purchase to any other device you use that uses your iTunes account.

You can also set iTunes on your computer and your other devices to automatically download new purchases. So when you buy on your iPad, you'll get the new music everywhere. On your iPad, that setting is found in Settings, iTunes & App Store, Automatic Downloads. In iTunes on your computer, it is found in the menu iTunes, Preferences, Store, Automatic Downloads.

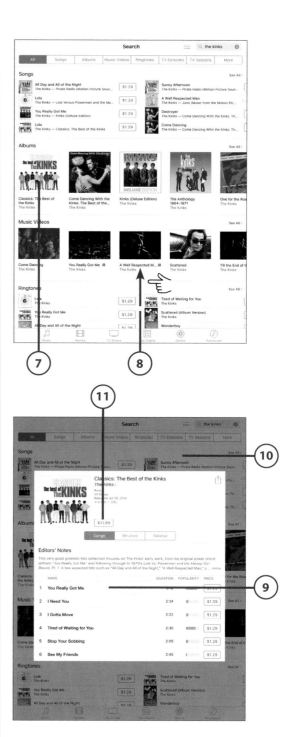

iTunes Match or Apple Music—No Syncing Needed

If you are using iTunes Match, you really don't need to worry about syncing between devices at all. All of the music you purchase will be available when you look in your Music app on iOS devices or iTunes on a Mac or PC.

If you use Apple Music, you have access to all the songs on all your devices. Your playlists and music you have marked as "My Music" would be available everywhere.

Sharing Purchases with Your Family

Family Sharing lets you share items you purchase from iTunes with other members of your household. One family member is set up as the organizer, and his or her iTunes account is the one that will be charged for all purchases.

Each member of the family sharing group can have their own Apple ID and iCloud account, which will be used for email, calendars, and other purposes. Purchases are made through the iTunes account of the organizer's Apple ID.

In addition, those who are part of your Family Sharing group will also have a shared photo stream in the Photos app, a special shared calendar in the Calendar app, a shared Reminder list in the Reminders app, and can see one another's location with the Find My Friends app.

Setting Up Family Sharing

1. The organizer should tap Settings to open her Settings app, and then tap iCloud.

2. Tap Set Up Family Sharing near the top of the iCloud settings side.

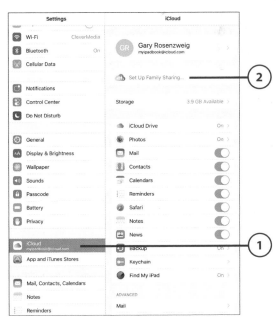

(3) Next, there is a quick series of screens telling you more about Family Sharing, asking you to read the legal agreement and to confirm your Apple ID and payment information. Tap Get Started to begin working with Family Sharing.

(4) After you complete these screens, you are now listed as the organizer for Family Sharing. You can tap your name to alter your settings.

(5) You can always turn off purchase sharing. Family Sharing can still be used for other features, such as the shared photos and calendar events.

(6) You can now tap Add Family Member to add another family member to the group.

(7) Type their Apple ID email address or choose it from your list of contacts.

(8) Tap Next.

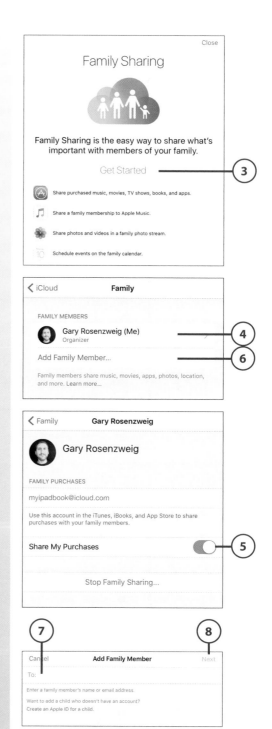

9 Tap Send an Invitation to send the invitation to the family member's iPad so they can confirm their membership in your Family Sharing group.

10 They will see a notification appear. If they tap it, they will be taken right to the Family Sharing section of the Settings app.

11 They need to tap Accept to join the group.

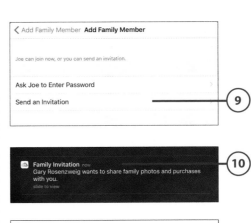

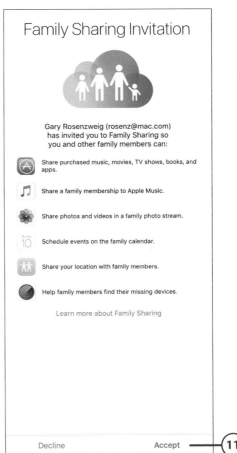

>>>*Go Further*
PARENTAL GUIDANCE

If a family member younger than 13 years old is added to your group, every time they try to make a purchase, the Family Sharing organizer will get a notification and will have to approve that purchase before it goes through. Also, children ages 13–17 can have this option turned on when they are added to Family Sharing.

The organizer can also tap on any adult family member's name in the Family Sharing settings and then flip the switch labeled Parent/Guardian to enable that adult to approve purchases made by children.

Having It All with Apple Music New!

A popular option for music lovers today is to subscribe to an unlimited music service. Apple now offers such a service, called Apple Music, which is built into the Music app on your iPad.

For a monthly fee, you can play music from a huge collection of millions of songs—nearly everything that is available in iTunes, with only a few notable exceptions, like The Beatles. You can listen to what you want, when you want, on your iPad, iPhone, and Mac. For a modest increase in the monthly fee, you can also share your music access with your family members.

Signing up for Apple Music is fairly easy, and Apple even allows you to try it for a while before you start paying for your subscription. After you are signed up, you can browse Apple Music and pick songs or whole albums to add to your collection in the Music app, and then play those songs any time you want.

Apple Music also includes a For You section that offers specially curated playlists and listening ideas based on your listening preferences and history.

Signing Up for Apple Music

You sign up for Apple Music in the Settings app.

1 In the Settings app, go to Music.

2 Tap Join Apple Music.

3 Tap the button to begin your trial period.

4 Select your plan. The Individual plan is just for you and works on all of the devices and Macs you have set up with your Apple ID. The Family plan also includes others you have set up with Family Sharing. Continue to follow the prompt to complete setup.

Cancelling

Signing up for the trial is low risk as you could always cancel your subscription before the trial period ends. Just tap on the ID button at the top of the Music app (looks like a circle with a head in it), select View Apple ID, then Manage under Subscriptions.

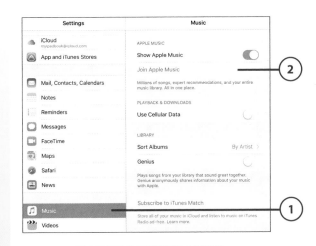

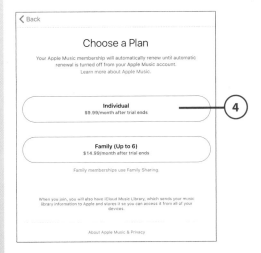

Using Apple Music

After you have signed up for Apple Music, using it is similar to playing songs you have imported from your computer or purchased from iTunes.

(1) In the Music app, tap New at the bottom of the screen. This shows you the latest music available in the service.

(2) Alternatively, you can go to For You to get recommendations based on your music collection and past listening.

(3) Use the Search button to access anything in Apple Music.

(4) Type any artist or song name to search.

(5) Make sure you select Apple Music instead of My Music. The latter only shows results you have already added to your collection.

(6) Tap the result that best matches what you are searching for.

(7) The results show artists, songs, albums, and playlists. If you see the item you want, tap it. In this case, tap an album.

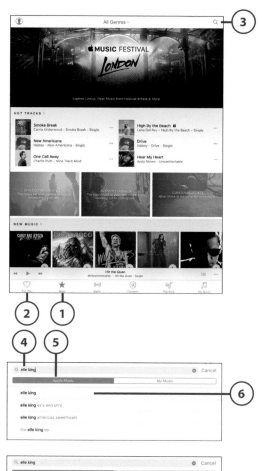

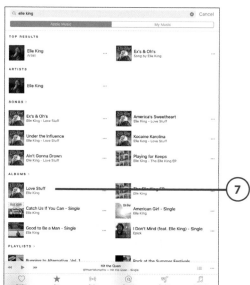

8 A plus button appears next to the album name. Tap it, and it turns into a checkmark. This indicates you have added the album to your collection. It now appears under My Music just as if you had bought it.

9 Alternatively, you can tap the … button to access some options on a per-song basis, including a + button for adding just that one song to your collection.

10 You can also just tap a song to play it immediately.

11 You may be wondering whether you can play Apple Music songs when you are not connected to the Internet. The answer is yes and no. If you tap the … button next to the album and select Make Available Offline, you will have a copy saved to your iPad to play any time. But you need to do that before you go offline, naturally. You can select this option for any song or album you have in your collection.

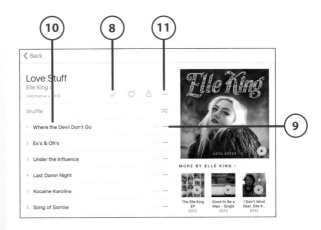

One-Time Setup

These steps are how you play music for the first time, or how to add music from Apple Music to your collection. After you do that, you can replay the songs from My Music just as if you had purchased them, as long as you remain a subscriber. You also now find these added songs on your other iOS devices and Macs.

>>>Go Further

TRY NEW THINGS

One big advantage to a subscription service like Apple Music is you can try new songs as much as you like. If you hear of a new artist, or catch a song on the radio, or hear something in a TV show, you can go to Apple Music and play the album just to see if you like it. That's not easy to do otherwise, as you would end up buying lots of albums that you only listen to once.

Listening to Podcasts

Podcasts are episodic shows, either audio or video, produced by major networks, small companies, and individuals. You'll find news, information, tutorials, music, comedy, drama, talk shows, and more. There is something covering almost any topic you can think of.

Subscribing to Podcasts

To subscribe to and listen to or watch podcasts, you use the Podcasts app from Apple.

1. Tap the Podcasts app icon on your Home screen.

2. Tap the My Podcasts button to look at the podcasts you've already downloaded. If you start off by looking at your library, you'll see an equivalent button labeled Store at the bottom left that takes you back to this screen.

3. Tap Featured to go to a screen with Apple's currently featured podcasts. Alternatively, if you know what you are looking for, you can tap the Search button at the bottom of the screen to search for a podcast by name or topic.

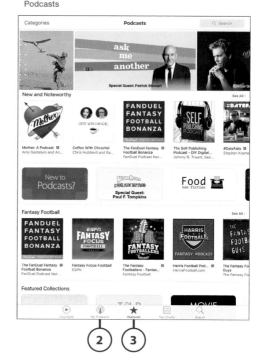

Podcasts

4 Tap a podcast to get more information about it. You can also swipe right to left to view more in the list.

5 Tap Reviews to see what others have to say.

6 Tap the Play button next to a single episode to play just that episode.

7 Tap Subscribe to subscribe to the podcast. This downloads the latest episode and also automatically gets new episodes as they become available.

8 Using the My Podcasts button from step 2, you can go to the list of podcasts you are subscribed to.

9 Tap the episode to watch or listen to it.

10 Tap the … button and select View Full Description to get more details about an episode. Other options allow you to mark it as played without listening, queue it for future play, or delete it.

11 Tap the settings button to set the sort order and auto-download preferences for the podcast. You would want a current events podcast to put the newest at the top, while a podcast that tells a story or is a learning series would be better suited for oldest on top.

12 Tap Edit to be able to delete podcast episodes from your library.

13 Tap the Edit button at the top left and then use the red buttons next to the podcast names to remove a podcast subscription.

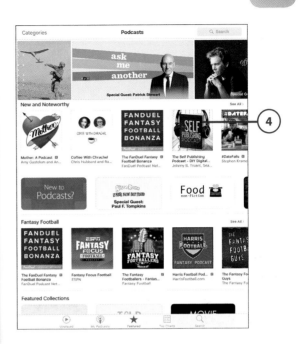

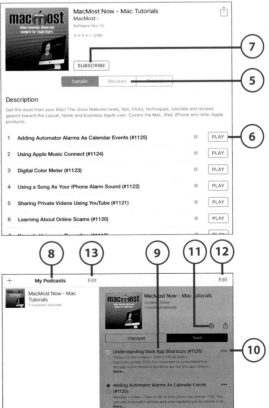

Playing Video

After you have movies, TV shows, and home videos on your iPad, you need to play them using the Videos app.

1. Tap the Videos app icon on your Home screen.

2. The Movies you have on your iPad display by default. Tap Movies, TV Shows, or Home Videos to switch lists. If you don't have videos in one or more of these categories, then that button may not appear at all. Other categories, such as Music Videos, might also appear if you have that kind of video content.

3. Tap a movie to view more information about it. Depending on the type of video, it may just start playing and you have to stop it to see the information. Movies show the information first, but Home Videos will just start playing.

4. Tap the Play button to start the movie.

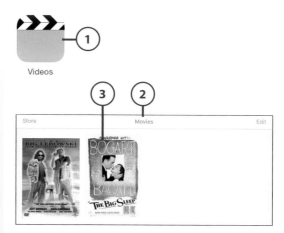

Any Video Alternatives to Apple?

You bet! There is a Netflix app for the iPad that Netflix subscribers can use to stream movies. Amazon also has an Amazon Instant Video app for subscribers to their service. Some companies, such as ABC, have also provided their own apps for viewing their shows on the iPad. You can also view video from any site that has video in standard MP4 formats. The site www.archive.org/details/movies has public domain movies and videos, often in MP4 format. The popular video site http://blip.tv also works well with the iPad.

5 After a movie is playing, tap in the middle of the screen to bring up the controls at the top and bottom of the screen.

How About My Home Videos?

If you shoot a home video with a video camera, or iPod touch or iPhone, you can bring that into iTunes on your Mac or PC and sync it to your iPad. They appear as Home Movies in the menu along the top of the Videos app.

6 Tap the Play/Pause button to pause the movie and then again to resume.

7 Adjust the volume with the volume control.

8 Drag the dot along the line to move to a different section of the movie.

9 Use the Back and Forward buttons to jump between chapters.

10 Tap the Done button to exit the movie and return to the movie information screen.

Changing the Orientation

For most video content, you can rotate your iPad to view in a horizontal orientation and use the Zoom button at the upper right to crop the left and right sides of the video so that it fits vertically on the screen. This is similar to watching a movie on a standard TV.

What About My DVDs?

If you can import CD music content into iTunes, you'd think you'd be able to import video content from your DVDs. Well, technically it is possible (although not necessarily legal) by using programs like Handbrake (http://handbrake.fr/) for your Mac or PC to import DVD content and then drag the resulting file into iTunes. You can then sync it with your iPad. These may also show up as Home Movies, since your iPad doesn't recognize them as official movie content.

>>>Go Further
BUYING AND RENTING VIDEO

Although buying video is similar to buying music, some significant details are different and worth taking a look at.

Copy Protection: Although music in the iTunes store recently became copy-protection free, videos are a different story altogether. Purchased videos can be played back only on the Apple devices you own that use your iTunes account. You can't burn videos to a DVD, for instance, or watch them on a TV unless it is hooked up to an Apple device. Rentals are even more strict because you can watch them only on the device you rent them on.

Collecting Movies: Thinking of starting a collection of videos by purchasing them from Apple? These videos take up a lot of space on your hard drive. An iPad, even a 128GB version, quickly fills up if you start adding dozens of movies. Fortunately, once you purchase a movie with iTunes, you can download it again later. So you can purchase many movies over time, but only put the ones you want to watch on your iPad. Movies you own will appear in your Videos app as well, even if they are not actually on your iPad. You will see a little iCloud download button appear next to them. You can tap that icon to start downloading that movie to your iPad from Apple's servers.

Time-Delayed Rentals: Rentals have some strict playback restrictions. After you download a rental, you have 30 days to watch it. After you start watching it, you have only 24 hours to finish it. This means you can load up your iPad in advance with a few movies to watch on an airplane flight or while on vacation.

TV Show Season Passes: You can purchase seasons of TV shows that aren't complete yet. When you do this, you are basically pre-ordering each episode. You get the existing episodes immediately but have to wait for the future episodes. They usually appear the next day after airing on network television.

Multi-Pass: In addition to season passes, you can also get a Multi-Pass, which is for TV shows that broadcast daily. When you purchase a Multi-Pass, you get the most recent episode plus the next 15 episodes when they become available.

HD Versus SD: You can purchase or rent most movies and TV shows in either HD (high definition) or SD (standard definition). Look for the HD/SD button to the right of the buy buttons on movie purchase pages. The difference is the quality of the image, which affects the file size, of course. If you have a slow connection or limited bandwidth, you might want to stick to SD versions of the shows.

Using AirPlay to Play Music and Video on Other Devices

In iTunes, with the Video app and many other apps that play music or video, you have the option to send the audio or video stream from your iPad to another device that is connected to the same Wi-Fi network, such as an Apple TV.

You need to enable AirPlay on those devices first. For instance, using the Apple TV (2nd generation models or newer), you need to go into settings on the device and turn on AirPlay. You also need to make sure that the device is using the same Wi-Fi network as your iPad.

Accessing AirPlay

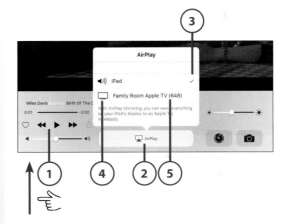

(1) While using almost any app, bring up the Control Center by swiping upward from the bottom of your screen. (See "Using Notifications and Control Center" in Chapter 1.)

(2) Tap the Airplay button to bring up a list of devices. Note that if you do not have any Airplay devices on your Wi-Fi network, you will not be able to select this.

(3) Your iPad will show as the first device. Use this to switch back to playing the media on your iPad if you have switched to something else.

(4) Next to each device, you will see either a screen icon or a speaker icon. This tells you whether you can stream video or just audio using that device.

(5) Tap on another device, and the music or video currently playing will start to play over that device.

AirPlay Everything

You can also use AirPlay to mirror your iPad's screen with an up-to-date Apple TV. In Control Center, you will see a Mirror switch appear under any video device you select. Use that to turn on mirroring and send your screen to the Apple TV. This is great for apps that do not have a specific video to present, like games or productivity apps. You'll just see your iPad's screen on the TV. Some video streaming apps, however, specifically block this.

Home Sharing

If you are using iTunes on your Mac or PC, you can play this iTunes content on your iPad if it is on the same local network.

1. In iTunes on your Mac or PC, choose Turn On Home Sharing from the File menu. You are prompted to enter your Apple account ID and password.

2. In the Settings App, tap Music.

3. Tap Sign In and enter the same Apple account ID and password used in step 1.

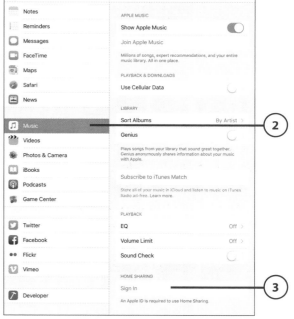

(4) In the Music app, tap the list type at the top. It usually reads Artists, Albums, Songs, or Genres.

(5) Tap Home Sharing.

(6) Then choose the name of the library you want to access. The content in your Music app changes to reflect the content in the iTunes library on your Mac or PC. You can now play songs from your computer without having to transfer them to your iPad first.

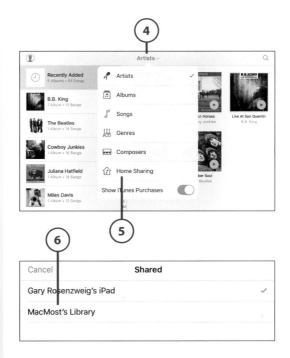

What if My Library Doesn't Appear?

Home Sharing is tricky. It requires that you use the same iTunes account IDs on both your iPad and on your Mac or PC. It also requires that you have the iPad on the same local network as your Mac or PC. In addition, network firewalls and other software may get in the way. It usually works effortlessly, but some users have reported trouble getting Home Sharing to work at all with their particular home network setup.

Listening to iTunes Radio

iTunes Radio is a streaming music service from Apple that is available in iTunes on computers and in the Music app in iOS. You choose a music genre, artist, or song, and then you hear a continuous stream of songs based on that starting point. That stream is saved as a "station," and you can return to it at any time. Meanwhile, you can create other stations with other starting points and switch between them. The music comes from Apple's servers and includes music you already own, as well as music you don't.

In addition, Apple has some specially curated station that you can enjoy as streaming radio. Plus, there is the DJ-hosted Beats 1 Apple radio station that broadcasts live 24 hours a day. You don't need to be a subscriber to Apple Music to listen to these stations.

Selecting a Station

Using iTunes Radio is very easy. You can choose from some sample stations or create your own.

(1) Tap the Radio icon at the bottom of the Music app. If this is your first time using iTunes Radio, you might get a welcome message and be prompted with a Start Listening button.

Log In

You must be signed in to your iCloud account to use iTunes Radio. You can sign in using the Settings app in the iTunes & App Stores section.

(2) The Beats 1 station is listed at the top. You can tap Listen Now to start streaming it to your iPad. If you don't like what you hear at the moment, keep in mind that Apple runs different programming all day long. So while this particular show may not be for you, one later in the day may be more appealing.

(3) You can listen to one of the Featured Stations that Apple provides. There are quite a few of them, so you have to scroll down to see them all.

4 To create your own station, browse your music and select an artist, album, or song. Look for the radio station button to the right of it and tap it. It looks like a dot with curves to the left and right.

5 It might appear that you are just playing a single song, but you can see in the scrolling description that it is "radio."

6 You can purchase the current song from iTunes.

7 Tap the star button, and you can choose Play More Like This or Play Less Like This. You don't need to do this for every song, but doing it for songs you feel especially fit your idea of this station, or don't fit in at all, helps fine-tune future songs played.

8 You can skip the current song.

9 To stop the station, tap the pause button. It changes to a play button so you can resume later.

After you have created a station, it appears as a recently played station on the main Radio screen, just above the present Apple stations in step 3.

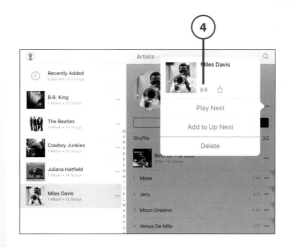

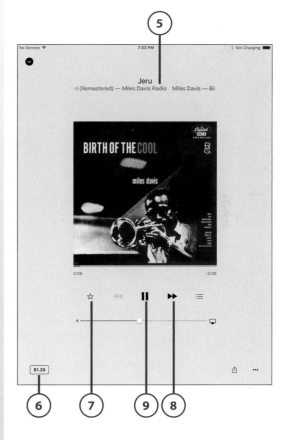

What About Bandwidth?

iTunes Radio streams music from the Internet. This means it uses bandwidth. If you are using your iPad with a mobile network or have limited bandwidth at home, that is something to be aware of. However, audio streams do not use as much as video streams, so you may be surprised at how little bandwidth an hour or so of music uses compared to watching a few YouTube videos.

And Now a Message from Our Sponsor

iTunes Radio is free, but sometimes includes commercials. Every so often you'll hear a sponsored message between songs on stations you create. Beats 1 occasionally has "sponsored by" messages. But if you have an iTunes Match account and are signed into it, as a bonus you get to listen to the station you created in iTunes Radio commercial-free!

Purchase and read
books with the iPad's
ebook reader.

In this chapter, find out how to purchase books from the iBooks store and how to read them on your iPad.

→ Buying a Book from Apple
→ Reading a Book
→ Using Reading Aids
→ Adding Notes and Highlights
→ Adding Bookmarks
→ Organizing Your Books
→ Using iBooks Alternatives

Reading Books

As an ebook reader, your iPad gives you access to novels, textbooks, and more, storing hundreds inside. Plus, you can purchase more books right from the iPad.

A single app, the iBooks app, allows you to both read and purchase new books. You can also download and add books from other sources, including the Kindle app.

Buying a Book from Apple

The first thing to do with the iBooks app is to get some books! You can buy books using the store in the app. You can also find some free books there.

1. Tap the iBooks app icon to launch iBooks.

2. If you have previously purchased and downloaded books, you see those when iBooks opens.

3. Tap one of the buttons such as Featured, NYTimes, Top Charts, or Top Authors to switch to the iBooks store.

Don't Want to Purchase from Apple?

You don't necessarily need to buy books from Apple. You can buy from any seller that sends you an ePub or PDF formatted file with no copy protection. If you receive the file on a computer, just drag and drop it into iTunes. It will add it to your books collection there, ready to be synced to your iPad.

You can also add PDFs you find on the web or receive in email to your iBooks library. While viewing a PDF on your iPad in Safari, tap once in the middle of the screen, and an Open in iBooks option appears at the top. While viewing a PDF attached to an email message, you can use the Share button to open it in iBooks. Many other third-party apps also allow sharing PDFs to iBooks this way. Text and ePub-formatted documents often work as well. When you open a document in iBooks, a copy is placed in your iBooks library.

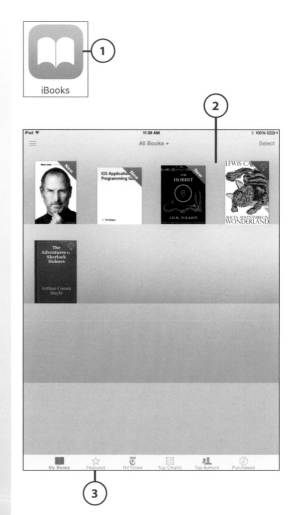

4 Swipe left and right to browse more featured books.

5 Tap the Categories button to go to a list of book categories.

6 Tap Top Charts button to see a list of bestsellers.

7 Swipe up to see more featured categories.

8 Use the search field to search for book titles and authors.

9 Tap any book cover to view more information about the book.

10 Tap the price next to a book to purchase it. The price button changes to Buy Book. Tap it again to continue with the purchase.

11 Tap the Sample button to download a sample of the book.

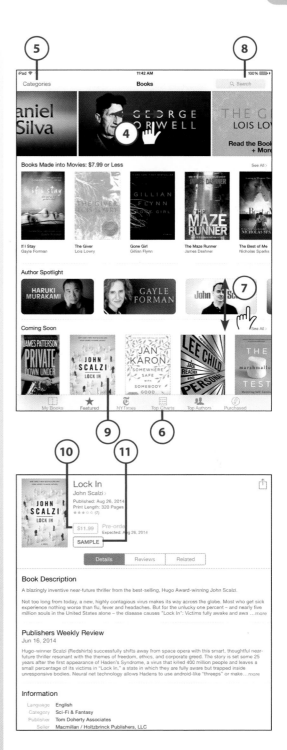

Reading a Book

Reading books is a simple process. Following are the basics of reading your downloaded books.

(1) Tap the iBooks app icon to launch iBooks.

(2) If you are still in the store section of the app, tap My Books at the bottom to go to your iBooks library. Then, tap a book to open it.

Can't Find Your Book?

Did you download a book only to discover that you can't see it in your Library? Try tapping the Collections button at the top of the screen and switching to a different collection. For instance, by default, PDF documents are put in the PDF collection, not in the Books collection.

(3) To turn a page, tap and hold anywhere along the right side of the page, and drag to the left. A virtual page turns.

(4) Tap and drag from the left to the right or simply tap the left side of the page to turn the page back.

(5) To move quickly through pages, tap and drag the small marker at the bottom of the page along the dotted line. Release to jump to a page.

(6) Tap the Table of Contents button at the top to view a table of contents.

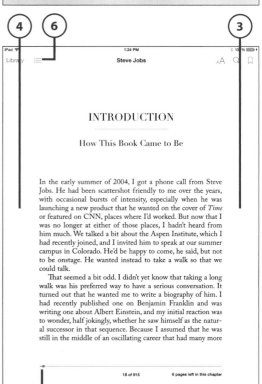

7 Tap anywhere in the table of contents to jump to that part of the book.

8 Tap the Resume button to return to the page you were previously viewing.

9 Tap the Library button to return to your books. If you return to the book later, you return to the last page you viewed. No need to stick a bookmark or piece of scrap paper into your iPad.

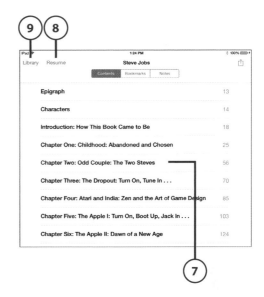

Using Reading Aids

iBooks has a variety of ways you can customize your reading experience. You can change the font size, the font itself, and even turn your iPad on its side to see two pages at one time.

1 While viewing a page in iBooks, tap the display adjustment controls at the top of the screen. If you don't see the controls, tap once in the middle of the screen to bring them up.

2 Drag the brightness control left or right. Dragging to the left makes the screen dim, which you might use if you're reading in a dark room. Dragging to the right makes it bright, which could make reading easier while outdoors.

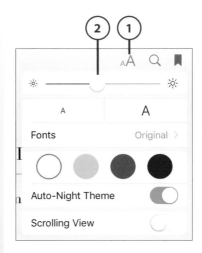

3 Tap the smaller "A" button to reduce the size of the text.

4 Tap the larger "A" button to increase the size of the text.

5 Tap the Fonts button to choose from a few font options.

6 Tap to select one of four color themes.

7 The Auto-Night Theme switch monitors the light around your iPad and switches to Night mode when it is dark.

8 Turn on Scrolling View to read your book as one long scrolling page.

9 Turn your iPad on its side to change to a two-page view. (Make sure your orientation lock is not on.)

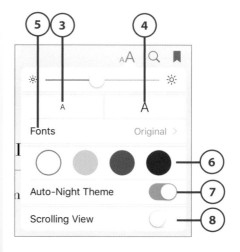

Where Did the Buttons Go?

If you tap in the middle of the screen, the buttons at the top and the dotted line at the bottom disappear. You can still turn the pages; you just don't have access to these buttons. To see the buttons again, tap in the middle of the screen.

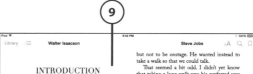

Adding Notes and Highlights

Each time you launch iBooks, your iPad returns you to the page you were last reading. However, you might want to mark a favorite passage or a bit of key information.

(1) Go to a page in a book in iBooks. (See the previous tasks in this chapter to find out how to access a book.)

(2) Tap a word and hold your finger there for about a second.

(3) Release your finger and you see six choices: Copy, Define, Highlight, Note, Search, and Share.

Define, Search, and Share

Tapping Define brings up a definition of the word. Tapping Search brings up a list of the locations of the word throughout the text. When you choose Share, you can send the excerpt you have selected to someone else using email, a text message, Twitter, or Facebook.

(4) Drag the blue dots to enlarge the section of text that is highlighted.

(5) Tap Highlight. Alternatively, you can tap a word and hold for a second and then immediately start dragging to highlight text.

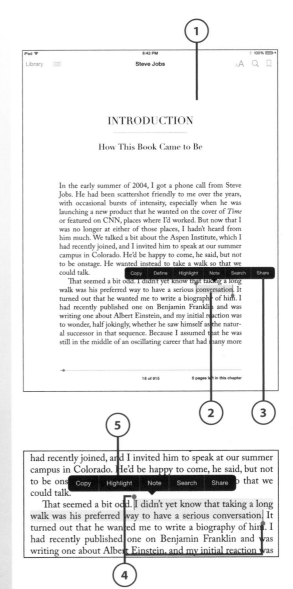

(6) The text is now highlighted.

(7) Tap the first button to change the type of highlighting. You can choose from various colors or a simple red underline.

(8) Tap the second button to remove the highlight completely.

(9) Tap Note instead of Highlight to bring up a yellow pad of paper and add a note.

(10) Tap in the note to bring up the keyboard and start typing.

(11) Tap outside the yellow paper to finish the note. It will then appear as a small yellow sticky note to the right side of the page. Tap it any time you want to view or edit the note. You can delete a note by removing all text in the note.

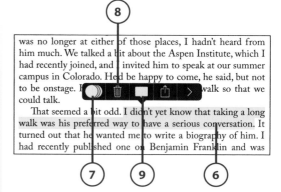

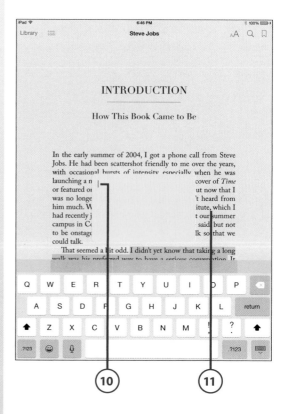

Adding Bookmarks

You can also bookmark a page to easily find it later.

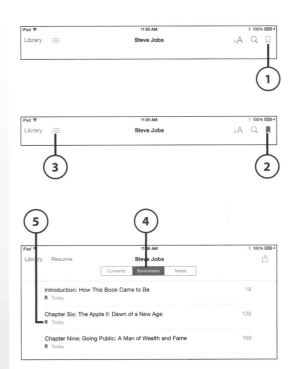

1. Tap the bookmark button at the top of a page to bookmark the page. You can bookmark as many pages as you want in a book. If you don't see the bookmarks button, tap once in the center of the screen to bring up the controls.

2. Tap it again to remove the bookmark from the page.

3. Tap the Table of Contents button to go to the table of contents.

4. Tap the Bookmarks button at the top of the table of contents to see a list of all the bookmarks, highlights, and notes you have added to the book.

5. Tap any bookmark, note, or highlight to jump to it.

Organizing Your Books

Like to read a lot? You aren't alone. Many people gather massive collections of ebooks on their iPads. Fortunately, iBooks includes a few great ways to organize your ebooks.

1 If you are on the iBook store screen, tap My Books to view your library. If you are viewing a book, tap Library in the upper-left corner to return to the book library.

2 The heading at the top of the screen shows which collection you are viewing. Tap it to see a list of collections.

3 Tap a Collection name to jump to that collection. You can think of collections as different bookcases filled with books.

4 Tap New Collection to create a new collection.

5 The New Collection option changes to an editable text field, and the keyboard appears. Type the name of the new collection.

6 The Collections list now features your new collection. Tap Done. If you ever want to delete or rearrange collections, the Edit button at the top of this list allows you to do that.

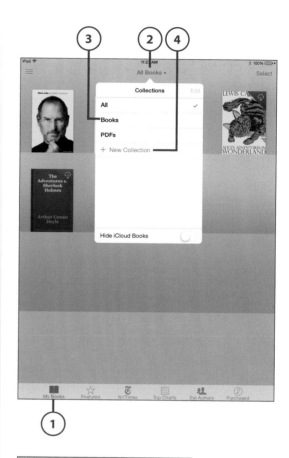

Books in the Cloud

When you view your Purchased Books collection, you will see all the books you have bought in the past, even if that book is no longer on your iPad because you removed it. These books will have a little iCloud icon in the upper-right corner; when you select one, it will download. If you then delete the book, you can always re-download it by tapping on the Purchased button at the bottom of the Collections screens, selecting Not on This iPad from the top, and tapping the download button next to that book.

7 The new collection doesn't have any books in it yet, so selecting it now only brings up a blank list. Instead, tap on All or Books to return to your list of books.

8 After you have returned to your list of books, tap Select to start selecting books to move to the new collection.

9 Tap on several books to select them. You'll see a checkmark appear in the bottom-right corner of each book.

10 Tap Move. (While in this mode, you can also tap Delete, which removes the books from your iPad.)

11 Tap the name of your new collection to move your books there.

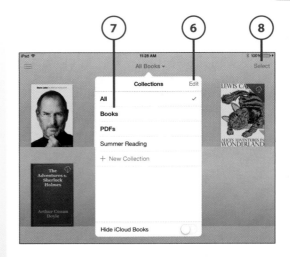

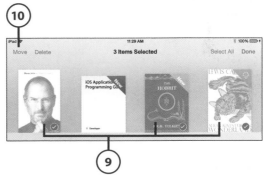

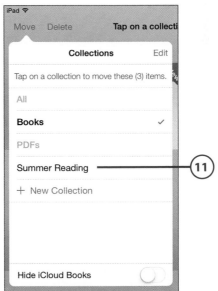

(12) Bring up the Collections list again and switch to your new collection.

(13) The books you selected to move will now appear here.

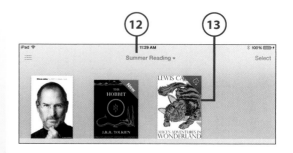

(14) To re-arrange your books inside a collection, tap and hold any book. The book's picture will get a little larger and start to follow your finger. Drag it around on the screen and release to place it before or after another book.

(15) Tap the button at the top left to switch to list view.

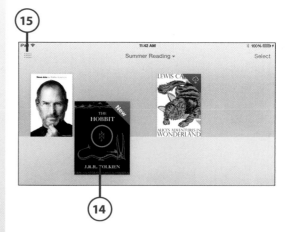

(16) The list view allows you to sort your books by author or category.

(17) Tap the button at the top left to return to the bookshelf view.

Another Way to Delete

You can also delete books in list view by swiping from left to right across the title of a book. A Delete button appears to the right. Tap it to delete the book.

Using iBooks Alternatives

You can purchase and read books from other sources in addition to Apple. The Kindle app allows you to buy books from Amazon.com, or read ones you have already purchased on a previous device. You can also find many small independent publishers and authors in Amazon's catalog that aren't available in iBooks.

You can use the App Store app to search for and install the free Kindle app. See "Purchasing an App" in Chapter 10 to learn how to get third-party apps.

(1) Tap the Kindle icon to launch the Kindle app. You see a screen that displays your library. There are two modes: Cloud and Device. Cloud shows all ebooks you have purchased from Amazon. Device shows the books you have already downloaded onto your device.

(2) Tap a book to open it.

3 Tap the middle of the page to bring up controls at the top and bottom.

4 Tap the Font button to change the font size, brightness, and background.

5 Tap the right side to flip to the next page.

6 Use the slider at the bottom to quickly move to other pages in the book.

7 The button at the top left allows you to jump to chapters or sections.

8 You can add your own bookmarks just like in iBooks.

9 Tap the Search button to search text in the book.

Cloud Versus Device

The Kindle app has a Cloud/Device control at the bottom of the screen. You can tap on a book on the Cloud screen to download it to your device. You can tap on it again, after it has been downloaded, to read it.

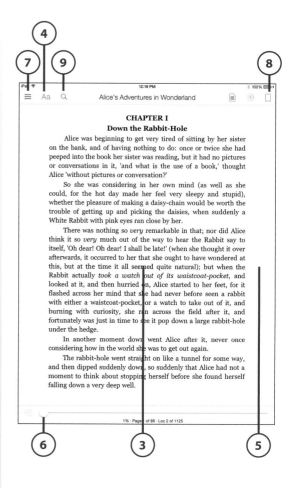

More eBook Alternatives

If you like to buy your books from Barnes & Noble, you can also get the Nook app. This lets you read books that can be purchased in the Nook store. If you own a Nook and have already bought books, you can access those books and load them onto your iPad.

Another App you can get is the Google Play Books app. This works with books purchased in the Google Play store, which is similar to the Amazon Kindle store or the iBookstore. You can choose whether you want to buy from Apple, Amazon, Barnes & Noble, or Google.

Free Books

You can fill your iBooks library with free books from many sources. Tap on Top Charts in iBooks, and you see the top free books in the list on the right. As you search, you also see many books with a GET button instead of a price. These are also free. Another source of free books is the website www.gutenberg.org—the books are in the public domain, and you can download them for free. After selecting a book, pick the EPUB format download. Safari actually gives you an option to Open in iBooks. Select that option to add the free book to your iBooks library.

Track your
appointments
and events.

Store and
search
all your
contacts.

Take notes and
create lists.

Set reminders.

In this chapter, we learn how to add and look up contacts and calendar events. We also look at the Notes and Reminders apps.

→ Adding a Contact

→ Searching for a Contact

→ Working with Contacts

→ Creating a Calendar Event

→ Using Calendar Views

→ Creating Calendars

→ Creating Notes

→ Creating Checklists in Notes

→ Adding Photos and Sketches to Notes

→ Setting Reminders

→ Setting Clock Alarms

Organizing Your Life

Whether you are a well-connected businessperson or just someone who has lots of friends, you can use the iPad to organize your life with the default Contacts, Calendar, Notes, and Reminders apps. Let's take a close look at some of the things you can do with these apps.

Using the Contacts App

The primary way iPad users store their contacts is to use Apple's iCloud service. This places your contacts database on Apple's servers, making them available to you on any iOS device or Mac you use. You can even access them from a PC with Apple's iCloud.com website. It also keeps all these devices in sync; so any time you add or edit a contact, the change will show up everywhere. The Contacts app on your iPad is how you access and modify your contacts.

Adding a Contact

Let's start by adding a new contact from scratch.

Contacts

(1) Tap the Contacts app icon to launch the app.

(2) Press the + button near the top of the screen. A New Contact form and keyboard appear.

(3) Type the first name of the contact. No need to use Shift to capitalize the name because that happens automatically.

(4) Tap the return key on the keyboard to advance to the next field and type the last name for the contact. If you are adding a company instead of a person, skip the first and last name fields and use only the Company field. The contact will be listed under the company name.

(5) To add more information, like a phone number, tap the green + button next to the field name.

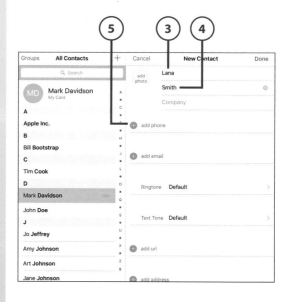

6 Type the phone number.

7 If you ever want to remove some information from the contact, you can use the red – buttons.

8 You can add more than one phone number per contact. Some contacts may have many: home, work, mobile, and so on.

9 Tap Add Photo to add a photo from one of your photo albums or take one right now using your iPad's camera.

Don't Worry About Formatting

You don't need to type phone numbers with parentheses or dashes. Your iPad formats the number for you.

10 You can add one or more email addresses to the contact as well. These will be used in your Mail app when you compose a new message. You will only need to type the person's name, or choose them from a list, instead of typing their email address.

11 You can add one or more physical addresses for the contact.

12 You can select a specific ringtone for the contact that is used when they call you via FaceTime. You can also set a specific Text tone for Messages.

13 You can swipe up to see more fields. You can even add custom fields and notes to a contact.

14 Tap the Done button to finish.

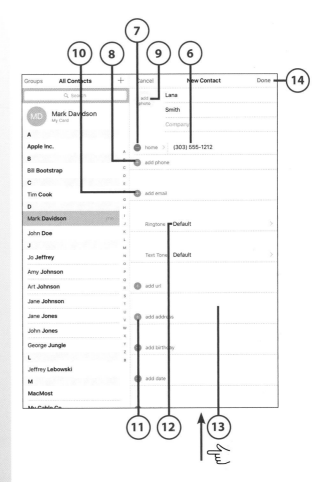

Siri: Call Me Ray

You can set a nickname field in a contact. When you do this, and the contact happens to be yours, Siri will call you by that name. You can also tell Siri: "Call me *name*" and it will change your nickname field even if you are not in the Contacts app at the moment.

You can also set relationships in your contacts by saying things like "Debby is my wife."

Searching for a Contact

If you didn't have a lot of friends before, I'm sure you gained quite a few since you got a new iPad. So how do you search through all those contacts to find the one you want?

(1) Tap the Contacts app icon to launch the app.

(2) Tap in the Search field. A keyboard appears at the bottom of the screen.

Other Ways to Find Contacts

You can also drag (or flick to move quickly) through the contact list to find a name. In addition, the list of letters on the left side of the Contacts app enables you to jump right to that letter in your contacts list.

Siri: Show Me

You can also use Siri to find a contact. Try these phrases:

"Show me John Smith."
"Show me my contact."
"Show me my wife."

3 Start typing the name of the person you are looking for. As soon as you start typing, the app starts making a list of contacts that contain the letters you've typed. Keep typing until you narrow down the list of names and spot the one you are looking for.

4 Tap the name to bring up the contact.

5 Tap the Cancel button to dismiss the search.

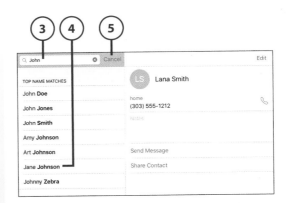

Working with Contacts

After you have contacts in your iPad, you can do a few things from a contact in the Contacts app.

1 Tap and hold the name to copy it to the clipboard buffer.

2 Tap and hold the phone number to copy it to the clipboard buffer.

3 Tap the phone icon to call the number. Tap the message button to send a text message to the contact using that phone number. You can also tap Send Message near the bottom of the contact. See "Conversing with Messages" in Chapter 8.

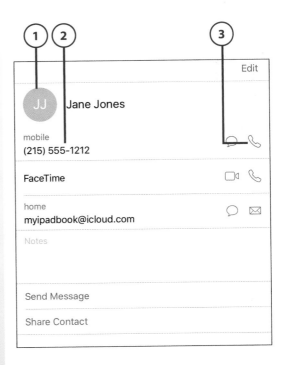

4. Tap the FaceTime button to start a video chat with the user, providing they are also on an iOS device (or a Mac) and have set up FaceTime. You can start a FaceTime video call, or tap the phone-like button for an audio-only call.

5. Tap the email address to start composing a new email in the Mail app.

6. Tap to the right of Notes to add more information without entering Edit mode.

7. Tap Share Contact to send the contact information via a text message, email, or using AirDrop.

8. Tap Edit to enter Edit mode, which gives you the same basic functionality as entering a new contact.

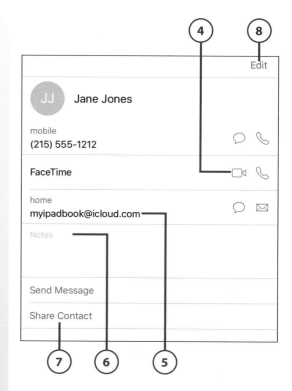

Using the Calendar App

Now that you have people in your Contacts app, you need to schedule some things to do with them.

Calendars, like contacts, are stored using Apple's iCloud service. So, your calendars will sync over the Internet to your other iOS devices and even your Mac, as long as you use the same iCloud account for each device.

Let's look at some things you can do with the Calendar app.

Creating a Calendar Event

Calendar

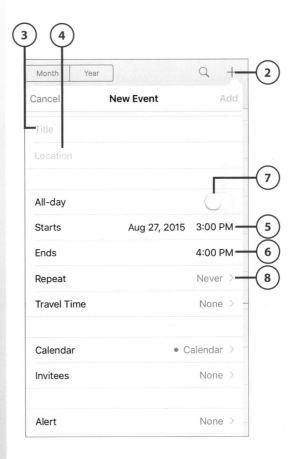

1. Tap the Calendar app icon on the Home screen.

2. Tap the + button at the upper right.

3. Enter a title for the event.

4. Enter a Location for the event, or skip this field.

5. Tap the Starts field to bring up a control for setting the starting time.

6. Tap the Ends field to bring up a control for setting the ending time for the event.

7. If the event covers the entire day, or a series of days, then slide the All-day switch on. The Starts and Ends fields will now be dates only, and won't include a specific time.

8. Tap Repeat to set an event to repeat every day, week, 2 weeks, month, or year.

9 Tap Invitees to send an email invitation to another person for this event, if your calendar system allows this. If you and the other person are both using iCloud, they will get a notification of the event and have the option to accept or decline. If they accept, the event will be added to their calendar. You will then be able to look at your event's invitation list in this same location and see if they have accepted or declined.

10 Tap Alert to set the time for a notification alert to appear. This can be at the time of the event, or before the event, such as 5 minutes, 15 minutes, or even as much as a week before.

11 In addition, if you set Travel Time, your alert will be adjusted so you have enough time to get to the event's location.

12 Tap Add to complete the event.

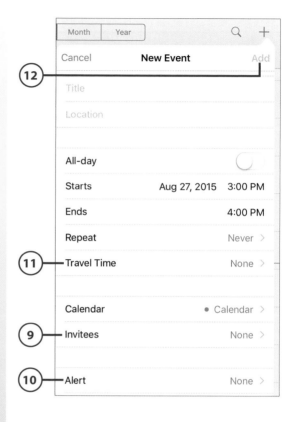

Siri: Creating Events

You can use Siri to create new events even when the Calendar app is not on your screen.

"Schedule a doctor appointment for 3 PM next Wednesday."
"Set up a meeting with John tomorrow at noon."
"Cancel my dentist appointment."

Deleting Events

To delete an event, scroll to the bottom of the event information while editing it to reveal a Delete Event button. This button also appears when you tap the event in any of the Calendar views. There is no real need to delete past events from your calendar—they take up almost no space and could be useful as a record of your past appointments.

Using Calendar Views

There are three main ways to view your calendar: Day, Week, and Month. Let's take a look at each.

Exploring Day View

The Day view is broken into two halves: the left side shows a timeline from morning until evening. Events are shown as blocks of color in this vertical timeline. The right side shows information for the event selected, if any.

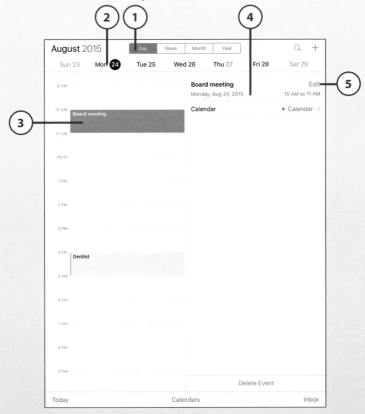

1. Tap Day to enter Day view mode.
2. You can tap any day shown at the top to jump to the list of events for that day. You can also drag left and right here to see previous days and upcoming ones.
3. Tap any event shown to view information about that event.
4. The information appears on the right.
5. You can tap Edit to edit that event and change any aspect of it, or delete it.

6 You can drag up and down to view the entire day.

7 Tap Today to jump to the current day, in case you have moved to another day and want to return quickly.

8 Tap Calendars to select which calendars are shown. This is useful if you have set up multiple calendars in iCloud, or have subscribed to public calendars.

9 Tap Inbox to view any invitations you may have received via email or messages. You can accept or reject them. Accepted invitations will be added to your calendar.

10 Tap + to add a new event.

Year View

There is also a Year view, as you may have already noticed since there is a Year button at the top of the screen. This shows you 12 very small monthly calendars, with colored-in spaces on days where you have events. You can use this view to quickly navigate to an event in a different week or month. Or, you can use it to see when the days fall in the week.

Exploring Week View

To get a view of all the events for the week, switch to Week view. This gives you seven days across, but less space to preview each event. You can still select and edit events.

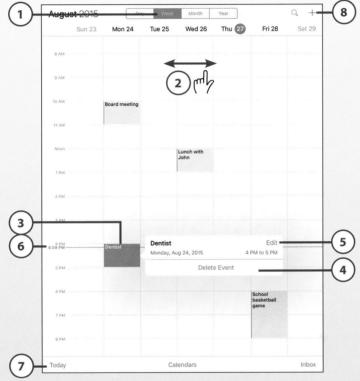

1. Tap Week to go to the Week view.

2. You can move to the previous week or the next by tapping and dragging in any blank part of the calendar. You can also drag vertically to see earlier in the morning or later in the evening.

3. Tap an event to view more information about it.

4. The information appears in a box to the left or right of the event.

5. You can tap Edit to edit the event right here. The familiar editing interface will appear in an expanded box while you remain in the Week view.

6. You can see the current time represented by a red line.

7. Tap Today if you have navigated away from the current week and want to get back.

8. Tap + to add a new event while remaining in Week view.

Exploring Month View

To see the "big picture," you may want to use Month view. This gives you a grid of seven days across and six or more weeks vertically. While this view is similar to a monthly calendar, it doesn't necessarily have to show a single month. It can be used to show any group of six consecutive weeks.

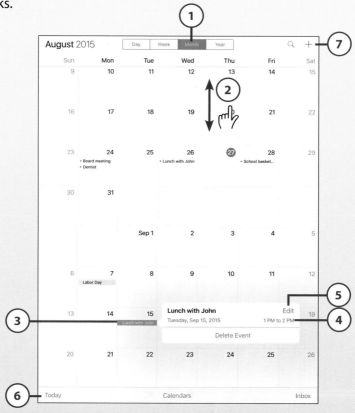

1. Tap Month to enter Month view.

2. While in Month view, you can tap and drag in blank areas to scroll up and down.

3. Tap an event to view more information.

4. The information appears in a box, like in Week view.

5. Tap Edit to edit the information right here in Month view. The editing interface will appear inside an enlarged box.

6. Tap Today to return to the current day if you have scrolled away from it.

7. Tap + to add a new event right here in Month view.

Siri: Checking Your Schedule

You can use Siri to see what events you have coming up.

"What do I have going on tomorrow?"
"What is on my calendar for this week?"
"When is my dentist appointment?"

Creating a Calendar

You may have noticed in the previous tasks that you can select a calendar when you create an event. You can create multiple calendars to organize your events. For instance, you may want to have one for work and one for home.

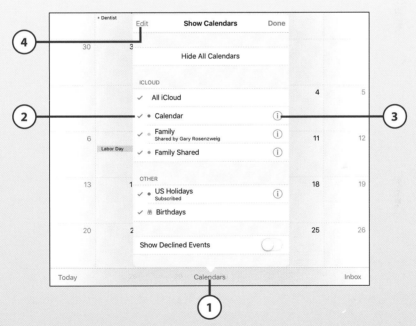

1. From any calendar view, tap the Calendars button at the bottom center.

2. You can scroll up and down this list and disable or enable calendars by tapping on the checkmarks. A calendar without a checkmark is hidden and won't appear in your views.

3. You can also view and change information about a calendar, such as changing the color used as a background for events. You can also share calendars with other iCloud users.

4. Tap Edit to go into editing mode.

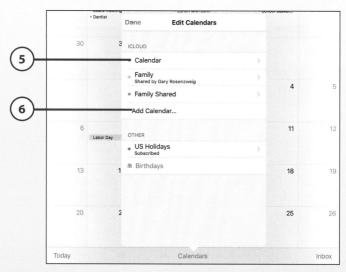

(5) In Editing mode, you can also select calendars to change their color and which other people they are shared with.

(6) Tap Add Calendar to create a new calendar.

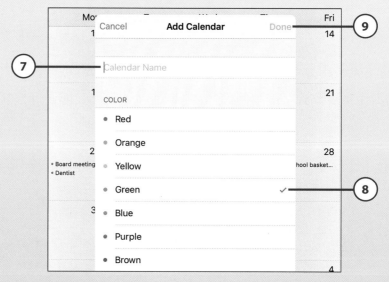

(7) Give the new Calendar a name.

(8) Set the color for the calendar.

(9) Tap Done.

Deleting a Calendar

You can delete a calendar by following the previous steps 1–4 and then selecting a calendar to edit. Scroll to the bottom below the list of colors and choose Delete Calendar.

Default Calendar

Which calendar will be used when you create a new event? The default calendar is a setting you can find in the Settings app, under Mail, Contacts, Calendars, way near the bottom of the list of preferences on the right.

>>>*Go Further*

SHARING CALENDARS

When you edit a calendar's information, you can also use the Add Person button that appears above the list of colors to share a calendar with a specific iCloud user. Below the colors list, you can choose to set the calendar to "public" and then share an Internet link that others can use to subscribe. For instance, you can create a schedule for your soft-ball team and make it public, and then put a link to the calendar on the team's website. Anyone can subscribe to this calendar, but only to view it. By default, others can edit it, but you can turn off Allow Editing by tapping the i button for the calendar, and then View & Edit next to the person's name with whom you are sharing it.

Using the Notes App

Another organization app that comes with your iPad is the Notes app. Although this one is much more free-form than a Contacts or Calendar app, it can be useful for keeping quick notes or to-do lists.

Creating a Note

① Tap the Notes icon on your Home screen.

② Notes opens up the note you were previously working on. To type, tap on the screen where you want the insertion point, and a keyboard appears.

What's in a Name

The filename for a note is just the first line of the note, so get in the habit of putting the title of a note as the first line of text to make finding the note easier.

③ To start a new note, tap the Compose button at the upper right.

④ To view a list of all your notes, and to jump to another note, tap the Notes button.

⑤ Tap the name of the note you want to switch to.

⑥ Tap and type in the Search field to find text inside of notes. If you don't see the Search field, tap and drag down on the list of notes to reveal it just above the first note in the list.

Notes

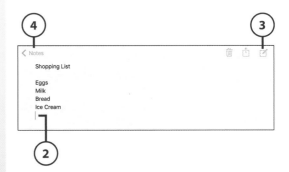

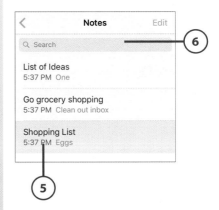

(7) Turn your iPad to horizontal
orientation, and you'll have a per-
manent list of notes on the left. In
this view, you don't need to tap
Notes, as you did in step 4, to see
the list.

(8) Tap the Trash button at the top-
right of the screen to delete the
note you are viewing.

(9) Tap the Share button at the
top-right of the screen to share
the note in a number of ways.
For instance, you can start a new
email message in the Mail app
using the contents of the note, or
print the note using AirPrint.

Notes Isn't a Word Processor

You can't actually use Notes for serious writing. There are only basic styles and no
formatting choices. You can't even change the display font to make it larger. If you
need to use your iPad for writing, consider Pages or a third-party word processing app.
If you want to make some text bold, italic, or underlined, you can tap and hold a word,
adjust the selection, and use the **B**/U button next to Cut, Copy, and Paste to apply a
simple style to the selection.

Notes in the Cloud

Notes are stored on Apple's iCloud server, just like calendar events and contacts. If
you are using the same iCloud account on your Mac, for instance, you should see
the notes appear almost instantly on your Mac, synced through iCloud. They will
also appear on your other iOS devices.

Creating Checklists in Notes New!

You can already see that Notes is useful for creating lists. Apple has built in a list function to make it even easier to use in this way.

(1) Start a new note, or continue typing in an existing one.

(2) Tap the checklist button when you want to start a list. You can have text before and after the list, it doesn't have to be at the top of the note or the only thing in the note.

(3) You'll see an empty circle appear on the line you are typing.

(4) Type the first item in the list.

(5) Hit Return on the on-screen keyboard and you can continue entering more items, each with an empty circle to its left.

(6) Tap the checklist button again when you want to resume typing normal non-list text.

(7) You can tap any empty circle in the list to fill it with a checkmark.

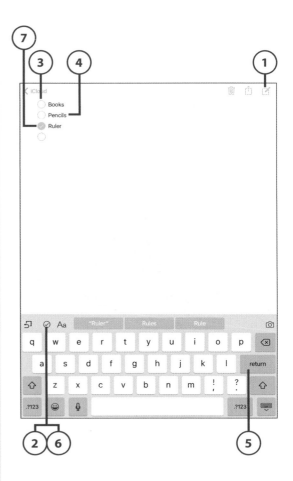

Notes vs. Reminders

Checklists in Notes are good for things like shopping lists, packing lists, party invitation lists, and so on. For to-do lists, use the Reminders app, which we will look at later in this chapter.

Adding Photos and Sketches to Notes New!

You can also insert photos from your photo library into notes, take photos with the camera, or draw sketches with your finger to include in your notes.

(1) Create a new note or use an existing one. Photos and sketches can co-exist with other text in any note.

(2) Position the cursor where you want to insert the photo or sketch.

(3) Tap the Photo button to choose a photo from your library, or take one with the camera. It is the same way you insert a photo into an email message or text message. You are asked to choose a photo from your library or shown the camera interface to take a picture.

(4) Tap the sketch button to enter the sketching screen.

(5) On this screen, you can draw anything you like using a few simple tools. Select the pen, marker, or pencil tool at the bottom.

(6) Select a color. You can swipe from left to right across the colors to see two more sets of colors.

(7) Tap and drag your finger to draw.

(8) The eraser tool enables you to clear marks you have made.

(9) You can use the undo and redo buttons to help draw.

(10) When you are done, tap Done to return to the note.

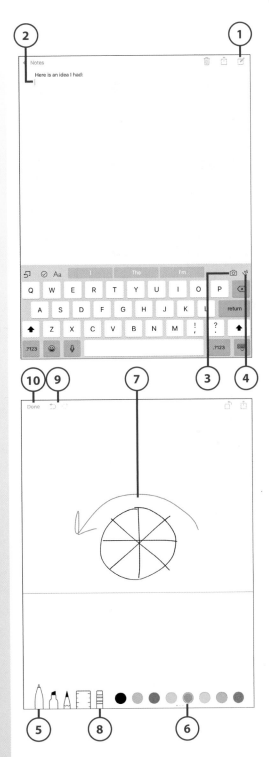

(11) The sketch appears in your note. Tap it to return to the sketch screen to edit it. If you tap and hold the sketch instead, you get Cut, Copy, Delete, and Share options.

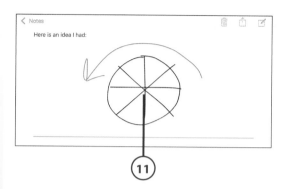

Multiple Sketches

You can add more than one sketch to a note. If you need to move a sketch to a different location in your note, or to a different note, tap and hold the sketch until you get the options menu. Then use Cut to remove it and later use Paste to place it elsewhere.

It's Not All Good

Don't See the Photo or Sketch Buttons?

These buttons only appear on more recent iPad models and only if your notes are being stored in the latest version of iCloud notes. For instance, if you share your notes with a Mac using an older version of OS X, or an iPhone using an older version of iOS, then you can't create sketches in your notes because they are not compatible with the Notes app on those other devices.

Using the Reminders App

Reminders is a to-do list application available on iPad, iPod touch, iPhone, and Macs. This app is for creating an ongoing list of tasks you need to accomplish or things you need to remember. These reminders can be similar to calendar events with times and alarms. Or, they can be simple items in a list with no time attached to them.

Setting a Reminder

(**1**) Tap the Reminders icon on your Home screen.

(**2**) Select the list you want to add a new Reminder to.

(**3**) Tap in a new line to create a new reminder.

(**4**) Type the reminder and close the keyboard when done.

(**5**) Tap the i button next to the reminder to bring up the Details dialog. If you don't see an i button, then tap any reminder item first.

(**6**) Tap here to edit the reminder.

(**7**) Slide the Remind me on a day switch to on to set a reminder alert.

(**8**) Set a time for the alert to occur.

(**9**) Add a note to the reminder if you want to include more details.

(**10**) Tap outside of the Details box when you are finished editing the reminder.

Siri: Remind Me

You can create new reminders using Siri like this:

"Remind me to watch Doctor Who tonight at 8 PM."
"Remind me to pick up milk when I leave work."
"Remind me to check my stocks every day at 9 AM."

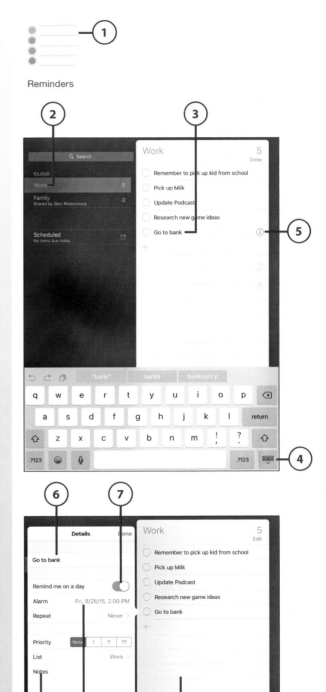

11 Tap the button next to the reminder when you have completed the task. It will remain in the list temporarily.

12 Tap Add List to add a new reminders list.

13 Tap Show Completed to see completed reminders.

14 You can also search for reminders by typing the title or something from the content.

15 Tap Edit to remove reminders.

16 Tap the red button next to a reminder to delete it.

17 Tap and drag the right side of the reminders to re-order them.

18 Tap Done when you are finished deleting and re-ordering the reminders.

19 You can also delete the entire list before leaving editing mode.

20 You can also share a Reminders list with another iCloud user before leaving editing mode. Tap Sharing, and you can add one or more people from your contacts or manually add people with their Apple ID. Shared Reminders lists will sync items to all people sharing it.

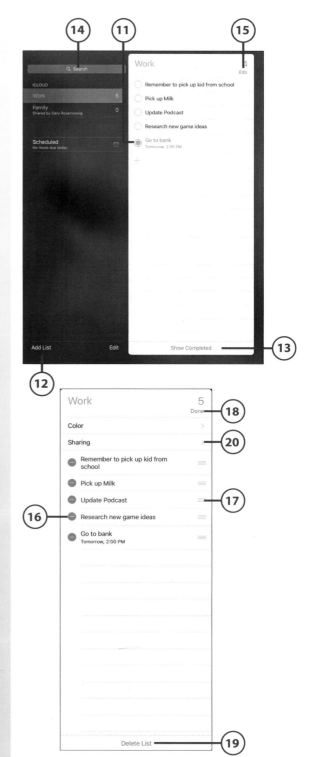

iCloud

Reminders sync by using the iCloud service from Apple. So, they are automatically backed up and should also appear on your Mac in the Reminders app, if you have OS X 10.8 Mountain Lion or newer. And if you use an iPhone, they should appear there as well.

Using the Clocks App

The advantage of using an alarm rather than a reminder is that an often-recurring alarm, like your morning wake-up call, or a reminder on when to pick up your child at school, won't clutter up your Reminders list or calendar.

Setting Clock Alarms

1 Tap the Clock app.

2 The main screen shows up to six clocks in any time zone you want. Tap a clock to have it fill the screen.

3 Tap an empty clock to add a new city.

4 Tap Edit to remove or rearrange the clocks.

5 Tap Alarm to view and edit alarms.

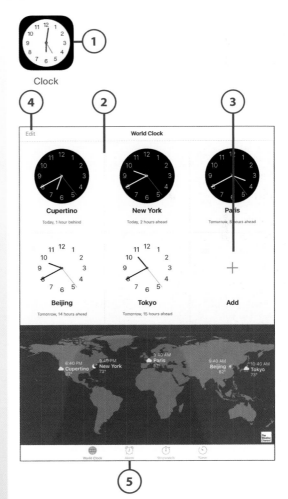

6 To add a new alarm, tap the + button.

7 Select a time for the alarm.

8 Select the days of the week for the alarm. Leaving it set to Never means you just want the alarm to be used once, as you might do if setting an alarm to wake you up early so you can catch a plane the next day. Otherwise, you can select from seven days of the week. So, you can set an alarm for Monday through Friday and leave out the weekend.

9 Tap Label to give the alarm a custom name.

10 Select a sound for the alarm. You can choose from preset sounds or your ringtone collection.

11 Leave the Snooze switch on if you want the ability to use snooze when the alarm goes off.

12 Tap Save to save all your settings and add the alarm.

13 The alarm now appears in the special Clock calendar. This alarm was set for Monday, Tuesday, Thursday, and Friday, so only those four days are indicated.

14 You can switch off the alarm, while leaving it in the calendar for future use.

15 Tap Edit on an alarm to edit or delete it.

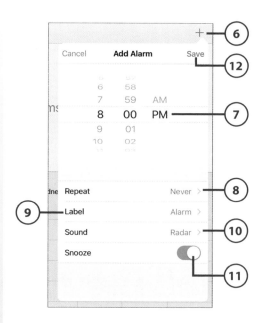

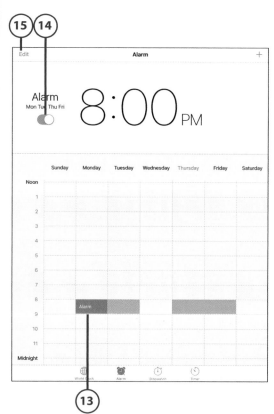

16 The alarm will sound and a message will appear when it is time. This will appear as a message in the middle of your screen. But even if your iPad is sleeping, it will wake up and display a message on the lock screen.

17 If you've enabled snooze, tapping here will silence the alarm and try again in 9 minutes.

18 To silence the alarm normally, assuming it has sounded while the iPad is asleep and locked, you need to swipe the lock switch. If the iPad was awake when the alarm went off, you simply get a button to tap.

Wake Up!
When you set an alarm, it will sound even if you lower your volume to nothing, mute the sound with the side switch or Control Center, and switch into Do Not Disturb mode. This way, you can't accidentally turn off an alarm just because you wanted to avoid other distractions.

Siri: Create Alarms
You can use Siri to create and delete alarms. Try these phrases:

"Set an alarm for weekdays at 9 AM."
"Create an alarm for tomorrow at 10 AM."
"Cancel my 9 AM alarm."
"Turn on my 9 AM alarm."
"Turn off my 9 AM alarm."

The Web is at your fingertips with iPad's Safari web
browser.

In this chapter, you learn about Safari, the browser built in to the iPad. You can use it to browse the Web, bookmark web pages, fill in forms, and search the Internet.

→ Browsing to a URL and Searching
→ Viewing Web Pages
→ Opening Multiple Web Pages with Tabs
→ Bookmarks, History, and Reading List
→ Deleting Your Bookmarks
→ Creating Home Screen Bookmarks
→ Viewing Articles with Safari Reader
→ Filling in Web Forms
→ Saving Time with AutoFill

Surfing the Web

The iPad is a beautiful web surfing device. Its size is perfect for web pages, and your ability to touch the screen lets you interact with content in a way that even a computer typically cannot.

Getting Started with Safari

Undoubtedly, you know how to get to web pages on a computer using a web browser. You use Safari on your iPad in the same way, but the interface is a little different.

At the top of the Safari browser is a toolbar with just a few buttons. In the middle, the largest interface element is the address field. This is where you can type the address (URL) of any web page on the Internet, or enter a search query.

Tips for Typing a URL

- A URL is a Universal Resource Locator. It can be a website name or a specific page in a website.

- For most websites, you don't need to type the "www." at the beginning. For instance, you can type **www.apple.com** or **apple.com**, and both take you to Apple's home page. You never need to type "http://" either, though occasionally you need to type "https://" to specify that you want to go to a secure web page.

- Instead of typing ".com." you can tap and hold the period button on the iPad keyboard. You can select .com, .edu, .org, .us, or .net.

Browsing to a URL and Searching

(1) Tap the Safari icon on your iPad to launch the browser. Unless you have rearranged your icons, it is located at the bottom of the screen, along with your other most commonly used applications.

(2) Tap in the field at the top of the screen. This opens up the keyboard at the bottom of the screen. If you were already viewing a web page, the address of that page remains in the address field. Otherwise, it will be blank.

Clear the Slate

To clear the field at any time, tap the X button located inside the field all the way to the right.

(3) Start typing a search term or a URL such as apple.com or macmost.com.

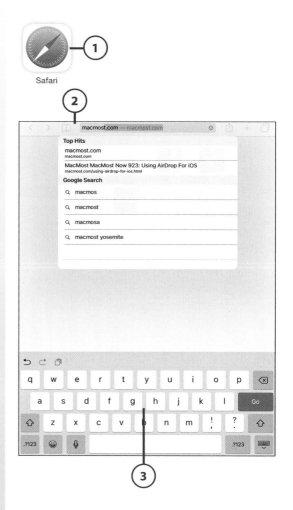

(4) The area to the right of where you are typing will fill with a complete address and description, trying to predict the URL you want. You can ignore this and keep typing until you have completed the URL. You can then skip to step 6.

(5) As you type, suggestions based on previous pages you have visited and past web searches from other users appear. To go directly to one of these pages, tap the page in the list.

Search This Page

Below the Google suggestions in the search suggestions drop-down menu is a list of recent searches and the occurrences of the phrase on the web page you are viewing. Use the latter to find the phrase on the page.

(6) Otherwise, tap the Go button on the keyboard when you finish typing. If you typed or selected a URL, you will be taken to that web page.

(7) Notice that the address field at the top of the screen shows you the domain name for the website you are visiting, but doesn't display the complete URL of the specific page of that site you are on.

If you typed a search term, or selected a search from the list, the term will remain at the top and you will get a page of search results.

(8) Tap on any result to jump to that page.

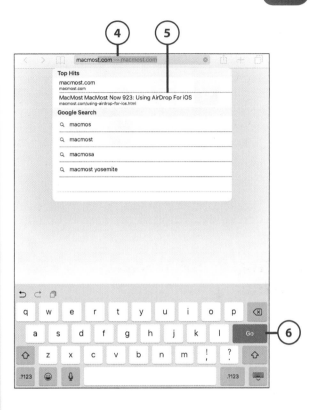

Siri: Search the Web

You can use Siri to search the web, even if you are not currently looking at the Safari screen. Sometimes Siri will also answer general questions by suggesting a web search:

"Search the web for iPad tutorials."
"Search for local plumbers."
"Search for MacMost.com."
"Search Wikipedia for Paris."
"Show me some websites about geology."
"Google Denver news."
"Search for iPad tutorials on MacMost.com."

Nothing Special, Please

Some websites present you with a special iPad version of the site. This is not as common as the special iPhone or iPod touch versions that many sites offer. If a website does not look the same on your iPad as it does on your computer, you might want to check to see if a switch is on the web page provided by the site to view the standard web version, instead of a special iPad version. You can also tap in the address field in Safari, and then drag down on the list of Favorites that appears to reveal a Request Desktop Site option. This is especially useful if a site has lumped the iPad together with the iPhone and provided a needlessly simplified version.

>>>Go Further
TIPS FOR SEARCHING THE WEB

- You can go deeper than just typing some words. For instance, you can put a + in front of a word to require it and a – in front to avoid that word in the results.

- You can use special search terms to look for things such as movie times, weather, flight tracking, and more. See https://support.google.com/websearch/answer/134479 for all sorts of things you can do with a Google search.

- Using iPad's Settings app, you can choose the search engine that Safari uses as its default. Tap the Settings icon and choose Safari on the left, and then look for the Search Engine setting. You can choose Bing, Yahoo!, or Duck Duck Go instead of Google, for instance.

- Using Google, you can search for much more than text on web pages. Look at the top of the search results, and you see links such as Images, Videos, Maps, News, and Shopping. Tap More and you can also search for things such as Blogs and Books.

- To explore the search results without moving away from the page listing the results, tap and hold over a link to see a button that enables you to open a link in a new tab, leaving the results open in the current tab.

- You can use many search settings with Bing or Google. These are not specific to the iPad but work on your computer as well when performing searches. Tap the settings button (looks like a small gear) in the upper-right corner of the search results page to choose a language, filters, and other settings. Set up a Bing or Google account and log in to save these search preferences and use them between different devices.

Viewing Web Pages

Whether you typed in a URL or searched for a web page, after you have one open on your iPad screen, you can control what you view in several ways. You need to know these techniques to view the complete contents of a web page and navigate among web pages.

(**1**) Navigate to any web page using either of the two techniques in the previous step-by-step instructions. When you arrive at the page, only the domain name shows at the top.

(**2**) When you are viewing a page, you can touch and drag the page up and down with your finger. As you do so, notice the bar on the right side that gives you an indication of how much of the complete web page you are viewing at one time.

(3) To zoom in on an area in the page, touch the screen with two fingers and move your fingers apart. This is called an unpinch. You can also move them closer together (pinch) to zoom back out. A double-tap restores the page to normal scaling. This works well on websites made for desktop computers, but mobile sites usually are set to already fit the screen at optimal resolution.

(4) You can also double-tap images and paragraphs of text to zoom in to those elements in the web page. A second double-tap zooms back out.

(5) While zoomed in, you can also touch and drag left and right to view different parts of the web page. You see a bar at the bottom of the screen when you do this, just like the bar on the right side in step 2.

(6) To move to another web page from a link in the current web page, just tap the link. Links are usually an underlined or colored piece of text; however, they can also be pictures or button-like images.

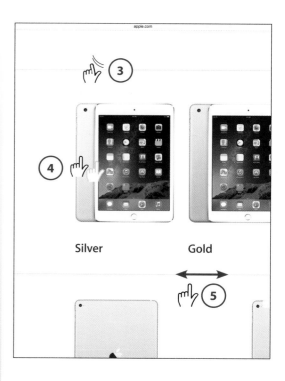

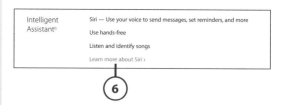

It's Not All Good

Where's the Link?

Unfortunately, it isn't always easy to figure out which words on a page are links. Years ago, these were all blue and underlined. But today, links can be any color and may not be underlined.

On the iPad, it is even more difficult to figure out which words are links. This is because many web pages highlight links when the cursor moves over the word. But with the touch interface of the iPad, there is no cursor.

Opening Multiple Web Pages with Tabs

Safari on the iPad enables you to open multiple web pages at the same time. You can view only one at a time, but you can hold your place on a page by opening a new tab to look at something on another page.

1. View a web page in Safari that has links to other pages, such as MacMost.com. Instead of tapping on a link, tap down and hold your finger there until a contextual menu pops up above your finger.

2. Tap Open in New Tab.

3. Alternatively, you can tap the + button at the top of the screen to open a new tab that shows icons linking to the websites you have put in your Favorites.

4. You see two tabs at the top of the screen now. The one on the right is in front of the one on the left and represents the page you are looking at below. You can tell which tab is the active one—it is in a lighter shade of gray than the others, and the Close Tab button (shown as an X) is visible.

5. You can switch tabs by tapping on the other tab; that tab now appears front of the one on the right, and the screen area below shows that page.

6. When you enter a new web address, search, or use a bookmark, it changes the page of the current tab, but doesn't affect the other tab.

7. You can close the current tab by tapping the X button to the left of the tab's name.

8. Tap the Tabs button at the upper right to see all your tabs presented on one screen.

9. Each tab will appear. You can now tap any tab to jump to it.

10. In addition, you'll also see the titles of tabs open on other devices that are using the same iCloud account. The size of these previews will shrink depending on how many tabs are open. You can tap these to open their pages on your iPad.

11. Tap Done to return to the tab you were viewing previously.

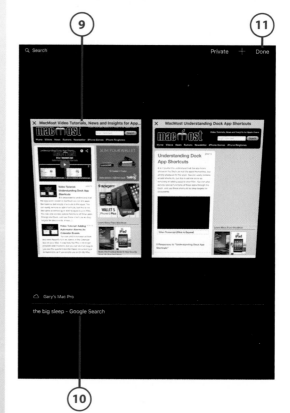

Private Browsing

When you use the tabs screen to select which tab to view, you also see a Private button at the top. Tap that and a new tab opens in private browsing mode. Web pages you view in this tab are not stored in your history. In addition, browser cookies are deleted after you close the tab. This does not hide your browsing behavior from your ISP or employer, but it could help you keep the surprise when buying a birthday present for someone who uses the same iPad.

Viewing Articles with Safari Reader

Web pages on the iPad can be vibrant and pretty. But sometimes the website tries to cram so much text and other junk onto a page that it can be painful to read. You can clear away all the clutter to reveal the text of a news article or blog post using the Reader feature.

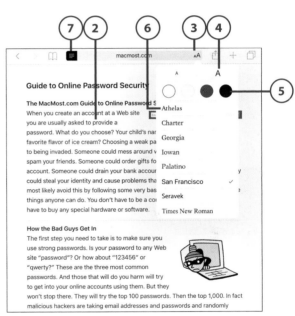

(1) Look for the Reader button in the address field. If it is there, that means you can tap it to switch to Reader mode for this article.

(2) In Reader mode, only the text and inline images of the article appear.

(3) Tap the text appearance button to the right of the web address to view options.

(4) Tap the large or small "A" buttons to make the text size larger or smaller.

(5) Tap the background color buttons to adjust to your liking.

(6) You can also select from a short list of fonts.

(7) Tap Reader again to return to the regular view of the page.

Bookmarks, History, and Reading List

You can always visit a web page by typing its address in the field at the top of Safari. But the app also has a way for you to get to your most frequently visited sites easily, find a page you recently visited, or save a page to read later.

Using Bookmarks and Favorites

Bookmarks allow you to save the web pages you visit most often and then access them with just a few taps. Favorites are bookmarks that appear at the top of the Safari browser for easier access.

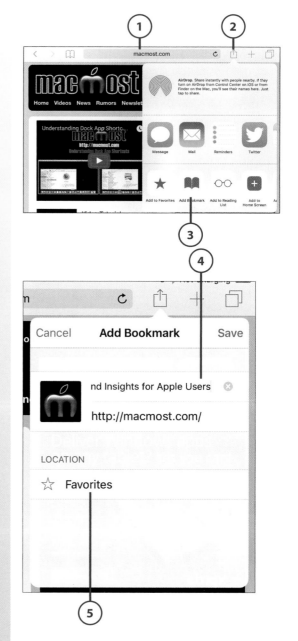

1. Use Safari to navigate to any web page.

2. Tap the Share button at the top of the screen.

3. Tap Add Bookmark.

4. Edit the title of the bookmark. The official title of the web page is prefilled, but you can use the keyboard to change it. You can tap the X to clear the text and start fresh.

5. Tap Location to place the bookmark in a bookmarks folder.

6 You can choose to place the bookmark in Favorites, so it will appear at the top of the Safari window where you can easily find it.

7 Or you can put it in Bookmarks, where you can select it from the Bookmarks menu.

8 Tap Save to finish creating the bookmark.

9 To use a bookmark, first tap the Bookmarks button. This opens up a sidebar on the left. In vertical orientation, this sidebar closes when you choose a web page to view. In horizontal orientation, the sidebar stays until you tap the Bookmarks button again.

10 Find the bookmark in the list and tap it to go to that web page. These would be any bookmarks you saved by using step 7.

11 If you put the bookmark in Favorites or another folder, such as in step 6, you have to tap that folder name first to dig down to find the bookmark.

12 When you create a new tab, the bookmarks you put in your Favorites folder will appear as icons for quick access to those pages. For more about tabs, see "Opening Multiple Web Pages with Tabs" earlier in this chapter.

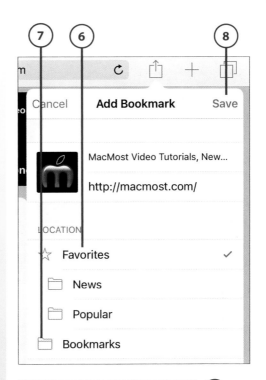

>>>Go Further

TIPS FOR BOOKMARKING WEBSITES

- The titles of web pages are often long and descriptive. It is a good idea to shorten the title to something you can easily recognize, especially if it is a web page that you plan to visit often.

- To create folders inside the Bookmarks folder, tap the Bookmarks button at the top of the Safari screen. Then choose the Bookmarks button at the top. At the bottom of that menu, tap Edit and then tap New Folder.

- You can create folders of bookmarks under Favorites. These appear as their own pop-up menu when you tap them, giving access to a subset of your bookmarks.

Using History

Safari keeps track of which web pages you have visited. You can use this history to find a page you went to earlier today, yesterday, or even several days back.

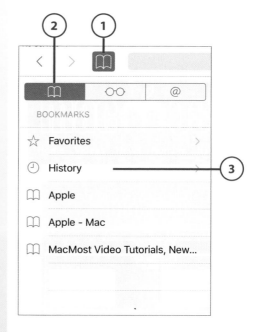

1. After using Safari to view several pages, tap the Bookmarks button at the top of the screen.

2. Tap the first tab at the top of this menu to view your bookmarks and history folders.

3. You may already be viewing your history at this point. If the top of this menu reads History instead of Bookmarks, then you are. Otherwise, tap the History item to go into your history. It is also possible that you have dug down into a bookmarks subfolder. If you see a label with a left-facing blue arrow at the top of the list, tap it to move up a level until you get to the main bookmarks list that includes Favorites and History.

(4) Tap any item in the list to jump to that web page.

(5) Previous pages you have visited are broken into groups by date.

(6) Tap the Clear button if you want to clear out your browsing history. For instance, are you about to hand your iPad to your spouse right after shopping for their birthday present?

History/Bookmarks

Safari treats both history and bookmarks the same. They are both just lists of web pages. Think of your history as a bookmark list of every site you have visited recently. If you think you may need to go to a web page later the same day or this week, you can always use your History instead of creating a new bookmark. Use bookmarks only for truly important pages that you know you'll need often or later on.

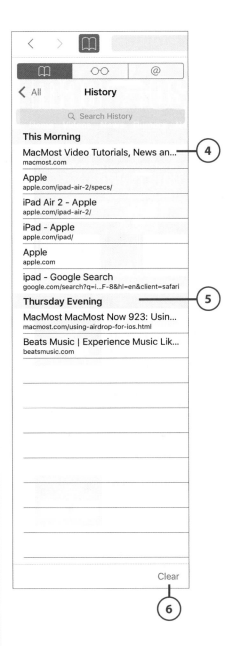

Deleting Your Bookmarks

Adding and using bookmarks is just the start. You eventually need to delete ones you don't use. Some might link to missing or obsolete pages, or some you simply no longer use.

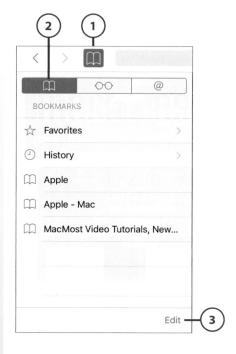

1. Tap the Bookmarks button at the top of the Safari screen.

2. Navigate to the Bookmarks section of that menu. If the bookmark you want to delete is in a folder, tap that folder to navigate into it so you can see the bookmark.

3. Tap Edit.

4. Tap the red button next to a bookmark.

5. Tap the Delete button to remove the bookmark. The bookmark is instantly deleted.

6. Tap Done when you finish deleting bookmarks.

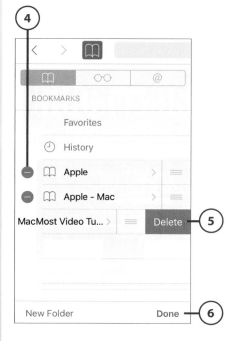

Sync Your Bookmarks

If you are using iCloud, your bookmarks should sync between all your iOS and Mac devices. Safari on your computer gives you greater control over moving and deleting bookmarks. So just do your wholesale editing on your computer and those changes should be reflected in your iPad's bookmarks as well.

Creating Home Screen Bookmarks

If a web page is so important to you that you want even faster access to it than via a browser bookmark, you can save it as an icon on your iPad's Home screen.

(1) Use Safari to navigate to any web page.

(2) Tap the Share button at the top of the screen.

(3) Tap Add to Home Screen. Note that the icon shown here will change to use the icon for that website or to a small screen capture of the site.

Managing Home Screen Bookmarks

You can arrange and delete Home screen bookmarks just like icons that represent apps. See "Arranging Apps on Your iPad" in Chapter 10 for details.

---

(4) You can now edit the name of the page. Most web page titles are too long to display under an icon on the Home screen of the iPad, so edit the name down to as short a title as possible.

(5) You can tap Cancel to leave this interface without sending the bookmark to the Home screen.

(6) Tap Add to complete adding the icon to the Home screen.

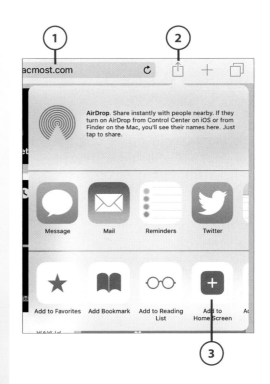

(7) Press the Home button to return to your Home screen (not shown).

(8) Look for the new icon on your Home screen that represents this bookmark. You may need to swipe through the pages of your Home screens to find it. Then, you can move it to any page or into a folder. The icon acts just like the app icons on your Home screen. See "Arranging Apps on Your iPad" in Chapter 10.

Website Icons

The icon for this type of bookmark can come from one of two sources. Web page owners can provide a special iPhone/iPad icon that would be used whenever someone tries to bookmark her page.

However, if no such icon is provided, your iPad takes a screen shot of the web page and shrinks it down to make an icon.

Building a Reading List

Your reading list is similar to bookmarks. You can add a page to your reading list to remember to return to that page later. When you do, it is removed from the Unread section of your reading list, but still appears in the All section.

(1) Find an article you want to read later.

(2) Tap the Share button.

(3) Tap Add to Reading List.

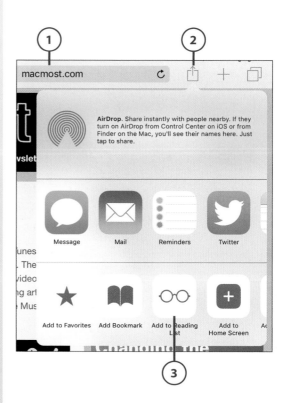

(4) To see your reading list, tap the Bookmarks button.

Take it Offline

Pages you add to your reading list are downloaded to your iPad so that you can read them later, when not connected to the Internet.

(5) Tap the Reading List button.

(6) Tap any item to view the page. Even if you are not connected to the Internet, the page will show because Safari stored the content when you added the page to the Reading List.

(7) At the bottom you see either Show All or Show Unread. This lets you switch between the two lists. Show All shows everything in your Reading List. Show Unread does not show items you have already opened from the Reading List.

Reading List Syncing

The Reading List also syncs across your iOS devices and Macs using iCloud. So you can add it on your Mac and then see it appear in your Reading List on your iPad.

Shared Links

In addition to Bookmarks and Reading List, there is a third button that looks like an @ symbol that appears only if you are signed into social media networks like Twitter or Facebook in the Settings app. Here you find shared links. Recently shared links from those networks appear in this list.

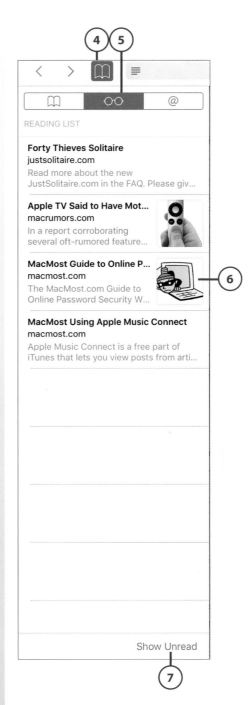

Working with Web Forms

The Web isn't a one-way street. Often you need to interact with web pages, filling in forms or text fields. Doing this on the iPad is similar to doing it on a computer, but with a few key differences.

The keyboard shares screen space with the web page, so when you tap on a field, you bring up the keyboard at the bottom of the screen.

Also pull-down menus behave differently. On the iPad, you get a special menu showing you all the options.

>>>*Go Further*

SCANNING YOUR CREDIT CARD

When encounter a web form that asks you to enter a credit card number, it can be a pain to have to enter all those digits. Instead, you can have your iPad read the number right from the card using your iPad's camera. Just tap in the credit card number field, and you see a Scan Credit Card button appear above the keyboard. Tap that and you are instructed to hold your card up to the camera. If the lighting is good and your number is clearly visible, it will be read by the camera and inserted into the field. If you don't see the Scan Credit card button, it could be because the web page isn't labeling its fields in a way that Safari can recognize. In that case, you need to enter the number manually.

Filling in Web Forms

(1) Use Safari to navigate to a web page with a form. For demonstration purposes, try one of the pages at http://apple.com/feedback/.

(2) To type in a text field, tap that field.

(3) The keyboard appears at the bottom of the screen. Use it to type text into the field. The features of the keyboard will depend on queues from the website. For instance, a site can set a text field to only accept numbers, so you'll see a numeric keyboard instead of a full keyboard.

(4) Tap the Go button when you finish filling in all the required fields.

(5) To select a check box or radio button, tap it just as you would click on it on your computer using the mouse.

(6) To select an item in a pull-down menu, tap the menu.

(7) The special iPad pull-down menu reacts like any other iPad interface. You can tap an item to select it. You can touch and drag up and down to view more selections if the list is long.

(8) A check mark appears next to the currently selected item. Tap that item or any other one to select it and dismiss the menu.

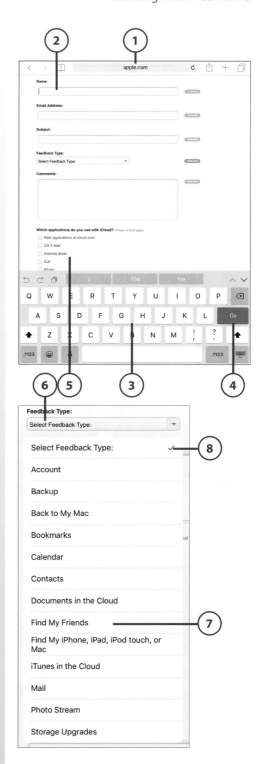

Special Menus

Some websites may use special menus that they build from scratch, rather than these default HTML menus. When this is the case, you get a menu that looks exactly like the one you get when viewing the web page on a computer. If the web page is well coded, it should work fine on the iPad, though it might be slightly more difficult to make a selection.

>>>*Go Further*
TIPS FOR FILLING IN FORMS

- You can use the AutoFill button just above the keyboard to fill in your name, address, and other contact info instead of typing on the keyboard. To enable AutoFill, go into your iPad Settings and look for the Passwords & AutoFill preferences under Safari. Also make sure your own information is correct and complete in your card in the Contacts application. See "Saving Time with AutoFill," later in this chapter.

- To move between fields in a form, use the flat left and right arrow buttons just above the keyboard that move to the Previous or Next field. You can quickly fill in an entire form this way without having to tap on the web page to select the next item.

Saving Time with AutoFill

When you go to websites and fill out forms, it can be annoying to type out basic information like your name and address, or your user ID and password. Furthermore, if you have to type your password every time you visit a site, or even on a daily or weekly basis, this encourages you to use simple, easy-to-guess passwords so you don't have to type long complex strings of characters.

The Keychain function built into Safari allows you to automatically fill in forms and login prompts. After you enter your information the first time, you never have to do it again for that website.

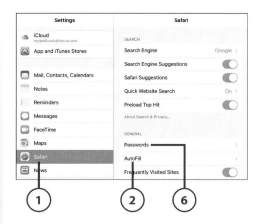

Setting Up AutoFill

To set up AutoFill in Safari, start by going to the Settings app.

1. Tap Safari in the Settings app.

2. Tap AutoFill.

3. Slide the Use Contact Info switch on, if it's not. Now any time you go to a web page with a form that asks for basics like name, address, or telephone number, AutoFill uses your contact information in the Contacts app to fill those fields automatically.

4. Tap My Info to tell Safari which contact in the Contacts app is you.

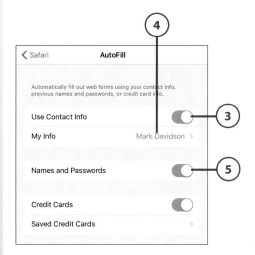

5. Slide the Names and Passwords switch on to have Safari remember user IDs and passwords when you log on to websites. As you will see in the next section, Safari prompts you each time you enter a new User ID and Password so you can decide the passwords that are saved.

6. After you have visited some sites and saved some passwords, you can access the list of saved passwords by going back to the main Safari settings screen and tapping Passwords.

7. Tap on any entry to view the ID, password, and the website it belongs to. This can come in handy if you need to view or copy and paste a password. For instance, you can grab your Amazon password to paste it into the Kindle app.

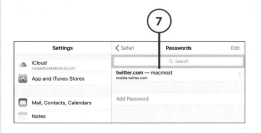

8 You can enter Edit mode to delete entries.

9 You can manually enter new passwords right here as well.

10 Safari can also remember credit card information. Those settings are found back on the AutoFill settings screen. Slide the Credit Cards switch to on for this information to be saved.

11 Tap Saved Credit Cards to see a list of your saved credit cards and to add new ones. When you add a credit card, include your name, the card number, the expiration date, and a short description. However, the security code for the card is not saved. Most websites will ask you for this even after Safari has autofilled in the information it has saved.

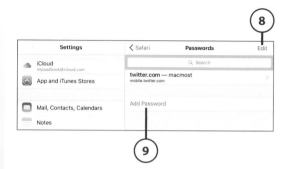

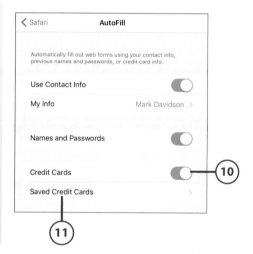

>>>Go Further
SAFETY AND SECURITY

If you add your passwords and credit card information for Safari to automatically fill in, isn't that incredibly insecure? Well, it is if you have not set a passcode for your iPad. The Settings app recommends this when you turn these options on.

You should set a passcode under Settings, General, Passcode Lock. Then, you should set the Require Passcode option to Immediately so as soon as you lock your iPad by closing the Smart Cover or pressing the sleep button, the passcode is required to use it.

Even with the security enabled, using a simple passcode like 1234 or letting it sit around unlocked still presents a problem. You don't need to use AutoFill on every website. You could use it for unimportant sites like games and forums, and avoid using it for bank accounts and social media sites.

The advantage to using AutoFill for passwords is that you can use a long, random password for an account rather than a short, memorable one. It is more likely that your account will be broken into remotely when you use a short, common password than someone stealing your iPad and using it to gain access to that website. And even if they do, you can simply change your important passwords if your iPad is stolen.

Using AutoFill

After you have AutoFill set up, using it is relatively simple. You can use it with a form that asks for basic contact information, or for a login form. The process is the same. Let's look at using it with a simple login form.

1. Enter an ID or password at a website.

2. If AutoFill is enabled, you may be prompted by Safari to save the password.

3. Tap Save Password to save the user ID and password.

4. Alternatively, you can tell Safari that you don't want to save the password for this site, and not to ask again.

5. You can also skip this for now. This is useful if you have multiple logons for a site and don't want to save the one you are using at this moment.

6 Log out and then return to the same website.

7 You'll notice that the ID and password are already filled in. The fields turn yellow to show that AutoFill has been used to fill them in.

8 Tap the button used by the site to complete the login.

9 If your ID and password don't appear at first, look for the Passwords button on top of the keyboard. This button will also allow you to select from multiple sets of IDs and passwords if you have more than one account at the site.

Changing Passwords

So what happens if you change passwords for a site? Simply use the keyboard to erase and retype the password when logging into that site the next time. AutoFill will prompt you, asking if you want to save the new password, replacing the old one in its database.

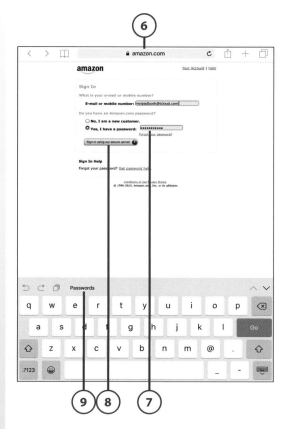

It's Not All Good

AutoFill Not Working?

AutoFill works because forms use typical names for fields: id, password, name, firstname, lastname, zip, and so on. If a website wants to get creative, or intentionally block AutoFill functions of browsers, then the site may obfuscate the names of fields to make it impossible for AutoFill to tell which field is which. Therefore, some websites might not work with AutoFill, while others do.

>>>Go Further

SAFARI EXTENSIONS

You can add new functionality to Safari with third-party extensions. For instance, you can use the popular 1Password app to insert passwords into login pages. You can use the Pinterest extension to pin web pages without leaving Safari.

To install an extension, first install the app from the App Store as you would any other app. (See Chapter 10 to learn how to find and install apps.) After you have installed an app that offers a Safari extension, tap the Share button at the top of Safari to start the process of activating it. This is the same button used to add a bookmark.

In the menu that appears, you see a list of ways to Share the page you are viewing, such as Message and Mail. You also have a list of more actions you can take with the page, such as Add Bookmark and Copy. Swipe either of these lists from right to left, and you see a More button as the rightmost item in the list. If the extension adds a way to share a web page, you find it by using the More button in the first list. Other extensions are behind the More button in the second list. Either way, switch the extension on to activate it.

After that, you'll find the extension along with the other items in either of these two lists as a button. For instance, with the Pinterest extension, you can tap the Share button, and then tap the Pinterest button to quickly add an image on the current page to one of your boards.

Send and
receive mes-
sages from
other
iOS and
Mac users.

Send and receive email from
your ISP or a variety of popular
email services.

In this chapter, you learn how to configure and use the Mail app to correspond using email and how to use the Messaging app to send and receive messages.

8

→ Configuring Your iPad for Email
→ Reading Your Email
→ Composing a New Message
→ Deleting and Moving Messages
→ Searching Email
→ Configuring How Email Is Received
→ Creating a Signature
→ More Email Settings
→ Setting Up Messaging
→ Conversing with Messages

Communicating with Email and Messaging

Now that you have an iPad with a battery that seems to last forever, you have no excuse for not replying to emails. You need to be comfortable using the built-in Mail app that enables you to connect with your home or work email using standard protocols such as POP and IMAP. You can even connect with more proprietary systems such as AOL, Exchange, Gmail, and Yahoo!. You can also send messages to your friends using Apple's iMessage system.

Configuring Your iPad for Email

It's easy to set up your email if you use one of the popular email services like Gmail, Yahoo!, AOL, or Microsoft. But if you use another kind of service, such as the email given to you by your local ISP or the company you work for, you need to enter more detailed information such as server addresses.

It is possible that your email account has already been set up for you. If you use Apple's iCloud as your email service, when you answered some questions while setting up your new iPad, you probably already gave your iPad your Apple ID and password and it set up your email automatically. You can use these steps to check to make sure that account is there, or add an additional account from another provider.

If you are using iCloud, Gmail, or any of the other services listed on the Add Account screen, all you really need to do is enter your email address and password. Your iPad will set up the account from those two pieces of information. But if you are using another type of email account, you need to enter several details about your account.

Set Up Your Email Account

1. Tap the Settings icon on your Home screen.

Settings

2 Tap Mail, Contacts, Calendars.

3 If you are using iCloud and set up your Apple ID when you first started your iPad, you should see your iCloud account listed. If this is your only email account, you don't need to do anything else.

4 If you have another email account you want to add, tap Add Account.

5 If you have an iCloud, Microsoft Exchange, Google, Yahoo! Mail, AOL, or Outlook.com account, tap the corresponding button. In the figure, we selected Google to access a Gmail account.

Other

If your email account is from a cable or DSL internet provider, or employers (depending on their system), you need to tap Other when setting up your account. Gather information like your ID, password, email server address, and account type (such as POP or IMAP) before starting. Check with your provider's support departments if you get stuck.

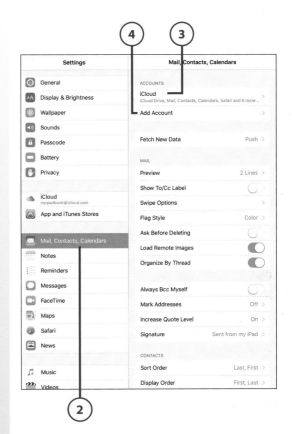

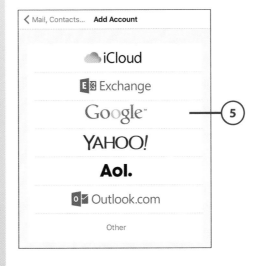

(6) The next screen varies depending on the service you are using. Here you can see Google's authentication screen. If you chose Yahoo!, you would see Yahoo's authentication screen, which looks different. Some account types, like AOL, simply offer a few text entry fields and no logo or other buttons.

(7) For Google's screen, start by entering your email address. Make sure you enter it perfectly, as this is your ID for logging into this email service.

(8) Enter your password for this email account.

(9) Tap Sign-In.

(10) The next screen shows you what services the provider offers. For instance, Google's accounts not only provide email, but also contacts, calendars, and notes. You can leave all these turned on, or turn some off if you prefer not to use a service from that provider on your iPad.

(11) Tap Save to continue.

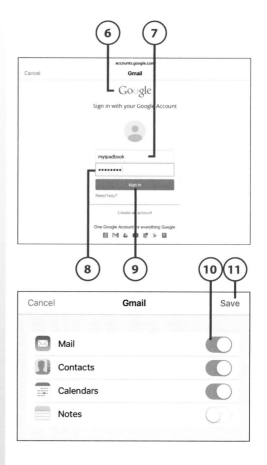

>>>Go Further
CHOOSING AN EMAIL PROVIDER WISELY

If you are using a cable or DSL provider, you might have an email address assigned to you by them. There are many good reasons to avoid using these email addresses and instead sign up for one such as Apple's iCloud or Google's Gmail service. The main reason is transportability. If you have a cable network email address now, you will lose it if you switch to another provider or you move out of your provider's territory. Another reason is that these ISP-provided email services tend to lack features like good junk mail filtering and the ability to send and receive email from multiple devices seamlessly.

Reading Your Email

You use the Mail app to read your email, which is much easier to navigate and type with your iPad turned horizontally. In horizontal mode, you can see the list of messages to the left while you view the message content to the right. In vertical mode, you view only one of these at a time. Let's start by reading some email.

1 Tap the Mail app icon on the Home screen.

Mail

2 On the left, you see a list of incoming mail. Tap a message in the list to view it.

3 On the right, you see the selected message.

4 If you want to check for new mail, drag the list of messages down and release. It will spring back up and ask the server to see if there are new messages.

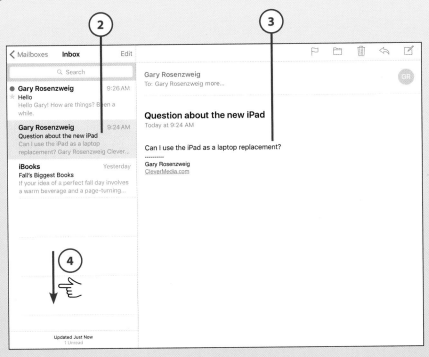

(5) Tap the name or email address of the sender.

(6) Tap Create New Contact to add the sender to your contacts.

(7) Tap Add to Existing Contact to add the email address to a contact you already have in your Contacts app.

(8) Tap the Folder button at the top of the message.

(9) Tap a folder to move the current message to that folder.

(10) Tap the Trash button at the top of the message to send the message directly to the Trash folder.

(11) Tap the arrow button at the top of the message to reply or forward the message.

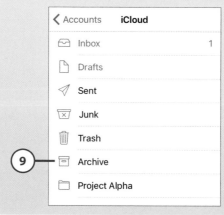

12 If you tap and swipe right to left or left to right across the message in the left sidebar, you get more options. Be careful not to swipe too fast; instead of options, you will quickly put the message in the trash.

13 Options include things like flagging or deleting the message.

Customization

You can customize this by going to the Settings app, selecting Mail, Contacts, Calendars on the left, and then Swipe Options. For instance, you can change the Swipe Right action from the default Mark as Read, to Archive.

14 If you tap More, you see a list of more options appear.

15 In addition to actions like Reply and Forward, you can also select Notify Me, which gives you an alert when someone else replies to this message thread (any message with the same title).

Multiple Inboxes

If you have more than one email account, you can choose to look at each inbox individually or a single unified inbox that includes messages from all accounts. Just tap the Mailboxes button at the upper-left corner of the screen and choose All Inboxes. You can also choose to look at the inbox of a single account, or dig down into any folder of an account.

How Do You Create Folders?

For most email accounts—particularly IMAP, Gmail, and iCloud accounts—you can create folders using the Mail app. Use the back arrow at the upper-left corner of Mail and back out to the list of inboxes and accounts. Choose an account. Then tap the Edit button, and you'll see a New Mailbox button at the bottom of the screen.

VIPs

You can make a contact a VIP when you select the sender's name in an incoming email. Then, their messages will continue to appear in your inbox as normal, but they will also appear in the VIP inbox. So if you get a lot of email and want to occasionally focus only on a few very important people instead of everyone, choose your VIP inbox rather than your inbox.

If you are using VIPs with your iCloud email accounts, you'll see the same VIPs for your Mac and other iOS devices using that iCloud account.

Composing a New Message

Whether you compose a new message or reply to one you received, the process is similar. Let's take a look at composing one from scratch.

(1) In the Mail app, tap the Compose button.

(2) Enter a To: address.

(3) Alternatively, tap the + button to bring up a list of contacts, and choose from there.

(4) Tap in the Subject field and type a subject for the email.

(5) Tap below the subject field in the body of the email, and type your message.

(6) Tap the Send button.

Siri: Sending Email

You can use Siri to send email by asking it to "send an email to" and the name of the recipient. It will ask you for a subject and a body to the message, and then display it. You can choose to send it or cancel. You can even do the whole thing through Siri by saying something like "Send an email to John Johnson with the subject hello and the body how are you doing."

Including Images

You can copy and paste inside a Mail message just like you can inside of any text entry area on your iPad. But you can also paste in images! Just copy an image from any source—Photos app, Safari, and so on. Then tap in the message body and select Paste. You can paste in more than one image as well.

>>>Go Further
HANDOFF TO YOUR OTHER DEVICES

Starting with version 8, iOS has a feature called Handoff, which helps those who use multiple iOS devices and Macs. If you are in the middle of composing an email on your Mac or other iOS device, and then you look at the lock screen on your iPad, you should see a small Mail app icon at the lower left. Tap that icon and swipe up, and your iPad will automatically launch Mail and bring up the message composition window with the contents of the message you were writing on the other device. Meanwhile, the other device will close the composition window.

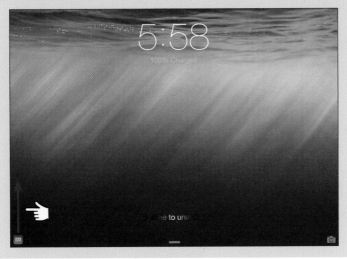

So, one device "hands off" the message to the other. You could be writing an email on your iMac and then grab your iPad and finish it there. Or vice versa. This also works with viewing Web pages in Safari and with Apple-created apps like Pages, Numbers, Keynote, and Maps.

There is a Handoff setting in the Settings app under General. It should be on by default. On Macs, there is a setting in System Preferences under General. But keep in mind that you'll need a pretty recent Mac running at least Mac OS X Yosemite for this to work. And both machines should be nearby with Wi-Fi and Bluetooth turned on. See the information at support.apple.com/HT204678 for setup help and troubleshooting.

Deleting and Moving Messages

While viewing a message, you can simply tap the Trash Can icon and move it to the trash. You can also move a group of messages to a folder or the trash.

1. In the Mail app, go to any mailbox and any subfolder, such as your Inbox.

2. If you are viewing a message, you can delete it by tapping the trash can icon.

3. You can also start the process of deleting a message or several messages by tapping the Edit button.

4. Tap the circles next to each message to select them.

5. They will be added to the middle of the screen in a neat stack.

6. Tap the Trash button to delete the selected messages.

7. Tap the Move button, and the left side of the screen changes to a list of folders. You can select one to move all the messages to that folder.

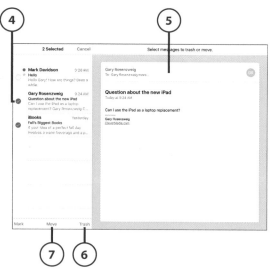

8 Tap the Cancel button to exit without deleting or moving any messages.

9 Alternatively, you can delete a single message by dragging just slightly right to left across the message in the list. This reveals Trash, Flag, and More buttons. If you drag all the way from the right to the left side of the screen, the Trash button enlarges and fills the space, and then the message is deleted with just this one gesture.

10 Tap the Trash button to delete the message. The More button allows you to reply, forward, flag, move, and perform various other actions on the message.

Oops—How Do I Undelete?

So you just tried to use step 9 to see what those buttons looked like, and you deleted the message by accident? You can always look in your Trash folder to select the message and move it back to the Inbox. But you can also give your iPad a quick shake, and you'll be prompted to undo the deletion.

Where's the Trash?

If you are just deleting the single message that you happen to be viewing, you can tap the trashcan icon at the top. But sometimes that icon isn't there. Instead, you may see an icon that looks like a file box. This is an Archive button. Some email services, like Gmail, insist that you archive your email instead of deleting it. To facilitate this, they provide a nearly infinite amount of storage space, so you might as well use that Archive button.

What About Spam?

Your iPad has no built-in spam filter. Fortunately, most email servers filter out spam at the server level. Using a service such as Gmail means that you get spam filtering on the server and junk mail automatically goes to the Junk folder, not your Inbox.

Searching Email

You can also search your messages using the Mail app.

1. The Search field is at the top of the messages list in the left sidebar in the Mail app. It won't be visible at first. To see it, tap and drag down the messages in the left sidebar.

2. Tap in the Search field.

3. Type a search term.

4. You see people and messages in the results. Select a message to view it from the search results.

5. Tap Cancel to exit the search and return to the mailbox you were previously viewing.

Search What?

Searches work on From, To, Subject fields and the body of the message. Any messages you have in your inbox will pop up right away, but any archived messages or ones stored in folders may or may not appear after a few seconds. The Mail app relies on your email server to return these results. Depending on what type of email server you have, it could take a while. Older results may not appear at all.

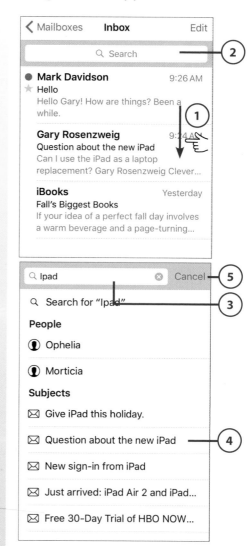

Customizing Your Email

You have more settings for email beyond the basic account setup. For instance, you can decide how you want to receive email, using either push delivery or fetch delivery (or manual). There are even more Email settings in the Settings app.

No Thanks—I'll Do It Myself

The Manual setting is useful if you don't want to be disturbed throughout the day as you receive email. These accounts will only be checked when you open the Mail app and look at the inbox for that account. Another reason to use Manual is to preserve battery as your iPad won't use Wi-Fi or your mobile connection as often. You also might want to use Manual if you are concerned about bandwidth, like when traveling internationally and only want to check email when using Wi-Fi.

Configuring How You Receive Email

When you receive email, it is either fetched, pushed, or delivered manually when you choose. Fetch checks for email at regular intervals, whereas push receives messages soon after they have arrived at your email service. Depending on what your provider supports, you can choose between these settings.

1. Go to the Settings app and tap on Mail, Contacts, Calendars.

2. Tap Fetch New Data.

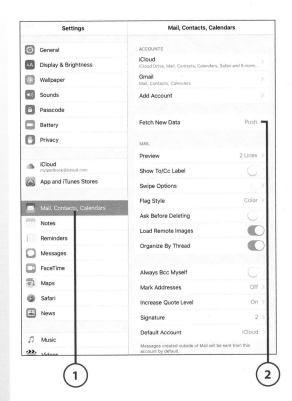

3 Turn on Push to use push email reception, if you use email accounts that can send email via push.

4 Otherwise, select how often you want your iPad to go out to the server and fetch email.

5 Tap one of your email accounts to customize the settings for that particular account. Note that even some subscribed calendars have the ability to be set to push or fetch.

6 For each account you can set your preferences to Fetch, Manual, or Push if available for that email account. Note that more options exist for some accounts, such as specifying which folders are pushed.

Siri: Checking Email

You can ask Siri for a quick list of new email messages by saying "check my email." You'll get a list from within the Siri interface, and you can tap on a message to read it in the Mail app. If you say "read me my email," Siri will read your new messages out loud to you.

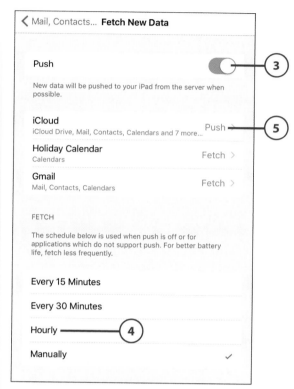

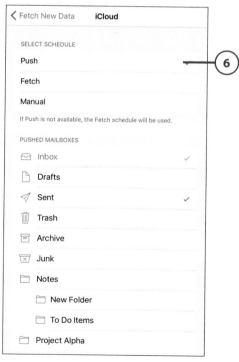

Creating a Signature

You can create a signature that appears below your messages automatically. You do this in the Settings app.

1. In the Settings app, choose Mail, Contacts, Calendars.

2. Tap Signature, which is way down in the list on the right.

3. If you have more than one email account set up, you can choose to have one signature for all accounts or a different signature for each account.

4. Type a signature in one of the signature text fields. You don't need to do anything to save the signature. You can tap the Home button on your iPad to exit Settings if you like.

Styles and Images in Signatures

You can make some text in your signature bold, italic, or underlined by selecting the text and tapping on the selection. In addition to Cut, Copy, and Paste options, you also see a "**B**/<u>U</u>" option. Tap that and you can style that selected text a bit. If you want to include an image in your signature, you can copy that image from another app and paste it in with the text. But try to refrain from pasting a photo or something large, as it may annoy your recipients to get a large image included with every message. A small company logo copied from your company's website might be more appropriate, although email etiquette points to keeping your signature simple and image-free.

Case-By-Case Signatures

You can have only one signature, even if you have multiple email accounts on your iPad. But the signature is placed in the editable area of the message composition field, so you can edit it like the rest of your message.

More Email Settings

You can change even more email settings in the Settings app. Tap the Settings app on your Home screen, and then tap Mail, Contacts, Calendars so we can take a look at some of them.

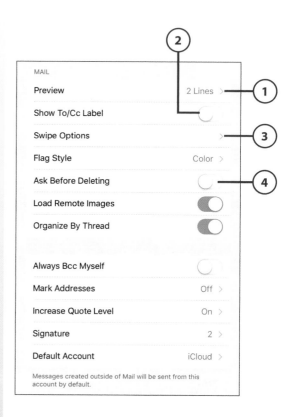

1. Tap Preview to choose how many lines of message preview to show when stacking messages up in the list view.

2. Turn Show To/Cc Label on to view "To" or "Cc" in each email listed so that you know if you were the primary recipient or someone who was just copied on an email to someone else.

3. When viewing messages in your inbox, you can swipe left or right across the message in the list to take an action. You can set this up here. For instance, you can set a swipe to the right to mark an email as read, or you can set it to archive the message and remove it from the inbox.

4. Turn Ask Before Deleting on to require a confirmation when you tap the trash can button in Mail.

5 Turn Load Remote Images off so that images referenced in an mail, but stored on a remote server, are not shown in the message body.

6 To group replies to a message under the original message, select Organize By Thread. This is handy when you subscribe to email discussion lists.

7 Turn Always Bcc Myself on if you want to get a copy of every email you send so that later you can move your copies of emails to your Sent folder on your computer. This might be a good idea if you are using an older email system. Modern email systems like iCloud and Gmail should save your sent messages to the server just like other messages.

8 Choose whether to indent the quoted text from the original email when replying to a message.

9 Tap Default Account to determine which account is used to send email by default if you have more than one account set up on your iPad.

10 In most apps from which you send emails, you can type a message and also change the account you use to send the email. To do this, tap on the email address shown next to From: and you get a list of all your accounts, including alternate email addresses for each account.

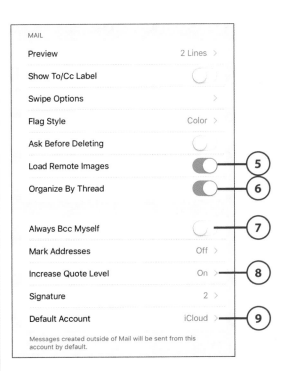

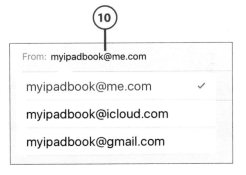

Why Not Show Remote Images?

The main reason to not show remote images is bandwidth. If you get an email that has 15 images referenced in it, you need to download a lot of data, and it takes a while for that email to show up completely. However, remote images are often used as ways to indicate whether you have opened and looked at messages. So, turning this off might break some statistics and receipt functionality expected from the sender (including from spammers).

Working with Messaging

Even though your iPad isn't a phone, you can send text messages. The catch is that you can only message others who are also using Apple's iMessage system. This would include anyone using iOS 5 or newer with an iPad, iPhone, or iPod touch, as long as they have signed up for the free service. Mac users can also send messages with the iMessage system.

Setting up Messaging

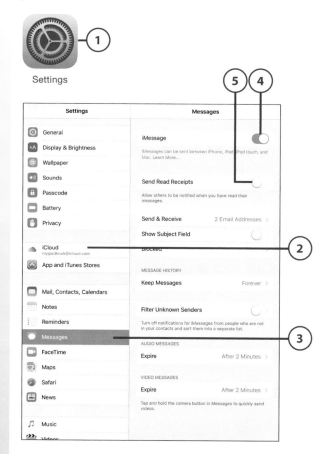

1. Tap the Settings app icon on your Home screen.

2. You need to be signed into iCloud with your Apple ID to use Messages. If you didn't do that when you set up your iPad, or when you set up iCloud email, you need to go to the iCloud settings and sign in or create an iCloud account.

3. Tap the Messages settings.

4. Make sure iMessage is turned on.

5. If you turn this option on, when someone sends you a message they will also get an indication when you have viewed the message.

6 You can use any valid email address that you own for Messages, even if it is not the same as your Apple ID email address. You can control which email addresses can be used to find you, adding more and removing others.

7 Apple's iMessage system can include a subject line along with the message, though most people don't use this.

8 Tap Blocked to add email addresses to block so individuals cannot send you messages.

9 Most people prefer to keep old messages around forever, to refer to them later. Text messages are small, so you don't have to worry about them using up any noticeable space on your iPad. But your iPad allows you to send audio and video messages as well, which do take up some space. You can choose to have those automatically disappear after you have listened to or viewed them.

10 You can opt to have messages received from senders not in your contacts list to be put in a separate list in the Messages app. You also won't receive notifications when someone not in your contacts list sends you a message.

11 Set how long to keep audio and video messages you receive. Typically, you want these to expire soon after you view them so that they don't fill up your iPad's storage space.

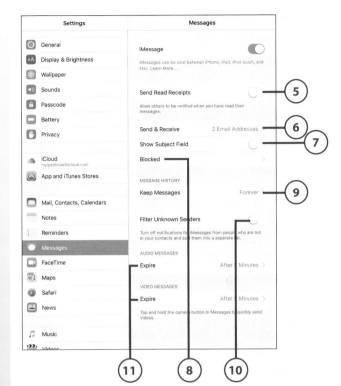

Stop Contacting Me!

There is an even easier way to block unwanted messengers when using the Messages app. You can tap on a Details button at the upper-right corner of the screen while viewing the conversation in Messages. Then an info button appears. It looks like an i with a circle around it. Tap that and you get additional options. Scroll all the way down in these options and a Block this Caller option will appear. Use this and you'll never get another message from that account again. Better still, it will block audio and FaceTime calls from them as well.

Conversing with Messages

After you have set up an account with Messages, you can quickly and easily send messages to others. The next time you launch Messages, you will be taken directly to the main screen.

Messages

(1)

1. Tap the Messages app icon on your home screen.

2. Tap the New Message button at the top of the screen.

3. In a new message, tap in the To field and enter the email address of the recipient. Note that they should already be signed up for iMessage or you will not be able to send them anything. Some iPhone users may use their phone number as their iMessage ID instead of, or in addition to, their email address. As long as the phone number is tied to an iMessage account, you can still converse with them using Messages on your iPad.

4. Tap the text field above the keyboard to type your message.

5. If you want to include a picture or video with your message, tap the camera button. This allows you to choose a picture or video from your photo library, or take a new one with your iPad's camera.

6. To the right of the message field is a microphone. Before you type anything, you can tap this to record a short audio message to send instead of text. But as soon as you start typing text, the microphone button is replaced with the word Send. Tap this Send to send your message.

7. You will see the conversation as a series of talk bubbles. Yours will appear on the right.

8. When your friend responds, you will see their talk bubbles as well.

9. A list of conversations appears on the left. You can have many going on at the same time, or use this list to look at old conversations.

10. Tap Edit to access buttons to delete old conversations.

11. Tap on the Details button to do various tasks such as adding them to your contacts, or starting a FaceTime video chat. You can also send your current location to the people you are messaging, which saves you time if you want to tell someone to meet you at your current location.

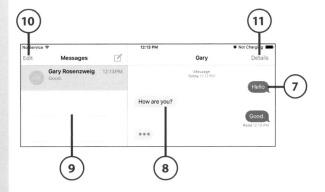

12 If you see a small bubble with three dots, it means that the other party is typing. You see this with other people using Apple's iMessage system, but if they are using a mobile phone with SMS or if their connection is poor, you may not see these indicators.

13 Tap and hold on any message to bring up more options. You can also drag right to left across the messages to reveal time stamps for each message that was sent to you.

14 Use the More button to bring up options like selecting and deleting individual messages in the conversation.

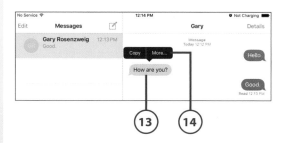

>>>Go Further
SMS ON YOUR iPAD

SMS, or Short Message Service, is the system of sending messages, sometimes called "texts," through your mobile carrier to other phone users. Unlike iMessage, SMS messages go through carriers like AT&T, Verizon, T-Mobile, and Sprint. So SMS is available on your iPhone, but not your iPad since your iPad isn't a phone and doesn't use these carriers for voice and messaging.

However, a feature called SMS Relay allows iPhone users to automatically forward SMS messages to their iPad and for their iPad to send SMS messages through the iPhone. This feature will appear if both your iPhone and iPad use the same iCloud account, and they are both connected to the same Wi-Fi network. You'll receive an initial prompt asking if you want to enable SMS Relay. After you confirm, you'll be able to converse using SMS on your iPad so long as your iPhone is connected to the same Wi-Fi network.

This enables you to send messages from your iPad to friends who have non-Apple devices and use SMS.

Siri: Sending Messages

You can use Siri to send messages. Simply tell Siri something like "Send a text message to Gary" and Siri will respond by asking you what you want to say in your message. Or, you can say something like "Send a message to Gary telling him I'll meet him after the movie," and Siri will create the whole message for you. You can review the message before it is sent for a truly hands-free operation. When you get a message, you can also ask Siri to "Read me that message" and you can listen to the message without ever glancing at your iPad's screen.

Browse your photos
on the iPad's brilliant
screen.

Take pictures
with the iPad's
cameras.

Take fun selfies
with Photo Booth.

In this chapter, we use the Camera and Photo Booth apps to take pictures. Then we learn how to view, edit, and share photos.

→ Taking Photos
→ Editing and Adjusting Photos
→ Taking Panoramic Photos
→ Using Photo Booth
→ Photo Sources
→ Browsing Your Photos
→ Viewing Your Photos
→ Sharing Your Photos
→ Viewing Albums
→ Creating Albums
→ Creating a Slideshow
→ Capturing the Screen

Taking and Editing Photos

In addition to replacing books, the iPad replaces physical photo albums. You can literally carry thousands of photos with you on your iPad. Plus, your iPad's screen is a beautiful way to display these photos. It can also replace your camera, as long as you don't mind its size.

In addition to photos you take using your iPad, you can sync photos from your computer to your iPad, or use the iCloud Photo Library. Then you can use the Photos app to browse and view your photos.

Working with Photos

All iPads after the first generation include two cameras you can use to take a variety of photos that you can then edit and adjust as you need. One camera is located on the front, and one on the back. The primary app for doing this is through the Camera app. Let's take a look at the things you can do with this app.

Taking Photos

Camera

1. Tap the Camera app icon on the home screen. This brings up the Camera app, and you should immediately see the image from the camera.

2. The camera app has six modes: Time-Lapse, Slo-Mo, Video, Photo, Square, and Pano. The first three are for video filming mode, and the other three take rectangular, square, and panoramic photographs. To switch between modes, you can tap and drag up and down in this area. Or, you could tap the word representing the mode you want, and it will switch to it. The option in yellow with a dot next to it is the mode you are currently using. Switch to Photo mode if you are not in that mode already.

Mode Support

Not all iPad models support each mode. Pano requires at least an iPad with a Retina display (like the iPad Air). Slo-Mo requires an iPad Air 2 or newer model.

3. Tap the button at the top right to switch between front and rear cameras.

4. Tap anywhere on the image to specify that you want to use that portion of the image to determine the focus and exposure for the photo. A yellow box appears at that spot.

5. After you have tapped on the image, and if you are using the rear-facing camera, you can zoom in. To do that, use your fingers to pinch apart.

6. Tap the HDR button to turn on High Dynamic Range Imaging.

7. Tap the time delay button to set a timer for 3 or 10 seconds. This allows you to set your iPad down on a stand or lean it against something and get into the shot.

8. Tap the large camera button at the right side of the screen to take the picture. Alternatively, press one of the volume buttons on the side of your iPad to take the picture. If you hold either button down, your iPad will continue to take pictures in rapid succession.

9. Tap the button at the lower right to go to the Camera Roll and see the pictures you have taken. You can edit and adjust the photo you have just taken, as you'll learn in the next task.

The Focus and Exposure Area

When you tap the screen as in step 4, the yellow box will appear. This area is now used for both focus and exposure. After you tap the screen, you can now tap and drag your finger up and down to make further exposure adjustments. You'll see the little sun icon next to the box move up and down along the line as you do so.

If you hold your finger down for a few seconds, the box will pulse and the text AE/AF Lock will appear at the top of the screen. This means the focus and exposure are now locked and will not change as you move your iPad to point it at something different.

High Dynamic What?

High Dynamic Range Imaging is a process where multiple pictures are taken in quick succession, each using a different exposure. Then the multiple images are combined. For instance, if you are taking a picture of a person with a bright sky behind them, one picture will do better with the person, and the other with the sky. Combining the multiple images gives you a picture that shows them both better than a single shot would.

When you use HDR, be sure to hold your iPad steady so each shot captures the same image. They will be taken a fraction of a second apart. So, HDR does not work well with moving objects or a moving camera.

It's Not All Good

You're Holding It Wrong

It is natural to hold your iPad vertically. You may use a majority of apps that way, so when it comes time to take photos or video, it is easy to forget and to continue to hold it vertically. This drives professional and amateur photographers crazy when they see a good photo ruined because a phone or iPad user forgot to turn the device before shooting the picture.

Although portrait photos have their uses, most pictures are best taken in horizontal orientation. Cameras are usually held horizontally, and when you view your photos on a computer screen or television, a horizontal photo will fit nicely whereas a vertical photo will need to shrink to fit, with vertical space wasted on the left and right. Never shoot video in portrait orientation

Editing and Adjusting Photos

You can start editing photos by tapping on the photo icon, like in step 9 of the previous task. Or, you can enter the Photos app and edit photos from there. We'll look more at the Photos app later in this chapter.

(1) If you don't see buttons at the top and bottom of the photo, tap the middle of the photo to bring up controls on the top and bottom of the screen.

(2) Use the thumbnails at the bottom to select a specific picture to view your photos. Or just swipe left and right through the thumbnails to flip through all your photos.

(3) If you are editing a photo you just took using the Camera app, you can tap Done to exit viewing this one image and jump back to the camera interface. Otherwise, continue on to step 4.

(4) Tap the Trash icon to delete the photo. Deleted photos appear for 30 days in a special Recently Deleted photo album, where you can rescue them if the deletion was a mistake. You can also tap and hold in the middle of a photo and then select Hide to hide the photo from Years, Collections and Moments views, though it is still shown in any album you have added it to.

(5) Tap the Share icon to send the photo to someone else via message, email, AirDrop, or a variety of other methods depending on which apps you have installed. This is also where you can copy the image so you can paste it into an email or another app.

(6) Tap the Favorites button to mark this photo as one of your best. You'll be able to find it quickly in the Favorites album in the Photos app.

(7) Tap Edit to enter Editing mode and bring up controls on the left side of the screen.

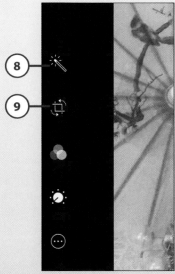

(8) Tap Enhance to have the app examine the brightness and contrast in the photo and try to bring out the best image.

(9) Tap the Crop button.

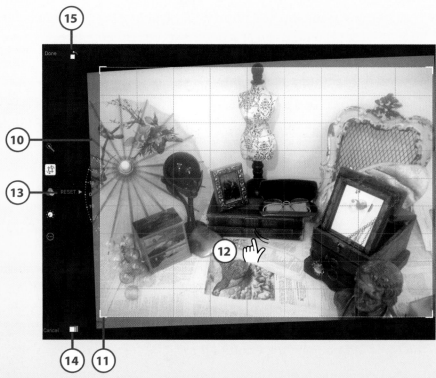

(10) In this example, notice that the image automatically rotates slightly. The accelerometer in your iPad recorded the orientation of your iPad at the moment you took the photo, so it can now straighten the photo to be level. Now you can tap and drag this angle up or down to rotate the photo manually.

(11) You can crop the photo by dragging any one of the four corners. Drag as many corners as you like to get the cropping just the way you want it.

(12) You can pinch in or out to zoom, or drag the photo to reposition it within the crop frame.

(13) Tap Reset to set the rotation to 0 degrees and the cropping back to the full image size. Tap here again to rotate the photo automatically as it first appeared after step 9.

(14) Tap this button to set the cropping rectangle to a specific size, such as 3:2 or square.

(15) Tap the Rotate button to rotate the photo by 90 degree increments. This is useful when a photo is upside down or the wrong orientation.

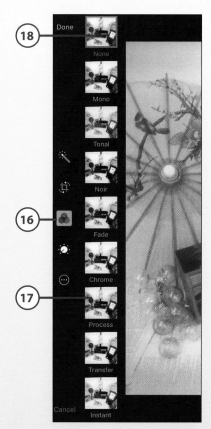 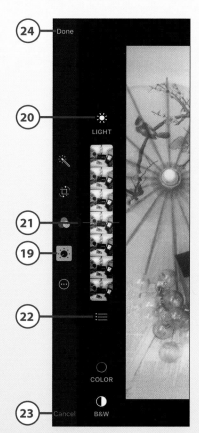

(16) Tap the filters button to apply a color filter to the photo.

(17) You can choose from one of the filters in the list and preview the changes immediately.

(18) You can always tap None to remove the color filter.

(19) Tap the color adjustments button.

(20) Tap one of the three color adjustment types: Light, Color, or B&W.

(21) Each type of adjustment has a filmstrip you can drag up and down to position the red line to indicate the level of adjustment you want. The main image on the screen shows you a preview of the result.

(22) You can dig deeper into each adjustment with the list button and modify only one sub-setting. For instance, you can adjust the contrast, brightness, or exposure.

(23) Tap Cancel to leave the cropping editor without saving the changes.

(24) Tap Done to exit the cropping editor and apply the changes to the photo.

>>>Go Further
EXTENDING PHOTO EDITING

You can add extensions to the Photos app that allow you to edit photos without leaving the app. When you install third-party apps such as **Camera+**, **Afterlight**, and **Fragment Prismatic Effects**, they add more functionality to photo editing. Look for a small button with three dots on the Photo app edit screen. You can see it just below step 19 in the screenshots. Tap that button, and then tap the More button to switch on an extension.

After it is switched on, tap the small three-dot button when editing a photo to select the extended functionality and apply interesting effects to your photo. Dozens, if not hundreds, of third-party apps will soon be available to give you all sorts of photo-editing fun.

Taking Panoramic Photos

If you have an iPad Air or an iPad mini with a retina display, the Pano option is available in the Camera app. This option allows you to take wide panoramic shots, covering a larger area than you could normally fit into a photo.

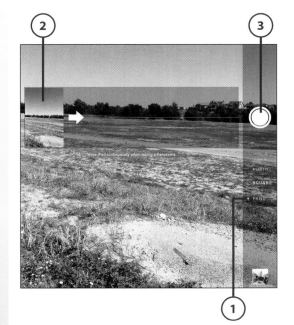

1. In the Camera app, slide the available capture types up until Pano is yellow.

2. Hold your camera in vertical orientation. Look at the rectangle in the middle of the screen. You will be filling this rectangle with images from the camera. Position it so the left side of the rectangle contains the portion of the scene you want to be on the left side of the finished panoramic photo.

3. Tap the camera shutter button, or the physical volume buttons, on your iPad to start taking the photo.

(4) Slowly and steadily turn your body and your iPad from left to right to allow the camera to take in more of the image. As you move, the rectangle fills up with the scene. Small parts of the top and bottom may remain empty if you tilt the iPad a little up or down. Try to keep these areas to a minimum, but a little of this is typically unavoidable.

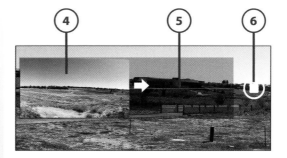

(5) You don't need to fill the entire rectangle. Most panoramic photos don't need to use the full horizontal area. Just get as much as you need to make a good photograph.

(6) Tap the shutter button again to finish.

(7) The result is just like a regular photo in your photo library, except that it is wider. You view it and edit it just like in the previous task.

>>>Go Further
PANORAMIC TIPS

- Before you start taking the panoramic, you can tap the arrow on the screen to reverse direction and take the photo from right to left.

- You don't need to restrict yourself to horizontal panoramas. You can hold your iPad in horizontal orientation and take a vertical one. This could be used to capture a skyscraper, or to get both the ground and a plane in the same shot.

- Panoramas don't have to be of scenery. For instance, you can capture a wide painting in an art museum even if there is not enough space to back up and get it in one shot. Or you can capture everyone sitting around a dining table in one shot.

- If there are moving objects in your panorama, such as soccer players running on a field, you might not get a clean shot. Sometimes a player who is moving fast might appear twice in the same panorama.

Using Photo Booth

In addition to the basic picture-taking functionality of the Camera app, you can also use the included Photo Booth app to take more creative shots using one of eight special filters.

Photo Booth

1. Launch the Photo Booth app.

2. You'll start by seeing all the filters you can choose from. Tap one of the filters to select it.

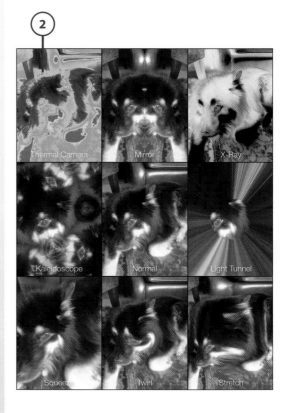

(3) Now you'll see just that one filter. In addition, you have some buttons. Tap on the button at the bottom right to switch between the front and rear cameras.

(4) Tap the button at the bottom left to return to the 9-filter preview.

(5) Tap the camera button at the bottom to take a picture.

(6) Some filters also allow you to tap the live video image to adjust the filter. For instance, the Light Tunnel filter enables you to set the position of the center of the tunnel.

A Kind of Flash

When you take a picture with the camera on the front of the iPad, you get a kind of flash effect from the screen. It simply turns all white for a second. This helps in low light situations.

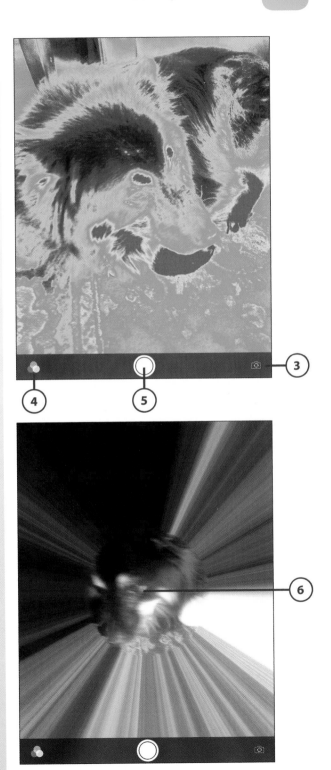

Photo Sources

Your iPad's Photos app can display photos from many different sources. You can then view them chronologically by Years, Collections, and Moments, as we'll look at in the next task. You can also organize them by albums that you create. Before we look at how to view your photos, it is important to understand where the photos come from. Here are all the possible sources:

- **Photos you take with your iPad's camera:** When you use the Camera app or the Photo Booth app to take a picture, it is added to your library with easy access through an album named Camera Roll.

- **Images from apps:** Many apps allow you to export images into your iPad's photo library. These will also be seen in the Photos app. Included in this category is when you take a screen shot. We'll look at that later in this chapter.

- **Synced from your computer:** iTunes on Mac and Windows computers can sync photos to your iPad. See "Syncing Photos" in Chapter 3. You can take pictures with a dedicated camera device, organize them on your computer, and then sync the ones you like to view on the iPad.

- **Transferred over a network:** You can use AirDrop on an iPod, iPhone, or Mac to send images to an iPad. You can also save images you see on the web or save images attached to emails or messages. Sometimes third-party apps allow you to access images stored on other photo services and transfer these to your photo library as well.

- **iCloud Photo Library:** You can choose to store all your photos on Apple's cloud server and access them from all your iOS devices and Macs. When you use this option, you can no longer sync with iTunes on a computer because the two methods are mutually exclusive. You can turn this on in the Settings app, under Photos & Camera.

- **Photo Stream:** If you enable Photo Stream, every picture you take is automatically sent to iCloud's Photo Stream where it also appears on your iPad, Mac, and even your Apple TV, if you have Photo Stream enabled on those devices. Think of this as a temporary email inbox for photos. Only the most recent 1,000 pictures from the last 30 days are stored in Photo Stream. You could take a picture on your iPhone and see it on your Mac and iPad, choosing to then move it to your main library if you want to keep it permanently. You can turn this on in the Settings app, under Photos & Camera.

- **iCloud Photo Sharing:** You can create iCloud photo albums and share them with others. Likewise, you can subscribe to someone else's shared album. Then you can view these shared album photos in the Photos app.

The big choice you need to make is whether to use iCloud Photo Library or sync photos using iTunes.

iCloud Photo Library is a great way to manage your photos as they will simply be available to you everywhere. But if you have a slow Internet connection at home, then you might want to stick with the old system of storing your photo library on your computer. Though this might be a good excuse to call your service provider and get a faster connection.

Browsing Your Photos

The Photos app on your iPad organizes your photos chronologically and breaks time into three levels: Years, Collections, and Moments. The photos taken on your iPad are combined with photos you synced from your computer or photos in your iCloud Photos Library. Let's take a tour of the Photos app to learn how to browse through your photos.

Photos

(1)   Launch the Photos app to view your photos.

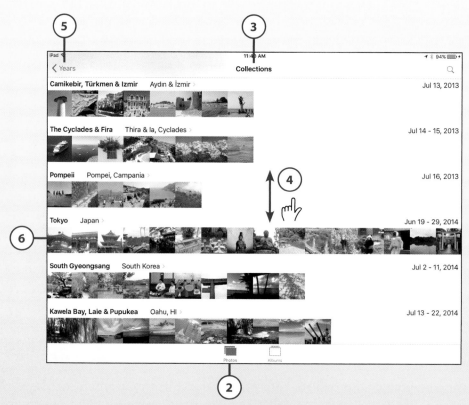

2 Tap Photos at the bottom to browse your photos.

3 You will resume viewing your photos at the same level you were viewing them the last time you looked. The three levels are: Years, Collections, and Moments. You can see which level you are at by looking at the top of the screen.

4 You can tap and drag vertically to scroll through your photos.

5 To move up a level, from Collections to Years, or Moments to Collections, tap the label in the upper-left corner. If you are viewing Collections, the label says Years to indicate that is the view you are moving back to.

6 Whichever level you are at, you can dig down to the next level by tapping one of the strips of photos. You can also tap and hold your finger over any photo until it pops out of the strip, and then release to jump right to viewing that photo.

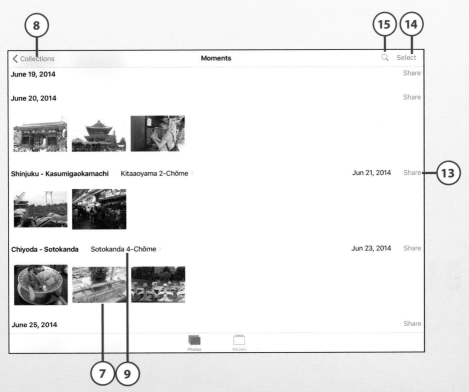

(7) At the Moments level, you see the individual photos. Tap one to view it. We'll look more in depth at viewing photos in the next task. Note that Moment groupings are based both on time and location. So photos taken at a park in the afternoon and then at dinner later that day on the other side of town could be grouped into different Moments.

(8) Tap Collections to go back up to the Collections level.

(9) At the Moments or Collections level, you can tap any location name to go to a map where the photos are arranged by location.

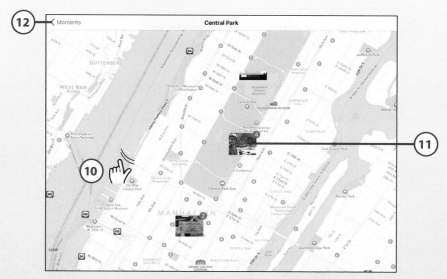

(10) The map resizes to contain all the photos in the Moment or Collection you are viewing. If the photos are all taken in the same city, you may get a city map. If they are taken across the world, you may see the whole planet. You can pinch to zoom, or tap and drag to move the map.

(11) Tap any single photo to view it, or tap a group of photos to see a screen that shows each one and allows you to scroll through them.

(12) Tap at the top left to return to Moments or Collections.

(13) At the Moments level, you can tap a Share button next to any Moment grouping and share some or all of the photos through email, iCloud, Messages, or Facebook.

(14) You can also tap the Select button, and then you can select multiple Moments groups to share.

(15) Tap the Search button, and you can search by typing location or date terms like "Hawaii" or "October."

It's Not All Good

Where in the World Are You?

When you take pictures with a mobile phone like the iPhone, the location is automatically added to the photo. But most dedicated digital cameras, even expensive ones, do not have any GPS feature, so they don't know your location. iPads without a live Wi-Fi connection won't know, either. So your photo collection may have a lot of photos with no location information. These photos will not appear on maps and can't be accurately divided into Moments by location.

Viewing Your Photos

Whether you are viewing a photo you tapped on at the Moments level, such as in step 7 of the previous task, or you are viewing a photo in an album or from the Camera app, the interface is basically the same.

1. Tap in the middle of the photo to remove the buttons and text at the top and bottom of the screen so you can enjoy the photo. Tap again to bring the interface elements back.

2. Pinch out to zoom in on the photo. Once zoomed, you can tap and drag to see different areas of the photo.

3. When zoomed out to view the entire photo, you can swipe left or right to view the previous or next photo in the Moment or album.

4. Alternatively, you can tap or drag in the strip of photos at the bottom to move through the photos in the Moment or album.

5. Tap Edit to edit or adjust the photo. See "Editing and Adjusting Photos," earlier in this chapter.

6. Tap Moments to exit viewing this photo and return to the Moments level. If you are viewing a photo from the Cameras after taking a picture, you'll have a Done button at the right to return to the Camera screen, plus an All Photos button to the left to open the Photos app.

7. Tap the Share button to share via AirDrop, email, social networks, and a variety of other methods. See the next section for more information about sharing.

>>>Go Further
ZOOM AND ROTATE

Here are a few tips on how to navigate your photos as you view them:

- Pinch or unpinch with two fingers to zoom out and in.
- Double-tap a photo to zoom back out to normal size.
- While a photo is at normal size, double-tap to zoom it to make it fit on the screen with the edges cropped.
- If you pinch in far enough, the picture closes, and you return to browsing mode.

Sharing Your Photos

You can share photos while viewing an individual photo, such as in step 7 of the previous task. You can also share from the Moments screen by tapping Share next to any moment.

Let's pick up from step 7 of the previous task, as if you have just tapped the Share button while viewing a photo.

1. At the top of the Sharing screen, you see your selected photo—plus you can choose others in the same Moment or album to share. Tap any photo to include it. You'll see a checkmark on photos that you have set to share.

2. You can share via AirDrop, sending the photo to another iOS or Mac user near you. See "Sharing with AirDrop" in Chapter 3.

3. You can send the photos using either the Message or Mail apps.

4. You can also post directly to Facebook, Twitter, or Flickr, so long as you have configured these services in your Settings app.

5. You can copy a photo to use it in another app. You can also tap and hold in the middle of a photo while editing it, and select Copy.

6. AirPlay lets you show the photo on an Apple TV connected to the same Wi-Fi network.

7. You can send the photo to a printer on your network.

8. iCloud Photo Sharing lets you add the photo to an online shared album.

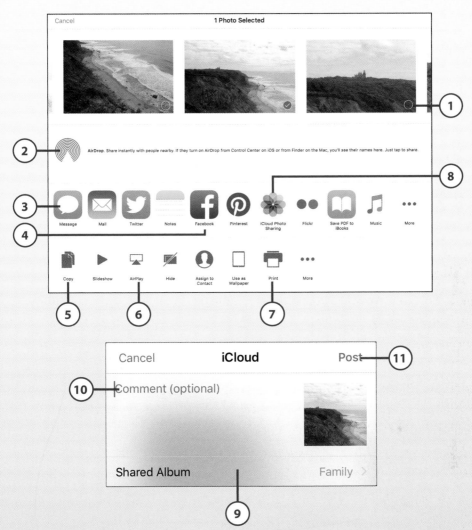

9 Set the online album where the photo should be placed. You'll also be given the chance to create a new album.

10 You can add a comment that will appear online with the photo.

11 Tap Post to send the photos to iCloud.

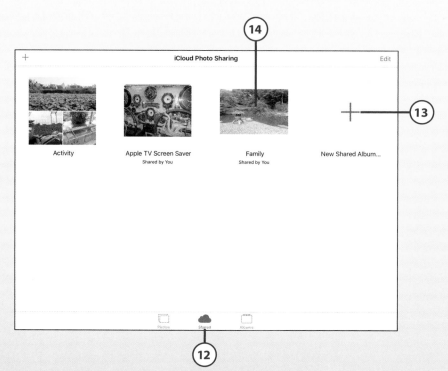

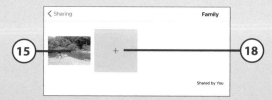

(12) You can see these online albums in the Photos app by tapping on the Shared button at the bottom of the Years/Collections/Moments screen.

(13) You can create a new shared album from this screen.

(14) Tap on a shared album to view it.

(15) You see all the photos in that album. Tap a single photo to view it.

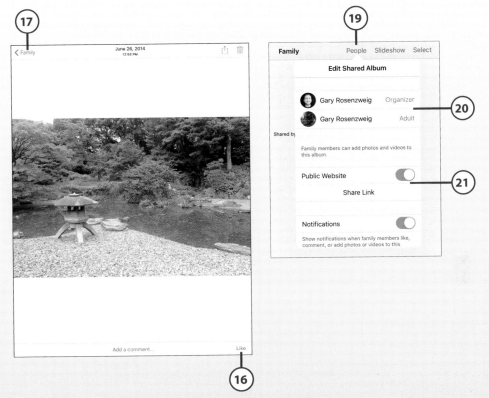

16 When looking at an individual photo, you can "like" the photo and add a comment.

17 Tap the name of the album in the upper-left corner to go back to the previous screen.

18 Tap the blank album with the + sign to create a new shared photo album. You'll be asked to give it a name and enter email addresses of people with whom you want to share the album.

19 While viewing a shared photo album that you have created, tap the People button to change the sharing options.

20 If this wasn't the Family album, then you'd see a list of people with whom the album is shared. Since this is a special Family photo album created by the Family Sharing feature, it is automatically shared by everyone in the family group. Other albums you create can be shared with anyone. An option here would be to allow you to invite more people to share it.

21 You can also turn on the Public Website option to let anyone view these photos. Then, tap the Share Link button to send people a link to the web page.

You can share your photos in many ways, and it is likely that more will be added in the future. What you can use depends on what you have set up on your iPad. For instance, if you have Messaging and Twitter set up, you can use the Message and Tweet buttons to share using those services.

Working with Albums

Using the chronological Years/Collections/Moments views of the Photos app is a great way to find the photos you want to view. But, if you would rather organize your photos yourself, you can do so by creating albums.

Albums can be made using the photo library software on your Mac, Photoshop Albums or Photoshop Elements on Windows, or by using file system folders on Mac and windows. When you sync to your iPad with iTunes, you'll see these albums using the steps that follow. Or, if you are using iCloud Photo Library, you can create the albums on any device, and the albums will also show up on all your other devices.

The important thing to realize about photo albums is that the photos aren't really *in* the album. Think of them as a list of references to photos, the same way a playlist in iTunes refers to songs stored in your music library.

A photo appears once in your photo library, and you can see it once in the Years/Collections/Moments views, but you can put a reference to that photo in multiple albums. For instance, you can have a photo appear in an album named "My Best Pictures" and also in an album named "Summer 2014." If you delete it from one or both, the photo is still in your library—it just doesn't happen to be in any album.

Viewing Albums

1. In the Photos app, tap the Albums button.
2. Tap on an album to expand it to see all the photos.
3. Tap any photo to view it.
4. Tap the album name to return from viewing the photo, and then tap the Albums button on the next screen to return to the list of albums.

Getting Back to the Album

After you finish digging down into an album, you can go back to the list of albums by tapping the Albums button, or a similarly named button, at the top left. But you can also pinch in all photos to group them in the middle of the screen and then release to move back to the albums list.

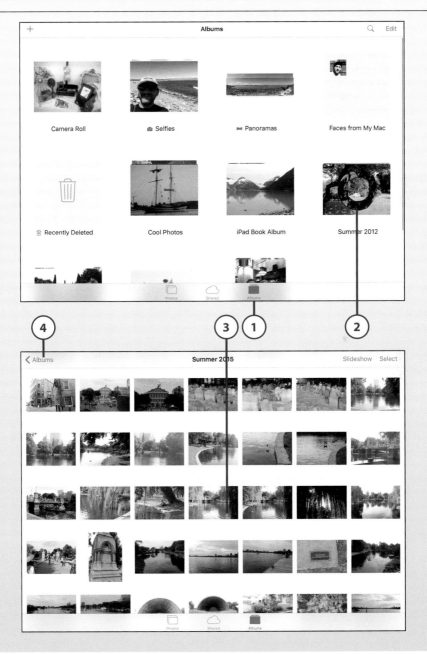

Creating Albums

You can create new albums on your iPad. If you are using iCloud Photo Library, these albums appear across all your devices. The process involves naming a new album and then selecting the photos to appear in the album.

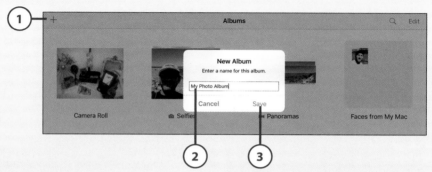

(1) In the Photos app, tap Albums at the bottom to view your albums, and then tap the + button to create a new album.

(2) Enter a name for the album.

(3) Tap Save.

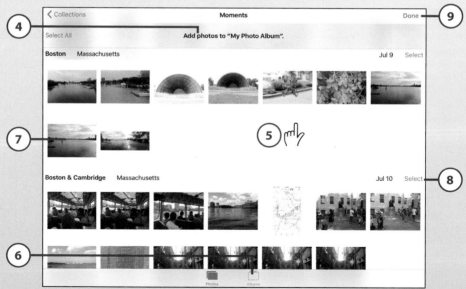

(4) Now you can start adding some photos to this empty album. You see all your photos appear in the Moments view, just as they did in step 7 of the task "Browsing Your Photos," earlier in this chapter.

5 Tap and drag vertically to flip through your photos to locate the ones you want to include in this new album.

6 If you prefer Albums view, you can tap Albums to switch to that view.

7 Tap photos to add them to the album. Tap again to undo the selection.

8 You can also select an entire Moment group of photos.

9 When you have added all the photos you want to the album, tap Done. You can always add more by viewing that album, tapping the Select button at the top, and then tapping the Add button at the top.

Special Albums

Many special albums are created automatically by the Photos app—most notably is the Camera Roll album with images you have just taken. There might also be a Recently Deleted album acting as a trash can or recycling bin, where you can rescue recently deleted photos. The Photos app also groups other items into albums automatically, such as Panoramas and Videos.

Creating a Slideshow

Another way to look at your photos is as a slideshow with music and transitions. You can quickly and easily create a slideshow with any group of photos in the Photos app that shows a Slideshow button at the top—for example, an album synced to, or that you created on, your iPad.

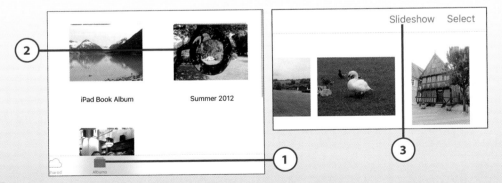

1 In the Photos app, tap Albums.

2 Tap an album to select it.

3 Tap the Slideshow button at the top of the album.

4 The slideshow immediately starts playing with default options. To customize it, first tap in the middle of the screen to bring up controls at the top and bottom.

5 Tap the pause button to stop playback while you adjust the settings.

6 Tap the Options button at the bottom right.

7 You can select from one of many themes for the slideshow.

8 You can change the music to one of many presets, or use a song from iTunes.

9 You can set the slideshow to loop.

10 Use this slider to change the speed.

11 Slideshows can be played on your iPad's screen, or on any connected AirPlay video devices, such as an Apple TV connected to the same Wi-Fi network.

12 Tap the Play button that took the place of the Pause button to start the slideshow.

13 Tap Done to exit the slideshow.

Stopping a Slideshow

Tap on the screen anywhere to stop a slideshow. This will take you into the album. Start with the current photo. Then you can continue to browse that album normally swiping left or right and using the strip of thumbnails at the bottom.

Capturing the Screen

You can capture the entire iPad screen and send it to your Photos app. This feature is useful if you want to save what you see to an image for later.

(1) Make sure the screen shows what you want to capture. Try the Home screen, as an example.

(2) Press and hold the Wake/Sleep button and Home button at the same time. The screen flashes and you hear a camera shutter sound, (unless you have the volume turned down).

(3) Go to the Photos app.

(4) Tap on Albums and then go to the Camera Roll album.

(5) The last image in this album should be your new screen capture. Tap it to open it.

(6) The screen shot will appear just like any other photo. You can edit it or delete it with the buttons on the top right and bottom right.

(7) Tap the Share icon to email the photo or copy it to use in another application. Or you can leave the photo in your photo library for future use.

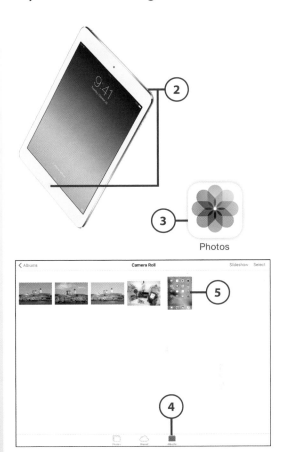

Photos

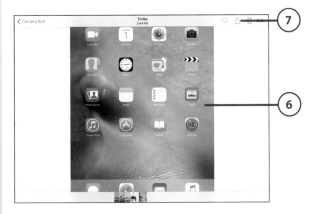

It's Not All Good

Sharing Slideshows

Want to share a slideshow via a social network or YouTube? You can, but not by using the Photos app's simple Slideshow feature. Instead, use iMovie. You can also use one of many slideshow and photo-sharing apps you can get in the App Store.

Search Apple's App
Store for thousands of
useful, educational, and
entertaining apps.

In this chapter, you learn how to go beyond the basic functionality of your iPad, and add more apps using the App Store.

→ Purchasing an App
→ Arranging Apps on Your iPad
→ Creating App Folders
→ Viewing Currently Running Apps
→ Quitting Apps
→ Viewing a Second App with Slide Over
→ Interacting with Two Apps At Once with Split View
→ Viewing Video with Picture-In-Picture
→ Finding Good Apps
→ Using iPhone/iPod touch Apps
→ Getting Help with Apps
→ Monitoring and Managing Your Apps

The World of Apps

Apps that come with your iPad and Apple's office apps, Pages, Numbers, and Keynote are just the tip of the iceberg. The App Store contains hundreds of thousands of apps from third-party developers, with more added each day.

You use the App Store app to shop for and purchase new apps—although many are free. You can also rearrange the app icons on your Home screen pages to organize them.

Purchasing an App

Adding a new app to your iPad requires that you visit the App Store. You do that, not surprisingly, with the App Store app on your Home screen.

(1) Tap the App Store icon on your Home screen.

(2) If this is the first time you have used the App Store, you see the featured apps at the top of the screen. Otherwise, tap the Featured button at the bottom.

(3) Swipe left or right to view more featured apps. You can do the same for the sections below, which often change to feature different types of apps.

(4) Swipe up to scroll down and see more featured apps.

(5) Tap Top Charts to see the top paid apps and top free apps.

(6) Tap Categories to see a list of app categories. Another way to see apps by category is to tap the Explore button at the bottom of the screen.

(7) Tap any category to go to the page of featured apps in that category.

App Store

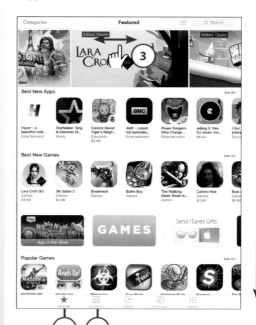

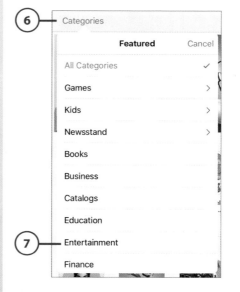

8 Use the search box to search for an app by keyword.

9 The button at the top lets you filter between iPad apps and iPhone apps. Apps that are optimized to work well with both screen sizes will appear in both.

10 Select whether you want to see apps that are free or both free and paid.

11 Select a category to narrow down the search results.

12 Choose how you want the results to be ordered: relevance, popularity, ratings, or release date.

13 Tap here to see the apps you have saved to your wish list.

14 Tap an app to read more about it and see screenshots, other apps by the same company, and user reviews.

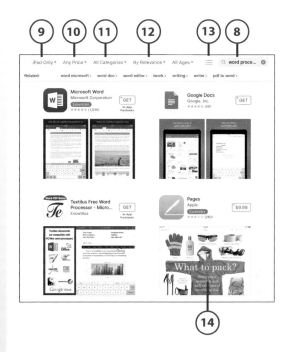

Redeem Codes

If you go to the bottom of the Featured page in the App Store, you will see a button marked Redeem. Use this to enter any redemption code you get for a free app. You may get a code because someone sends you an app as a gift. Developers also send out a handful of these codes when they release a new app or app version.

Automatically Download New Apps

If you go to the Settings app, look for the iTunes & App Store category. There you can turn on automatic downloads for apps, as well as music and books. Once you turn this on, purchasing an app on your Mac or PC in iTunes, or on another iOS device with the same Apple ID, will automatically send this app to your iPad as well.

(15) Tap on the price on the left under the large icon to purchase an app. It changes to a Buy App button. Tap it again. If you have already purchased the app, the button will say Open, and you can launch the app by tapping the button.

Purchased Apps

If you have purchased the app in the past, but don't currently have it on your iPad, you will see a cloud/download button that lets you download the app again. You do not pay again for an app you have already purchased.

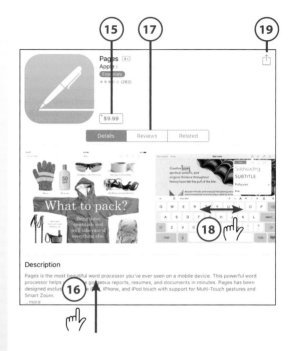

(16) Swipe up to read the description of the app.

(17) Tap Reviews to look at reviews for the app.

(18) Scroll left and right to flip through the screenshots for the app.

(19) Tap the Share button to send a link to the app to friends via email, Messages, and so on. You can also pay for and send a non-free app to a friend as a gift, or add a non-free app to your wish list to remember it for future consideration.

(20) When you purchase an app, it starts installing, and you can watch the progress from the app's information page in the App Store app or from the location of the app's icon on your Home screen.

Loading…

Redownloading an App You Already Purchased

Once you buy an app, you own it forever—at least as long as you keep using the same Apple ID. At the bottom of the App Store app, you see a button marked Purchased. Tap that to see a list of all apps you have bought, even if you have removed them from this iPad, or maybe never even downloaded them in the first place. Perhaps you previously bought an app on your iPhone or iPod touch. You can quickly jump to any of these apps and download them to your iPad without paying for it a second time.

>>>Go Further
FREE, PAID, AND FREEMIUM

Some apps in the App Store are free, and others you need to pay for before downloading and installing. But some apps are free for the basic version, and then you need to make in-app purchases to use advanced functions or buy more content. These are called "freemium" apps.

It is up to the developer of the app to design the method of making purchases. Most apps show you a preview of the function or content and then include a purchase or buy button. Before any app can charge your iTunes account for an in-app purchase, you will see a standard Confirm Your In-App Purchase prompt.

Confirm Your In-App Purchase

Do you want to buy one Just Jigsaw Puzzles Collection: The Masters for $1.99?

Cancel   Buy

Photo apps may use in-app purchases to charge you for additional filters or effects. Drawing apps may charge for new brushes or tools. Some free apps have advertising and allow you to make an in-app purchase to be able to use the app ad-free.

Often games will have a variety of items you can purchase to alter gameplay. But instead of a long list of in-app purchases, they simply charge you for in-game currency such as tokens, gems, or gold. Then you can use these to purchase items inside the game.

There's no risk in trying free apps that offer in-app purchases. If you find that the purchases in the app are not worth it for you, simply do not purchase anything. If the app isn't useful, you can delete it without spending a penny.

Organizing Apps on Your iPad

It doesn't take long to have several pages of apps. Fortunately, you can rearrange your app icons in two ways. The first is to do it on the iPad Home screen and allow apps to appear on multiple pages of the screen as each page fills up. In addition to spreading your apps across multiple pages, you can also group them together in folders so that several apps take up only one icon position on a screen.

Arranging Apps on the Home Screen

1 Tap and hold an icon until all the icons start to jiggle.

2 The icon you are holding is a little larger than the others. Drag it and drop it in a new location. To carry the icon to the next page of apps, drag it to the right side of the screen.

3 Delete an app from your iPad by tapping the X at the upper left of the icon. Note that the X does not appear over all apps, as the default set of apps that come with your iPad cannot be removed.

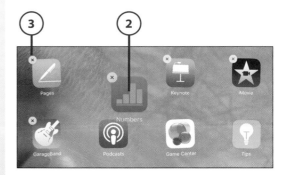

4 When finished, press the Home button (not shown).

Deleting Is Not Forever

If you sync your iPad to iTunes on a computer, you do not delete apps forever. All apps remain in your iTunes library on your computer unless you remove them. So, you can get rid of the app from your iPad and find it is still on your computer if you want to select it to sync back to your iPad. You can always re-download an app from the app store that you purchased previously, without paying again. If you don't think you'll need an app for a while, you can delete it and then add it back again later.

>>>Go Further
WHAT ELSE CAN I DO?

Here are a few more tips that might make your app housekeeping easier:

- You can release an app and then grab another to move it. If the apps still jiggle, you can keep moving app icons.

- You can drag apps into and out of the dock along the bottom where you can fit up to six apps. Apps in the dock appear on all pages of your Home screen.

- You can drag an app to the right on the last page of apps to create a new page of your Home screen.

Creating App Folders

Grouping apps in a folder enables you to de-clutter your Home screen if you find you have too many apps competing for space on the screen.

1. Identify several apps that you want to group together. Tap and hold one of those apps until the icons start to jiggle.

2. Continue to hold your finger down, and drag the icon over another one you wish to group it with.

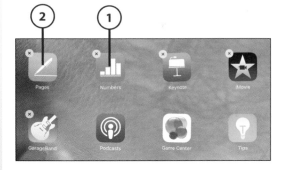

(3) An app folder appears and enlarges to fill the center of the screen.

(4) Change the name of the app folder.

(5) Press the Home button once to dismiss the name editor, and again to return to your home screen (not shown).

(6) You now see the app folder on your home screen. You can drag other apps to this folder using steps 1 and 2.

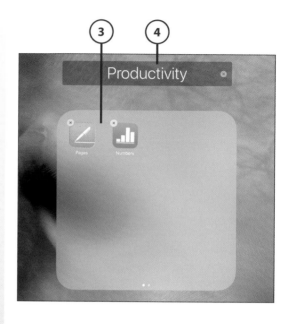

Working with Folders

After you have created an app folder, you can access the apps in it by first tapping on the folder and then tapping the app you want to launch. Tapping and holding any app in the folder gives you the opportunity to rename the folder, rearrange the icons in the folder, or drag an app out of the folder.

>>>*Go Further*

WORKING WITH APP FOLDERS

Here are a few more things you can do inside app folders:

- To remove an app from a folder and put it back into a position on the Home screen, tap and hold the icon until it jiggles. Then drag it out to the surrounding area outside of the folder.

- Inside app folders, you can have more than one page if you have more than nine apps stored in it. You can swipe left and right to move between pages while the folder is open.

- While apps in the app folder are jiggling, you can move them around inside the folder and off to the left or right to move them between pages inside the folder.

- You can move app folders around your Home screen and between Home screen pages just as you can with an app icon.

Working with Apps

You can have many apps running at once on your iPad. In fact, after you launch an app, it remains running by default even if you switch back to the home screen and run another app. With iOS 9, you can even view a second app at the same time you're running another one, or set up video to run picture-in-picture with another app.

Viewing Currently Running Apps

Apps running in the background use little or no resources. You can think of them as paused apps. You can switch back to them at any time, and most apps resume right where you left off.

1. Double-press the Home button (not shown).

2. This gives you a new view, called the Recents list, that shows all your currently running apps in a 3D series of pages. The app you currently are using appears to the right, and the previous app that you used is in the middle. This lets you easily switch between the current app and the previous app.

3. Swipe left and right to see more items in the list. The further to the right in the list the app is located, the longer it has been since you last used it.

4. Icons for each app also appear at the top. You can tap on these icons just as you can tap on the screens.

Moving from App to App with a Gesture

If you have several apps running, you can quickly move between them by using four-finger gestures. Just swipe left or right with four fingers at the same time. This will move you from app to app without needing to go back to the Home screen, or use the list of recent apps.

Quitting Apps

Although it is rarely necessary to completely quit an app, you can do it in one of two ways. This forces the app to shut down if it has frozen, or if you simply want to start the app fresh to see an introduction sequence or work around problems the app may be having.

1. Press the home button twice to see the list of your currently running apps (not shown).

2. Swipe to the left or right so the app you want to force to quit is in the center of the screen.

3. Tap the preview of the app and swipe upward quickly until your finger is almost at the top of the screen; then let go. The app will quit and be removed from the list.

>>>Go Further
DELETING ACTIVE APPS

A second method works when the app is the one currently onscreen.

Press and hold the wake/sleep button on the top of your iPad for about three seconds. You will see the "Slide to power off" control appear.

Don't use the "Slide to power off" control or press the Cancel button. Instead, hold the Home button down for several seconds. This quits the app and returns you to your Home Screen; or for some apps, it restarts the app.

The app also remains in the list you see when you double-press the Home button since it is one you recently used, even though it is not currently running.

Viewing a Second App with Slide Over New!

Ever wish you could check your email while surfing the web? Or write something in the Notes app while reading the News app? New in iOS 9 is the ability to view more than one app at a time on the iPad. The first of three methods for doing this is called Slide Over. As an example, start in Safari.

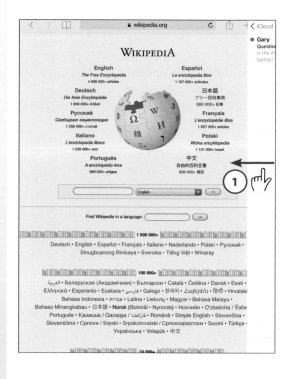

1 Tap and swipe in from the right side of the screen. It may be easier to touch just outside of the visible area of the screen so your finger moves from off the screen to on the screen. Then continue moving, and you will see the Slide Over screen appear. Stop when you are about a third of the way across the screen.

2. An app appears on the right side of the screen, taking up about a third of the space.
3. The app you were previously using remains on the other part of the screen, but is inactive. If you tap it, you dismiss the Slide Over app and return to your original app.
4. You can also tap and slide the handle on the left side of the Slide Over portion of the screen to go back to your original app.
5. To switch which app is shown in Slide Over, tap and drag down from the top of the screen on the right side. Start your finger just outside the screen for this to work.
6. You get a list of app icons. Only apps currently running and compatible with Slide Over are shown. Tap and slide vertically to see all the items in the list.
7. Tap an icon to have that app fill the Slide Over portion of the screen.

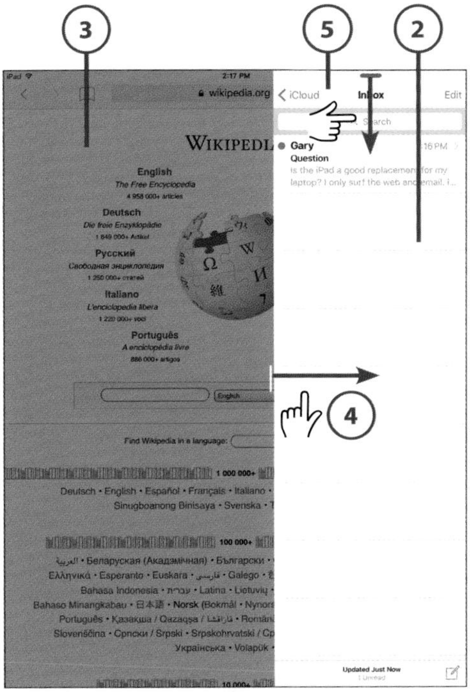

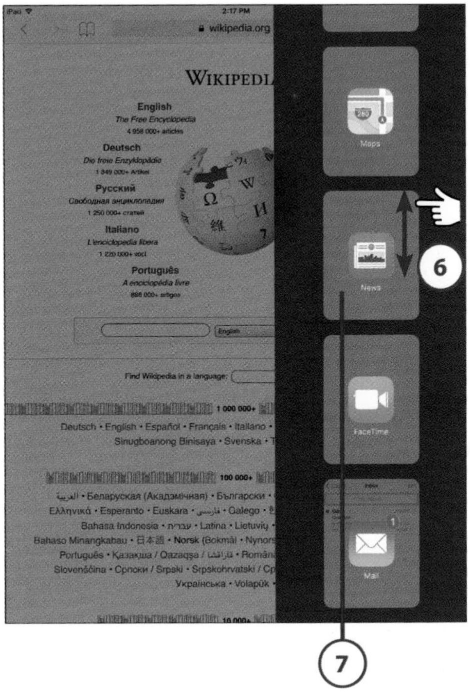

Limitations

Apps running in the Slide Over portion of the screen look and act differently from when they are running full screen, naturally. For instance, Mail shows you the list of messages in an inbox or the contents of a single message. But there is no room for both.

>>>Go Further
SLIDE OVER REQUIREMENTS

Slide Over requires a fairly new iPad model: The iPad Air or newer, the iPad mini 2 or newer, or an iPad Pro. In addition, for an app to work in Slide Over, it must be designed with that feature in mind. So many Apple-created apps like Mail, Calendar, Notes, News, and so on, work with it. However, most third-party apps do not.

Interacting with Two Apps at Once with Split View New!

Another way to interact with more than one app at a time is to use Split View. This mode seems to be similar to Slide Over, but there are two important differences. The first is that you can interact with both apps, not just the one brought over from the right. The second is that both apps take up equal space on the screen.

Split View works best when you are in horizontal orientation. So start by holding your iPad horizontally and bring up Safari.

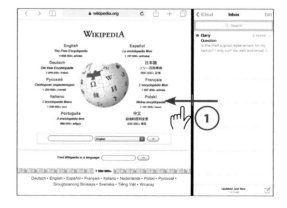

1. Start Split View the same way you start Slide Over, by dragging from outside the right side of the screen to the left. Stop about a third of the way to leave the app in Slide Over mode. But this time, tap and drag the handle again until you get to the middle of the screen.

Best on a Pro

This works particularly well if you have an iPad Pro. The Pro was designed to be about twice the screen size of an iPad Air. So using Split View is like having two iPads.

(**2**) The new app appears on the right. You can interact with it the same way as with Slide Over. In vertical orientation many apps on the right still only use about a third of the screen, while in horizontal mode they use half of it. This may change in future versions of iOS 9.

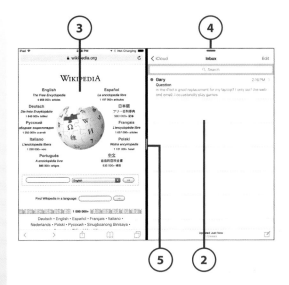

(**3**) The original app is now on the left, and you can interact with it as well.

(**4**) You can drag from the top of the right side down to view other apps to replace this one, just like with Slide Over.

(**5**) You can drag the center handle to the right or left to allow one of the two apps to take over the whole screen.

>>>Go Further

SPLIT VIEW REQUIREMENTS

Split View requires an even newer model of iPad than Slide Over. You need an iPad Air 2, iPad mini 4, iPad Pro, or newer models for this.

In addition, both apps must be compatible with Split View in order for it to work. This is because both apps need to know how to behave when they only have half a screen to work with. Most third-party apps won't work with Split View, but many Apple-created apps will.

Viewing Video with Picture-In-Picture New!

A third method for multitasking is specific to video. While you are watching video in some apps, like Safari, you can keep the video playing on the screen while you move to another app. As an example, we look at a video on a web page.

1. Start on a web page that has an embedded video.

2. Sometimes you need to start the video to see the controls.

3. Look for this Picture-in-Picture control. If you don't see it, it means that the video isn't being presented in a format that is compatible with picture-in-picture on your iPad. Tap this button.

4. The video is replaced with a "This video is playing in Picture in Picture" message.

5. The video moves to a corner of the screen.

6. Now you can leave this app. For instance, tap the Home button to go to your iPad's Home screen.

7. The video remains. You can tap and drag it now to move it elsewhere on the screen. You can also pinch it in or out to resize it.

8. Tap the Close button to remove the video from the screen.

9. Tap the Play/Pause button to toggle playback.

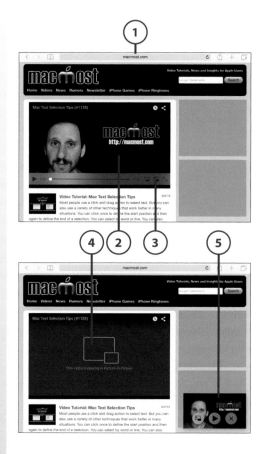

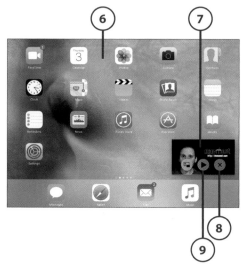

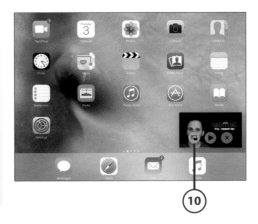

10 Tap the Return button to return to the app where the video originated. You can continue to move from app to app, and the video remains on the screen until you dismiss it. You can also drag it off to the left or right side to reduce the video to only a small "tab" that can be tapped to bring the video back onto the screen.

Finding Good Apps

Finding good apps might be the biggest problem that iPad users have. With more than a million apps in the App Store, it can be hard to find what you want, so here are some tips.

1 Check out the featured apps in the App Store (not shown). Be wary because they tend to be heavy on apps by large companies with well-established brands.

2 In the App Store app, find an app close to what you want and then check out the Related section.

3 Look for trial versions, which often have names with "Lite" or "Free" at the end. Search for the name of the app and see if other versions turn up. Use free versions of apps to determine if it is worth paying for the full or enhanced version.

4 Tap on Reviews.

5 Read reviews, but don't trust them completely. Casual users are not always the best at providing balanced reviews.

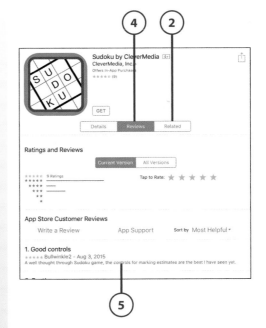

>>>Go Further

USING RESOURCES OUTSIDE THE APP STORE

Many good resources for finding apps aren't part of the App Store. Following are a few suggestions:

- Search using Google. For example, if you want another spreadsheet app, search "iPad App Spreadsheet."

- After you find an app that you want, try another Google search using the name of the app followed by the word "review."

- Find sites that feature and review apps. Many are out there, but be aware that some sites are paid by developers to review an app, so the review might not be the most objective.

- The author provides a list of recommended apps at http://macmost.com/featurediphoneapps.

Using iPhone/iPod touch Apps

Most apps in Apple's App Store are built for both the iPhone (and iPod touch) and iPad. Both devices run iOS, but the iPhone has a much smaller screen than the iPad. If a developer has created an app specifically for the iPhone's screen, and not the iPad, you can use a special feature of the iPad to enlarge the app to make it fill most of your display.

1. To enlarge the app, tap the 2x button at the upper-left corner.

2. If the app looks blurry when it's enlarged, tap the 1x button to return to normal size.

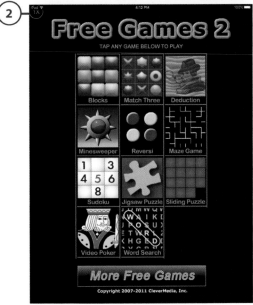

Getting Help with Apps

Apps are developed rapidly by both large and small companies. And apps are difficult to test because of Apple's restrictions on app distribution. So it is common to find bugs, have problems, or simply need to ask a question.

(1) Check in the app to see if you can contact the developer. For example, in the Word Spell game app, there is a FAQ/Feedback button that takes you to a page of frequently asked questions and contact information.

(2) If you don't find a way to contact support in the app, launch the App Store app and search for the app there.

(3) Select the app to view its information.

(4) Go to the Reviews section.

(5) Tap the App Support button.

>>>*Go Further*

REVIEWS VS. DIRECT CONTACT

You may be tempted to leave a review for an app and ask questions there, or ask the developer for new features or bug fixes. However, the developer does not have any way to respond to reviews in the App Store. In fact, the developer cannot even tell who is writing the review, so it would be impossible for them to ask more questions or communicate in any way. Be sure to contact the developer directly and not use reviews as a way to send a message. Only use reviews as a way to leave honest, helpful information for others who may be looking to purchase an app.

>>>*Go Further*

SHARING APPS

When you buy an app, it can be put on any iPad (or iPhone/iPod touch if it works there, too) registered to your iTunes account. So if you have an iPad and an iPhone, you can buy the app on one and put it on the other at no extra charge. You can use the Family Sharing feature of iOS to also share that app purchase with other members of your family. See "Sharing Purchases with Your Family" in Chapter 4 to learn more about Family Sharing.

Monitoring and Managing Your Apps

For most users, you don't need to do anything extra to keep your apps running smoothly. However, you do have a variety of tools that let you see how much storage space and battery power your apps are using, and whether they are accessing your location and other information.

Viewing App Storage Information

To see how much storage space each app is using on your iPad, go to the Settings app.

Settings

1. Tap the Settings app icon.
2. Tap General settings.
3. Tap Storage & iCloud Usage.
4. Tap Manage Storage under the Storage heading, not the iCloud heading.

5 You see a list of all your apps sorted by how much storage they are using. Tap any app for more details.

6 For the majority of apps, you will simply see another screen with the app size, version number, and total storage being used.

7 You always have the option to delete the app from your iPad, too, without needing to go back to the Home screen to do it.

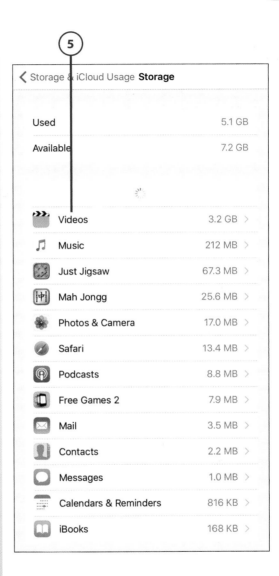

5

❮ Storage & iCloud Usage **Storage**

Used	5.1 GB
Available	7.2 GB

Videos	3.2 GB	❯
Music	212 MB	❯
Just Jigsaw	67.3 MB	❯
Mah Jongg	25.6 MB	❯
Photos & Camera	17.0 MB	❯
Safari	13.4 MB	❯
Podcasts	8.8 MB	❯
Free Games 2	7.9 MB	❯
Mail	3.5 MB	❯
Contacts	2.2 MB	❯
Messages	1.0 MB	❯
Calendars & Reminders	816 KB	❯
iBooks	168 KB	❯

❮ Storage   **Info**

JUST JIGSAW
Version 2.0.0
App Size: 63.5 MB   **6**

Documents & Data	3.8 MB

Delete App   **7**

8. For some apps, you get a list of content and a breakdown of how much space each item is using.

9. You can often swipe right-to-left to reveal a delete button for each item.

10. Another way to delete content is to use the Edit button, and then select items to be deleted.

Viewing Battery Usage

If you notice your iPad's battery life isn't as long as you think it should be, it could be because an app is using more than its share. You can check the battery usage for each app in the Settings app.

1. From the Settings app, tap on Battery.

2. Tap either Last 24 Hours or Last X Days to get an idea of how much battery each app has been using. If you haven't been using your iPad unplugged from power for a while, you might not see any apps listed at all.

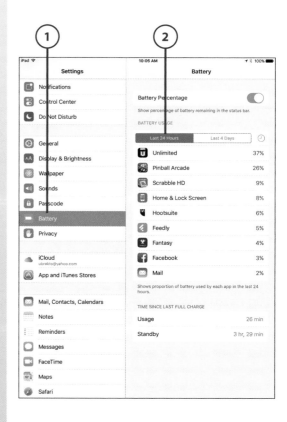

Days Vary

The number of days you see in Last X Days can vary based on your usage.

3 The list gives you an idea of which app may be an energy hog. Keep in mind that it is relative. In this example, the Marvel Unlimited app had just recently consumed the most battery power because I'd used it the most. However, I actually used the Pinball Arcade app for much less time, and it still consumed a significant chunk of battery power.

4 Tap the clock icon to see a list of how much time you've recently spent using each app.

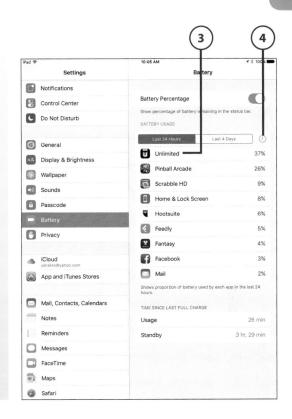

Viewing Location Usage

Another thing apps use is information. Of particular use is your location. This helps mapping and information apps to give you relevant results, for instance. You can see which apps use your location and how often they access it in the Settings app.

Locating Wi-Fi

Remember that your iPad can get your location even if you do not have a mobile wireless data plan. It looks at which Wi-Fi hotspots are near, and figures out your location from a database that knows where these hotspots are located.

(1) In the Settings app, go to the Privacy settings.

(2) Tap Location Services.

(3) Here you see a list of apps that access your location. Some apps access your location only while they are the app you are currently using. Other apps access that information even while they are running in the background. Keep in mind that this is about permissions, not usage. Just because an app has been given permission to access your location in the background doesn't mean it is always doing so.

(4) The little compass needle icons are color-coded to let you know how often your location is used by the apps. For instance, three apps show a gray icon, which means that they have used your location in the last 24 hours, but not recently.

(5) You can tap any item to revoke location access, or in some cases change it from Always to While Using.

What Is a Geofence?

The Location Services screen in the Settings app shows a hollow purple arrow next to an app that is using a Geofence. This simply means the app checks to see whether you are in a certain area. For instance, a shopping app may check to see if you are in the store. The MLB At the Ballpark app uses this to see if you are in the stadium, and will customize the information based on that fact.

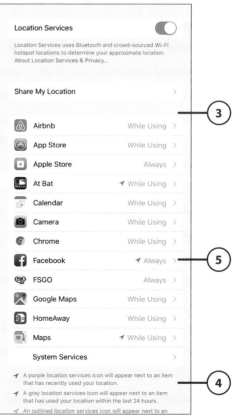

Viewing Information Sharing Permissions

Some apps communicate with each other. For instance, Keynote might have access to your photo library, or Skype may have access to your Contacts database. You are usually asked for permission when this first happens. For instance, the first time you insert an image into a Keynote presentation, a dialog pops up asking for you to grant permission for Keynote to access your photos.

You can view these connections between apps in the Settings app. You can also revoke these permissions.

(1) In the Settings app, tap Privacy.

(2) You see a list of apps that share information. Tap one of them.

(3) In this case, four apps have asked for permission to access the photo library. Some built-in apps that are part of iOS, like Contacts or Camera, won't be listed.

(4) You can switch off access to any app. Keep in mind that this could have consequences and the app might no longer be able to get the information it needs to operate.

Modifying Notifications Settings

When you start using an app, it might ask you if it is okay for it to send you notifications. These are little alert boxes in the middle of your screen, or messages at the top of your screen, that appear when something happens that the app wants you to know about. Apps need your permission to show you these notifications, which is why they ask. You can change your decision later by using the Settings app.

1. Open the Settings app and tap Notifications.

2. You see a list of all apps that send notifications. You can sort this list by most recent, or set a specific order by switching this to manual.

3. Tap an app to view its specific notifications settings.

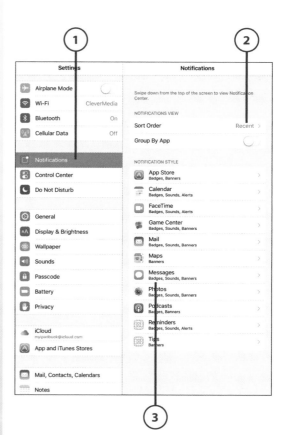

4 Choosing the None alert style means that neither a banner nor alert will appear.

5 Choosing Banners means that a drop-down banner appears when the app has a message, and it will go away on its own after a few seconds. These do not interrupt your work when they appear.

6 Choosing Alerts means that a box pops up in the middle of the screen when the app has a message, and you must dismiss it to continue.

7 Turning on Badge App Icon means that the app's icon shows a number over it when there is a message.

8 Many apps let you set the specific sound used. Tap Sounds to specify the sound the app uses.

9 Tap Show in Notification Center to choose how many alerts appear in the list in Notifications Center. You can also choose No Recent Items to indicate that you don't want to see them in the Notifications Center at all.

10 Show on Lock Screen means that alerts from this app appear, even when the iPad is locked.

11 Turn off Show Preview if you prefer that the small preview of the message does not appear with the alert.

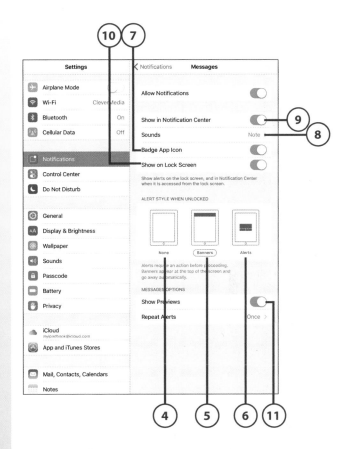

(12) Tap Repeat Alerts to configure whether the alert repeats after a few minutes, and how many times. It is useful to have an alert repeat in case you missed it the first time.

(13) If you want to completely disable an app's ability to send you notifications, you can do this quickly by just switching off Allow Notifications.

Apps Vary

Each app has its own set of settings, so take a few minutes to go through them all and see what options are offered. As you add new apps to your iPad, any that use the Notifications Center are added to this list, so it is a good idea to occasionally review your settings.

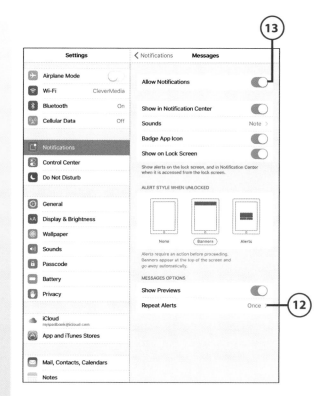

AARP has insights into
travel destinations, trips to
consider, and discounts.

Trade houses and
live like a local
using Intervac.

Translate your wishes into
most any language using
Talking Translator.

Use TripAdvisor
to explore great
places to eat,
sleep, and visit
when you travel.

Using Foursqure
to enhance all
aspects of your
travel

SeatGuru will
ensure your flight
is comfortable.

Compare airfares
and book flights
using Kayak.

Find your next
room, apartment,
or mansion for a
day, week, or year
on Airbnb.

Uber is an alternative to hiring
a taxi when you need to get
from here to there.

In this chapter, you learn to take advantage of some of the best iPad apps for planning and managing your travel needs.

→ Find interesting locations to visit and discounts using the AARP app.

→ Find travel accommodations with Airbnb.

→ Travel the world living like a local using the Intervac Home Exchange app.

→ Use Foursquare to enhance all aspects of your travel.

→ Use Kayak to create and manage your next trip.

→ Find your way using the Maps app.

→ Use SeatGuru to make your in-flight time as comfortable as possible.

→ Let Talking Translator help you communicate while traveling abroad.

→ Take advantage of others' travel experiences using TripAdvisor.

→ Get a ride using Uber or other travel apps.

Exploring the World with Your iPad

The iPad makes traveling easier and more enjoyable. Not only can you book your flight from your easy chair, but you can plan your itinerary, scope out amazing restaurants and markets, and find key things to do and sights not to be missed so that you take full advantage of your destination. And the great news is that most of the best iPad apps for travel are *free*!

Using the AARP App

AARP has built an awesome app that provides many interesting insights. The travel section of the app is useful. It zeroes in on several stunning travel ideas, and annotates them individually so that with a tap of your iPad, you can be planning your next trip.

(1) Search the App Store for the AARP app. Tap the Get button, and then tap Install to download it. Tap Open to open it. If you are not already a registered user, you must register at the AARP website (www.aarp.org) to access this app.

(2) After you register with AARP, you can use the same password and username to access the AARP app. Tap the icon for the AARP app on your iPad, and then sign in with your AARP username and password, or if you choose, tap register to be transferred to the AARP website to register.

Only One Sign-in Required

After you open the AARP app and sign in using your AARP username and password the first time, opening the app in the future takes you directly to the home page.

3 After reviewing a quick overview of the app, the AARP home page contains several interesting options to explore. Health, money, latest, work and retirement, care-giving resources center, life tools, and, of course, travel. Each of these segments is well thought out and contains a number of helpful articles.

4 For this task, explore the Travel section of the app. Tap the AARP travel icon.

5 In the Travel section of this app, you meet the AARP Travel Ambassador, Samantha Brown, a well-known travel show host.

6 You can find several additional pages of options by swiping your finger across your IPad from right to left to move on to the next page. AARP has chosen some enticing travel titles including Captivating Island Getaways, 9 Thrilling Drives Across America, New Air Travel Rules, 5 Must See Rome Sights, and more. There are a total of 70 different articles available at this time.

7 For this task, tap 9 Thrilling Drives Across America.

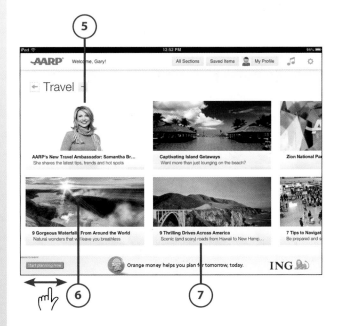

8) Tap the View Slideshow button to access the article.

9) The slideshow begins with Mauna Kea Summit Road in Hawaii. Swipe right to left to move along to the Dalton Highway in Alaska, Highway 1 in California, and on to many other breathtaking drives across the United States. This is an enticing app that can certainly stimulate your wanderlust.

Check Out AARP's Travel Website

Your one-stop shop for dreaming, planning, and booking your next trip is at http://travel.aarp.org. With the Trip Finder, click on the experiences you most want to have, and you get a list of potential destinations. Tapping Destination Guides takes you to information provided by Fodors about hundreds of destinations, with special points of interest, must-see attractions, and practical travel advice. You also have access to AARP member discounts for flights, rental cars, hotels, and cruises. One other area to check out is the Map Explorer, which lets you create a personalized itinerary for your trip.

Finding Interesting Accommodations with the Airbnb App

Thinking about taking a trip? Have a desire to experience things a bit differently from the norm? Try Airbnb! This app gives you access to a huge number of interesting options of places to stay when you are traveling. Through Airbnb you can rent everything from a couch, to a room, to an entire estate. We recently used Airbnb to book a house in New Orleans for 2 months. It was easy and we were able to find what appears to be the perfect fit for our needs (an extra bedroom so the children and grandchildren can join us and a place that will welcome Bubba, our dog).

1. Open the App Store by tapping its icon on your home screen.

2. Type **airbnb** in the Search field in the upper-right corner. Note that this app is designed for the iPad. Occasionally, you will want to access an app designed for iPhones on your iPad. See the note on this page for details.

Using iPhone Apps on iPad

Even though some apps are listed as "iPhone only," they will work just fine on the iPad. The app was developed for the size of the iPhone screen, so it will appear smaller on your iPad. You can tap the 2x button to make an iPhone app larger to fill your iPad screen. Regardless of the size of the app, it works the same on either device.

3 You can use the options on this screen to review the details about this app and read reviews from other users. Tap Get when you are ready to download and install the app. Tap Open to open the app.

4 The opening page gives an overview of Airbnb that you can access by swiping to the left. I chose to tap Skip in the upper-right corner to go directly to the App.

(5) The opening page shows several options for travel using Airbnb. You can tap any to see options in that city or area.

(6) Here you see several ways to access information on Airbnb. I tapped Search for just what was available for my upcoming trip to New Orleans.

(5)

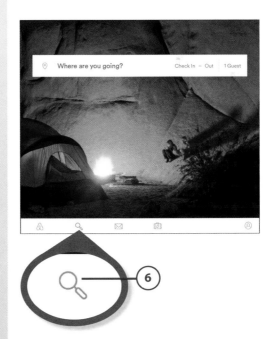

(6)

(7) In the Search box, I typed **New Orleans**. Various locations related to New Orleans appeared in the search results. I tapped New Orleans, LA United States to see the broadest selection of results.

(8) My results showed more than 1000 different options for staying in New Orleans were avalable.

(9) You can further refine your search by tapping the map option at the top.

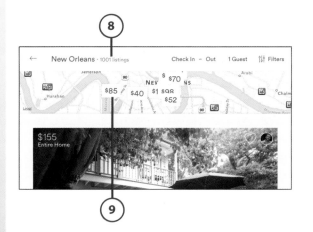

10 The map shows options for rent by location, as well as prices.

11 Tap Filters at the top right to drill down your search even further.

12 The Filters page enables you to search for the dates you want to travel, the type of listing you are looking for, price, and just how many guests it needs to accommodate. As you scroll down, you can further search for amenities, beds, bedrooms, and bathrooms. Using these filters, you can narrow down the properties to see only the ones that fit your criteria. (I chose January 15, 2016 to March 15, 2016, a whole house, for four guests.) Then tap Apply Filters to see what is available.

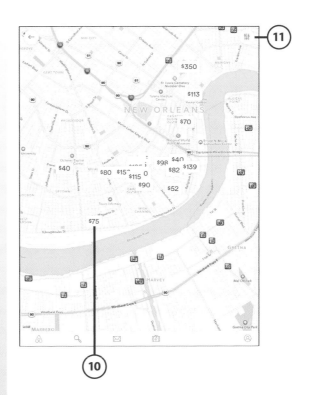

10

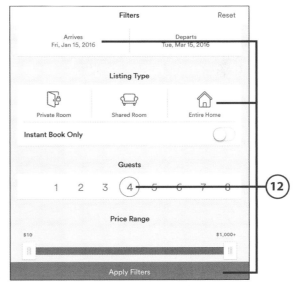

13 I found 8 homes that met my criteria and chose to take a closer look at the New Happiness option, listed for $2,685. I scrolled up the listing to view further details.

14 After tapping a listing, scroll down to find a thorough description, many photos, a biography of the owner, and reviews. The property I chose has 11 five-star reviews.

15 I scrolled down to the Reviews section and tapped See More to see what people had to say about their stay in this home.

16 There were 11 reviews for this rental. The reviews are listed in chronological order from most recent to oldest. Each gave a good description of what to expect when renting this home. Tap the X to close the review list.

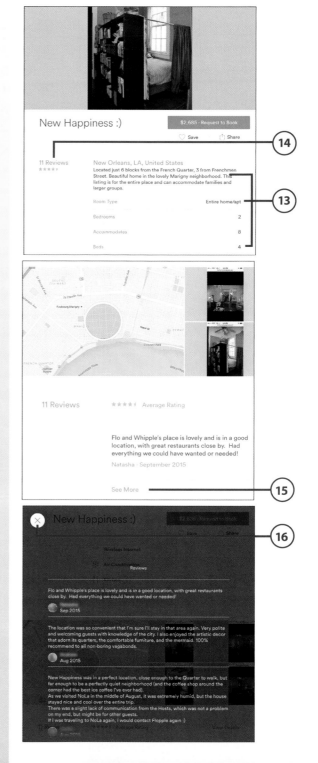

17 Tap See All Amenities to be sure that the property has wireless Internet and other things you find essential to a long-term stay.

18 If you find the property meets your needs, tap Request to Book at the upper right to move forward.

19 After requesting to book, Airbnb reviews all aspects of your choice to ensure it is truly what you are looking for.

20 Scroll down to access payment options.

Making Contact

After you have signed up, there will be an opportunity to contact the owner to follow up and be certain that the rental you have chosen will meet your needs.

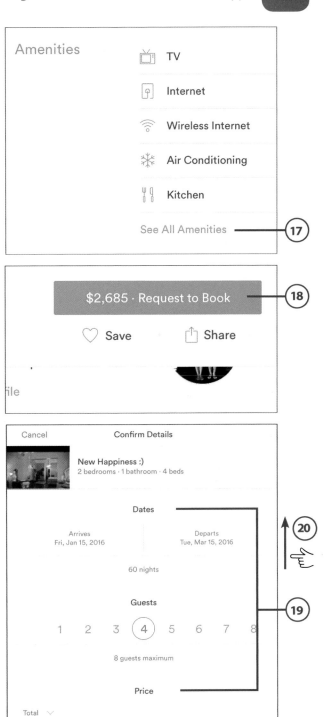

Amenities

TV

Internet

Wireless Internet

Air Conditioning

Kitchen

See All Amenities — **17**

$2,685 · Request to Book — **18**

♡ Save   ⬆ Share

Cancel   Confirm Details

New Happiness :)
2 bedrooms · 1 bathroom · 4 beds

Dates

Arrives
Fri, Jan 15, 2016

Departs
Tue, Mar 15, 2016

60 nights

Guests

1   2   3   **4**   5   6   7   8

8 guests maximum

Price

Total ⌄

Using Foursquare to Enhance Your Travel Choices

Foursquare has retooled to become a force in the Internet search and research business. It offers a vast number of well-researched places to eat, drink, and visit while you are traveling. Additionally, there are many reviews that provide insight from other travelers. The format is easy to use and visually stunning.

1. In the App Store, search for the Foursquare app. Tap Get, and then tap Install to load the app. Tap Open to start using Foursquare.

2. When you open Foursquare the first time, it asks permission to use your current location. Tap OK to allow, or tap Don't Allow if you prefer not to let the app know your location. Foursquare is able to offer you more relevant results if you allow the Location setting.

3. Next, Foursquare asks permission to turn on notifications. Tap OK to allow the app to send you an email whenever someone you know makes a post. Tap Not Now if you prefer not to be notified.

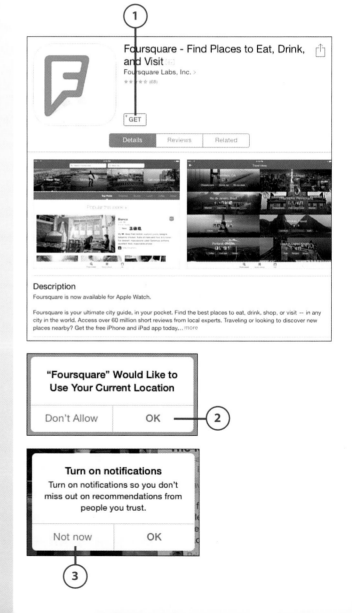

Location Settings

If you choose not to allow Foursquare to know your location, you can always go to the Settings app and allow it later. It can be helpful to allow this if you are in an unfamiliar place trying to find local venues. Tap the Settings icon on your home screen. Tap Privacy on the left side of the screen. Tap Location Services at the top of the right side. Swipe up from the bottom of the screen until you see Foursquare, and then tap the switch to turn on Location Services for that app. You can turn it off later if you don't want the app to always know your location.

(4) Along the top of the main Foursquare screen, you see several options from top picks to coffee to shopping, and many more. Slide the bar to the left to see all categories.

(5) Swipe up from the bottom to see categories including Trending this month, Recommended by experts, Best restaurants in the area, and more. For the purpose of this example, let's look at the restaurant Iron Roost.

(6) The Iron Roost Foursquare page begins with the vital information including address, hours of operation, and telephone number.

(7) At the bottom of the screen, swipe up to see several impressive photos of the food at the Iron Roost.

(8) Next, tap the middle area with the map for more information about the restaurant.

9 Tap the symbol on the map to get an expanded view of just where the restaurant is located.

10 Tap View Menu to see what is offered at the Iron Roost. The next page shows the menu at this restaurant.

11 Tap the arrow at the top left to return to the details.

12 Swipe up from the bottom of the screen to see more information about the restaurant.

Exchanging Homes Is a Great Way to See the World

Exchanging homes with like-minded folks around the world is quite possibly the best way to experience a foreign country. Home exchangers can live like a local, shop in local markets, cook as if a local, get to know neighbors and friends of the homeowner, and in many cases, become lifelong friends with the people they exchange with.

Using Intervac Home Exchange

The two oldest, and most popular, home exchange sites are www.usa. homelink.org and Intervac. For this task, I have chosen to take a look at the Intervac app. Although you can search the site to get an idea of what options might be available, to actually initiate an exchange you must join and list your own home as an option for exchange. There is a fee for joining. The amount depends on the type of membership you choose. The following task provides a look at this cool and inexpensive way to see the world.

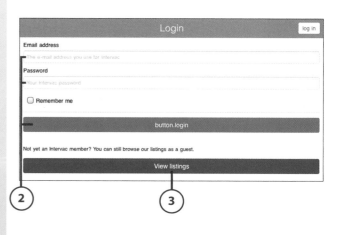

1. Search the App Store for Intervac. Tap Get, and then tap Install to download and install the app. After it has loaded, locate the Intervac app icon on your iPad, and tap it to start.

2. The email address, button. login, is for existing members to access their accounts.

3. Tap the View listings button to access the visitors view of the exchange options available. A variety of options appear.

Any Fees?

The only fee involved for Intervac is the fee to join (generally paid by credit card directly to Intervac). Intervac provides a vehicle to connect people interested in exchanging homes. From that point, the exchange is coordinated by the two families participating in the exchange.

4 Tap the green Select country bar near the top of the screen to restrict your search to the country you are interested in visiting.

5 Scroll down the list of countries to make your choice of listings to view by country, and then tap Next. For this task, I chose France.

6 The France options are listed randomly; I chose to tap the first Paris listing.

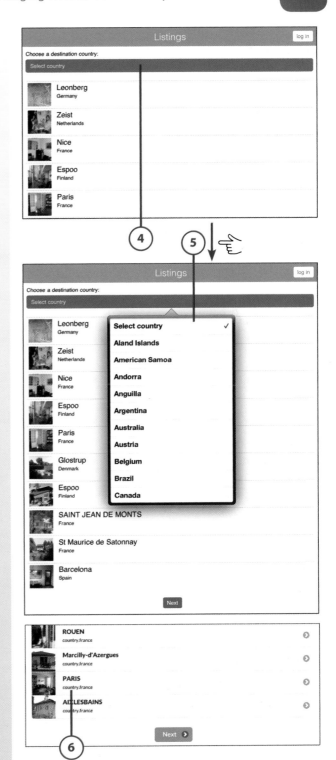

(7) The first photo of this apartment in Paris appears. Details about the listing are seen at the bottom of the page. Tap the green View All Photos button to see all the photos for this apartment.

(8) The next page includes many photos that the apartment owner has chosen to show. This is a great opportunity to get a feel for this location as a potential exchange.

As a visitor using this, you can get a general feel for the home exchange options available through Intervac. A visit to the website gives you the options to refine your search by date and those who are interested in visiting. I would suggest taking a look at the website prior to signing up—there is a fee involved to be a member.

What About Our Stuff???

Our take on this is it's quite similar to a nuclear stand-off. Yes, they are living in your house and using your "stuff" but equally, you are living in their house and using their "stuff." My wife and I have personally participated in many exchanges and never had a problem. As an added bonus, we now have friends throughout the world.

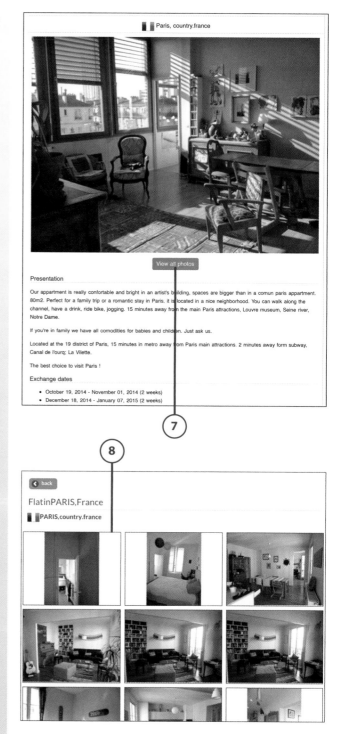

Arranging Travel Using the Kayak App

Kayak has the ideal app to help you find the best way to travel to your next destination. Through Kayak's app, you can book flights and hotels, reserve cars, and maintain your travel details all in one place. Kayak searches the travel options of many airlines and then refers you directly to the airline to make the purchase. A notable exception is Southwest, which doesn't participate in any of these apps. If you want to fly Southwest, you need to use its website to search for flights.

(1) Search the App Store for Kayak. Tap Get, and then tap Install to download it. Open Kayak by tapping its icon on your screen.

The Real Deal

One of the great things about being retired is the ability to travel "when the spirit moves," rather than at specified times—when budget allows. The opportunity to fly at nonpeak times becomes a reality that can greatly enhance your ability to take advantage of travel deals that others might miss.

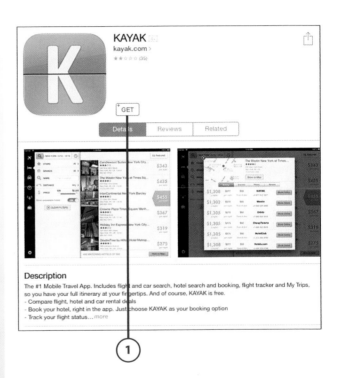

(2) The example in this task shows searching for a round-trip flight from New York's JFK airport to San Francisco, departing April 10 and returning May 10. There are several easy ways to modify your search. You can choose different dates, locations, and cabin options.

(3) One option is to choose seating other than economy. Your choices range from economy to first class; tap the CABIN line to access other seating options.

(4) After you make all your choices, tap Find Flights to find your outbound flight.

Apps Change Frequently

The images you see here are how these apps appeared at the time this book was written. App developers do occasionally update their apps by changing the way they look, moving buttons around, or adding new features. You might find that an app looks slightly different from what you see here, but unless the developer has given it a total overhaul, it should function basically the same way it did when these steps were written. So don't let that stop you from trying it out!

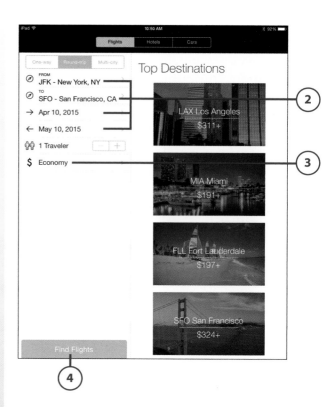

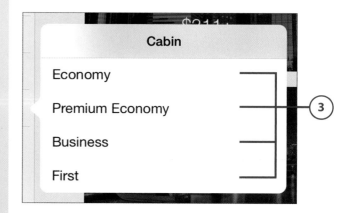

5 This search yields round-trip flights starting at $337 (Delta).

6 It is important to consider the time enroute for long flights. Kayak lists this information for each flight. It is better to spend your time exploring rather than sitting in an airplane.

7 In this example, the second Delta flight, departing JFK at 2:30 p.m. on April 10, was chosen along with the return flight departing San Francisco at 1:30 p.m. on May 10. You can see that each flight is non-stop and travels across the country in the shortest time.

8 The next screen contains a summary of your flight choice. The summary has two options for next steps: You can either tap the upper-right corner to email the information to yourself or fellow travelers, or tap Book Now to go to the airline website to buy the tickets.

9 For this example, tap Book Now to buy the tickets. At this point, you leave the Kayak app and go directly to Delta's website. When at the Delta website, you can proceed to buy your tickets, choose seat assignments, complete passenger information, as well as add on other optional items such as baggage fees and other extras.

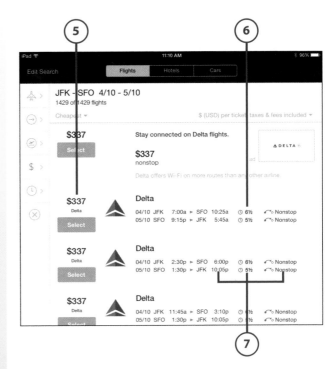

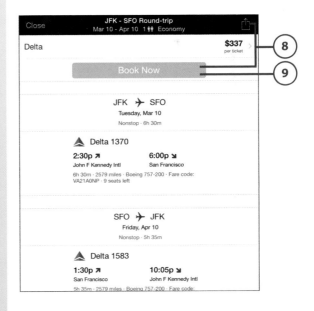

You can use this same process to search for hotels and car rentals to add to your itinerary, or you can book only hotels and a car rental if you don't need flights. Kayak also has a My Trips option that enables you to save your travel itinerary in one place. Time to pick a destination, book your flight, and start exploring!

Finding Your Way Using the iPad Maps App

The Maps app comes installed as part of the iOS operating system for your iPad (similar to Email and other built-in apps). There are many uses for this app, but it is particularly helpful when you travel. You can find your present location, get directions, check traffic, view the map from a satellite perspective, and search the area for various services, such as coffee shops, restaurants, gas stations, and more.

(1) Tap the Maps icon on your iPad.

(2) Tap the arrow at the bottom left of the page to see your present location.

Maps

Location Settings

Location services for Maps must be enabled for the Maps app to find your location automatically. Tap the Settings app on your home screen, and then tap Privacy on the left side. Tap Location Service at the top of the right side of the screen, and then slide the Location Services switch to ON. If you have allowed the Maps app to have access to your location, you should see it in the list below Location Services. Make sure its switch is set to ON. If it is not in the list, after you tap the location arrow in the lower-left corner of the Maps app, it asks to allow the app to have access to Location Services. Tap OK.

(3) Your location is indicated by a blue dot on the map.

4 To find directions, tap Directions in the upper-left corner.

5 If you allow Maps access to your location, Current Location is filled in the Start Field for you. If your current location is not your starting location for the directions you need, type in the address you are traveling from in the Start field. Type the address of your destination in the End field. In this example, the directions are for traveling from the current location to New York City.

6 Maps gives you the option to choose directions for car, walking, or bus.

7 This example chooses to get the best route by car. After you determine how you want to travel and where you are going, and have plugged that information into the start/end boxes, the Maps app automatically shows your potential routes.

8 Tap the Start button and Maps starts step-by-step directions. Tap End to stop the turn-by-turn directions.

9 The list on the left side of your screen provides a turn-by-turn summary of your directions.

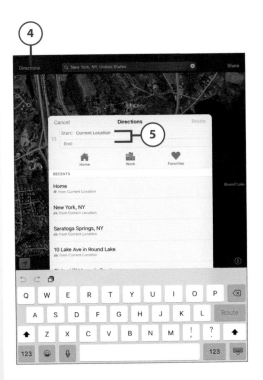

10 Tap the i at the bottom right to Hide Labels, Hide Traffic, show a 3D Map, or Report an Issue.

If you have a cellular-enabled iPad, it can also give you turn-by-turn directions. If you travel to an area that you are unfamiliar with, the iPad gives you the perfect way to familiarize yourself with the area from your hotel or apartment.

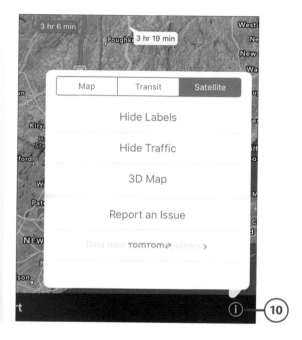

It's Not All Good

Maps Eat Data

Be aware that although having those turn-by-turn directions as you travel to a destination is convenient and reassuring, it also uses up your monthly data plan quickly. You will receive an email warning when you are nearing the maximum data allowed by your plan, and offer you the opportunity to pay for more data. It is recommended that you open your Settings app and tap Cellular Data in the list on the left side. On the right side, make sure Data Roaming is set to OFF to avoid any unexpected charges! You can save your data plan by simply planning and reviewing your route while you have access to Wi-Fi and not tap your monthly data plan for this convenience.

SeatGuru by TripAdvisor

Have you ever boarded an airplane, made your way to your seat, and settled in, only to find you have chosen the only row on the plane that doesn't tilt back? After you download SeatGuru from the App Store, those days will be over. The idea is to do your research upfront and get to know the aircraft you will be flying on before you buy your tickets and choose a seat. Using SeatGuru, you can choose the best possible seat to make your trip as comfortable as possible. Your days of selecting the worst seat on the plane are over!

1 Search for SeatGuru by TripAdvisor, an iPhone app, in the App Store. Tap Free, and then tap Install to download it. Open it by tapping its icon on your home screen. If you have downloaded it before, you'll see the iCloud download button as shown in the figure.

2 Tap on the Maybe Later link if you see no need to connect using Facebook; otherwise, tap Connect using Facebook for SeatGuru to log you in using your Facebook account and enable you to directly post photos and reviews to your Facebook page.

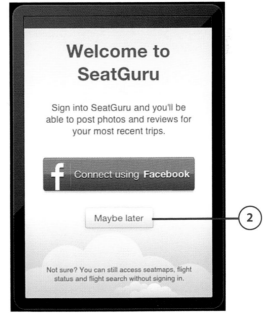

3 Tap the Get Seat Advice option.

4 If you know your flight number or airline, plug those in to find the type of aircraft you will be flying aboard.

5 If you are unaware of the flight number, you can tap the route or airline and search for the flight you are choosing.

6 After your flight info is entered, tap Find aircraft and an illustration of your plane's seat map opens.

7 This illustration indicates the great seats (green), lousy seats (red), seats with some drawbacks (yellow), and standard seats (white) available on your flight.

8 Tap a specific seat number to see a description of the pros and cons of that seat.

9 In this example, tap seat 26B, and the characteristics of this seat are shown. This is great information, particularly if you plan a long flight where comfort might be a priority.

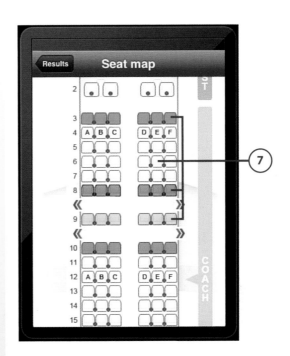

(10) The seat map key offers other types of information on seating that can be found using SeatGuru.

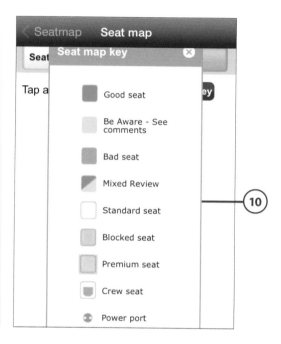

Communicating in a Foreign Country Is Easy When You Use Talking Translator

Talking Translator is an amazing app that enables you to speak into a microphone in your native tongue and instantly have the phrase translated into another language. You are allowed five free translations per day; after that, you need to purchase further translations. This is a remarkable app that can greatly enhance your ability to communicate in a foreign country.

To try out this app, do the following:

1. In the App Store, search for Talking Translator. Tap Get, and then tap Install to download it. After it is installed, tap the Talking Translator icon on your iPad's home screen to open it.

2. The opening page gives you a few options to review, including Continue, Leave Feedback, Buy, or Activate.

3. For this task, tap Continue, which takes you to the free translations.

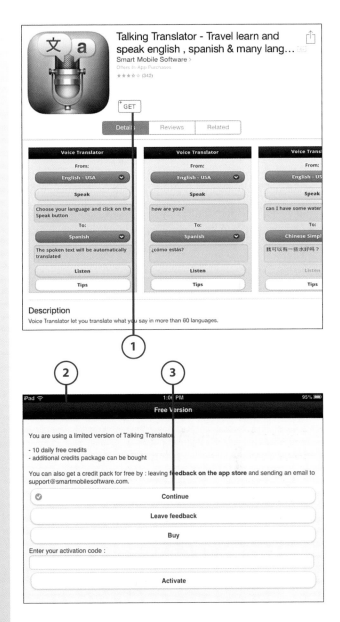

④ The next page requires you to choose your native tongue. For this task, choose English USA. As you can see, there are many languages to choose from.

⑤ Next, choose the language into which you want your phrase translated.

Apps Change Frequently

The images you see here are how these apps appeared at the time this book was written. App developers do occasionally update their apps by changing the way they look, moving buttons around, or adding new features. You might find that an app looks slightly different from what you see here, but unless the developer has given it a total overhaul, it should function basically the same way it did when these steps were written. So don't let that stop you from trying it out!

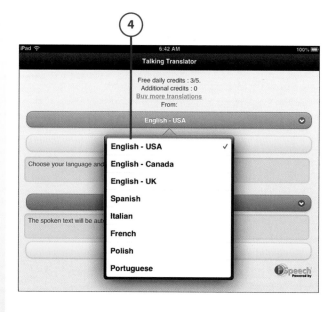

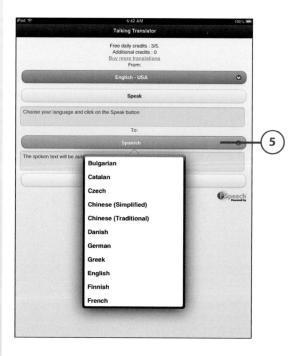

6 For this task, choose to have English USA translated into French.

7 Tap Speak and choose a phrase you commonly need to translate when abroad, such as "Please help me find the nearest bathroom."

8 To do this, tap the red dot at the bottom of the app. As soon as the dot begins to flash, speak into the microphone. The app writes what it heard you say. It is important to make sure that the app has captured your exact question.

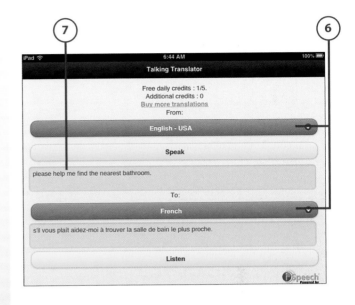

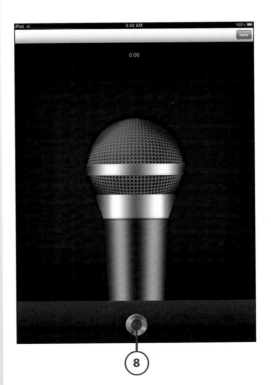

(**9**) Talking Translator shows your phrase written in French.

(**10**) Tap listen to hear your phrase.

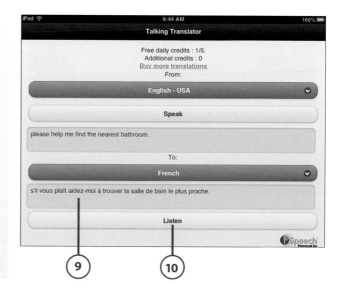

Getting Travel Advice from Others Using TripAdvisor

Whether you travel a few miles or thousands of miles from home, TripAdvisor serves to enhance that experience. With just a few taps, you have access to restaurants, hotels, things to do, and the thoughts of many people who have preceded you at your chosen destination. With TripAdvisor, you also have the ability to save your favorites.

1. To start, search the App Store TripAdvisor Hotels Flights Restaurants. Tap Get, and then tap Install to download and install the app. Tap the icon for the app on your Home screen to open it.

2. The first few slides ask you several questions about accessing your location, notifications, and ways to sign in. Tap Skip in the upper-right corner until you get to the main page of TripAdvisor.

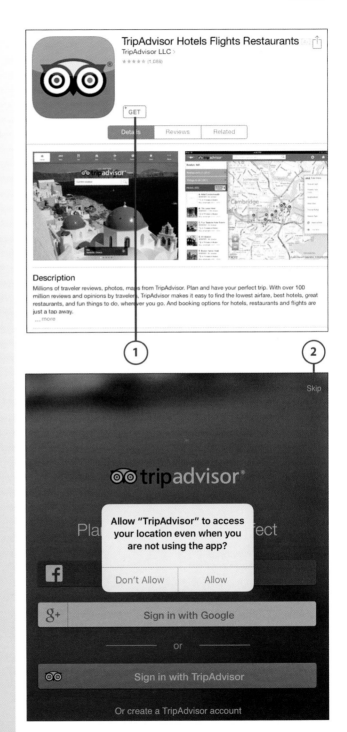

3 You can see the options you can explore through TripAdvisor along the left side of the screen. Tap the button that corresponds to what you want to explore.

4 For this example, I tapped Restaurants and typed **San Francisco** for the location to search.

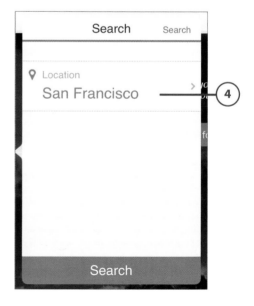

(5) The restaurant page now enables you the opportunity to refine your search by cuisine, price range, and locations within the city by tapping the Filter button.

(6) In this example, I chose all cuisines, all prices, all neighborhoods, and all dining options.

(7) At the time of this search, 5,214 restaurants were listed in San Francisco. You can tap the map to find the location of restaurants near your present location.

(8) Tap on The Bimini Twist insert to see further details.

Location Settings

To change your location settings, open the Settings App from your iPad's home screen, and then tap Privacy on the left side. Along the right side, be sure that TripAdvisor is set to ON. This ensures that should you choose Current Location, your iPad can find you.

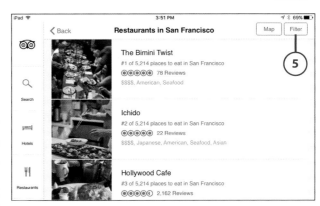

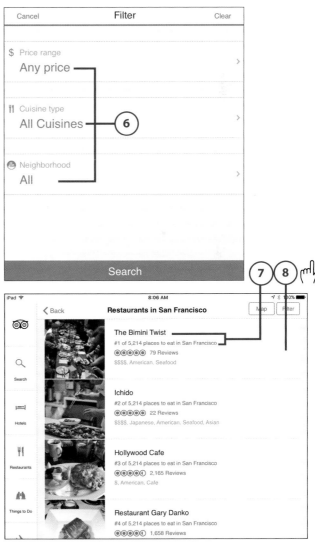

9 If you find the information interesting, you can tap Reviews, Photos, or Visit Website to see what others are saying or get even more information.

10 After you find a restaurant or hotel that you want to check out, tap the Save button to add it to your favorites.

You can tap Reserve with OpenTable to make a reservation (not shown).

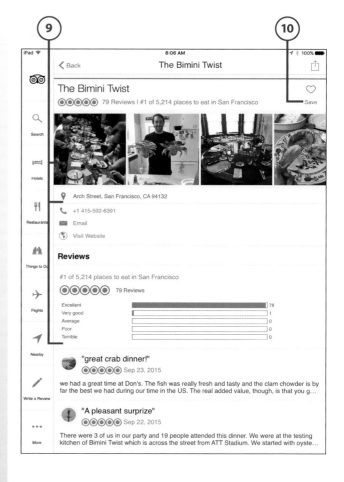

Getting a Ride Using the Uber App

You can now use your iPad to get from one place to another, including from the airport to a destination or home. Uber has become a transportation phenomenon. Now, with a few taps, you can request a ride, type in the car of your choice (similar to a cab service but with more options), watch as your driver arrives in minutes, pay with your mobile device, and usually save money. Note: You will need to either be in an area that has wireless capability or have an iPad that works on cellular.

As we are writing this, Uber is located primarily in major cities, but we fully expect that this service will expand quickly.

1. Open the App Store by tapping its icon on your home screen, and then type **Uber** in the Search field in the upper-right corner.

2. To locate Uber in the App Store, you first need to change the type of apps from iPad Only to iPhone Only at the top of the search results screen. When you see the Uber app in the search results, tap it. You can use the options on this screen to review the details about this app as well as read reviews from other users.

3. Tap Get when you are ready to download and install it, and then tap Open.

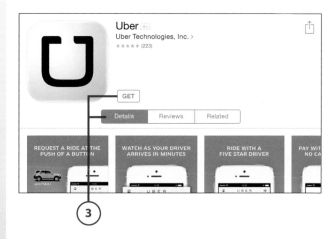

Using iPhone Apps on iPad

Even though some apps are listed as "iPhone Only," they will work just fine on the iPad. The app was developed for the size of the iPhone screen, so it will appear smaller on your iPad. You can tap the 2x button to make an iPhone app larger to fill your iPad screen. Regardless of the size of the app, it works the same on either device.

4. Tap Register to create an account, or tap Sign In if you already have an Uber account.

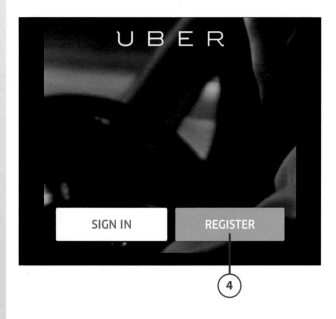

(5) You can create an account by completing your email address, adding your mobile phone number, and creating a password. As noted, Uber will use this information to send you ride confirmations and receipts. Tap Next in the upper-right corner.

(6) Create a profile with your name and photo to help the driver identify you at pickup. Type your name in the fields, and then tap the picture button to add a photo of yourself for the driver to see. You can take a new photo or choose one from your photo library. When finished, tap Next.

(7) Now you can enter arrangements for making payment for your ride. This can be done using a credit card or via PayPal (a secure way to make payment on the internet). I chose to use my PayPal account.

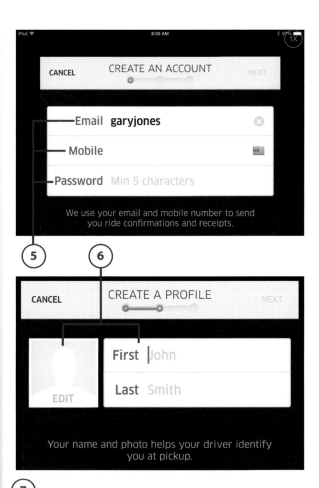

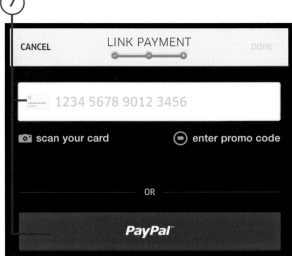

8 After you have decided your method of payment, Uber asks that you approve future payments using your chosen account. Tap Agree to continue.

9 If you have not already done so, Uber will ask that you turn on Location Services. This enables Uber to use your built-in GPS to determine your location as you use its service.

Location Services Settings

Locations Services is turned on using the Settings app. Tap the Settings app icon on your Home screen. Tap Privacy on the left side. Tap Location Services on the right side. If Location Services is turned off, slide the switch to on (green). Look in the list below Location Services and locate Uber. Turn on Location Services by sliding the switch to on (green). You can turn this on or off anytime by coming back to these settings.

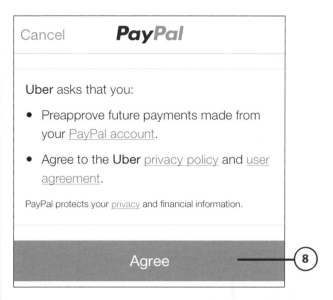

Cancel　**PayPal**

Uber asks that you:

- Preapprove future payments made from your PayPal account.

- Agree to the Uber privacy policy and user agreement.

PayPal protects your privacy and financial information.

Agree ——— **8**

LOCATION SERVICES DISABLED

Please turn on location services in Settings →Privacy →Location Services.

OK ——— **9**

(10) Uber sends you a text you are required to answer by responding "GO." You are asked to allow Push Notifications so that Uber can send you messages concerning your ride(s).

(11) Using your iPad's GPS, Uber shows your location on a map and gives you the opportunity to set pickup location.

(12) You need to decide what type of vehicle you want to pick you up. The choices range from uberX, the cheapest option (a common car), to an SUV, the most expensive option. Not all locations have the same car options. In some larger cities, Taxi is an Uber option as well.

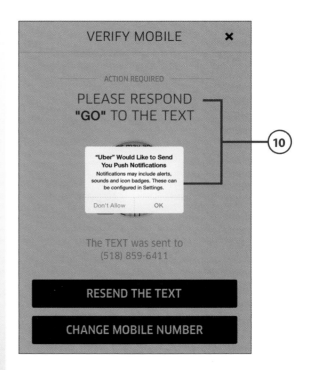

13 I tapped uberX, and the next page confirms my predetermined payment option. Tap Change to choose another type of payment.

14 Tap Fare Quote for details on your fare with this car.

15 The approximate pickup time is also indicated.

16 I tapped Fare Quote and entered San Francisco International Airport as my destination. The estimated quote for my uberX car to take me to the airport is between $49 and $63.

17 You'll see a note that some variability in the fare as a result of traffic, weather, and other factors is possible. Tap the X in the upper-right corner to return to the Confirmation page.

18 Tap Request uberX to complete the pickup request. You receive a confirmation of the request and an approximate time your car will arrive. Additionally, you are given the name, photo, and phone number of the person who is picking you up.

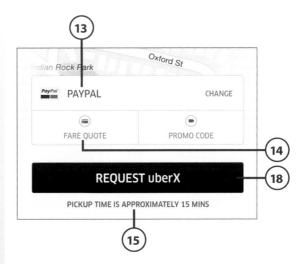

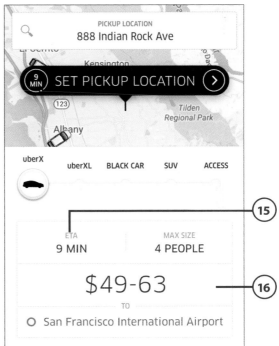

>>>Go Further

MORE USEFUL TRAVEL APPS

There are many more apps for travel that we cannot cover in this book, so here's a list of some others to check out the next time you get ready to take a trip.

- **Airports by Travel Nerd**—This offers a great deal of information on more than 50 airports worldwide, including maps, airlines by terminal, shops and restaurants, ground transportation, and information you need to have before taking off and landing.

- **Lyft**—Try Lyft for a friendly, affordable ride whenever you need one.

- **Minube**—This provides a user-generated travel guide that provides plenty of insight into places you may be traveling.

- **PackPoint Packing List Travel Companion**—This app analyzes the weather in the region you are traveling and helps you pack accordingly.

- **Sound Sleeper**—Having trouble sleeping due to unfamiliar sounds while you are traveling (or have a grandchild that's having a hard time getting to sleep)? This app offers 14 soothings sounds, from a car ride to the ocean to rain, that can be played to help you fall into restful sleep.

- **XE Currency Converter**—This app helps you to determine the value of currency in a foreign country.

Use Open Table to find restaurants, make reservations, and rate your favorites.

Explore Yelp to find great restaurants and places to shop for food.

Visit Escoffier's Cook Companion for an encyclopedia of cooking information.

Search for thousands of awesome recipes with Epicurious.

Use Safari to find awesome food-related websites and search for great recipes.

In this chapter, you learn to use your iPad and the many apps available to make great meals, find awesome restaurants, and make reservations from your easy chair.

→ Match awesome recipes with the food you have at hand.
→ Access a number of helpful tools for the cook in your family.
→ Find great recipes using your iPad's Internet browser.
→ Create and manage restaurant reservations using Open Table.
→ Use Yelp to search out a great restaurant wherever you travel.

Enhancing Your Next Meal with Your iPad

Having the opportunity to experience great food is one of the pluses of having an iPad. You can check out a new recipe in your own kitchen, discover a restaurant, and find farmer's markets with fresh vegetables. You can also explore sites that provide great insight into those who cook and sites that give you the tools to become a great cook. The great news is that most of them are *free*.

Also, when your schedules begin to loosen, or you get more vacation time, or you decide to retire, the option of traveling to far-off places and experiencing other cultures may become a reality. Whether checking out a recipe or restaurant, finding farmer's markets, or traveling, your iPad can be your best friend.

Finding Recipes

A large number of food-related apps are available in the App Store. Apps such as Big Oven, All Recipes, and several Food Network apps are just a few. I have chosen to take a look at the Epicurious app—just one of the culinary apps that will stimulate your creative juices when planning a meal, or simply putting together dinner based on what's in your refrigerator.

Apps Change Frequently

The images you see here are how these apps appeared at the time this book was written. App developers do occasionally update their apps by changing the way they look, moving buttons around, or adding new features. You might find that an app looks slightly different from what you see here, but unless the developer has given it a total overhaul, it should function basically the same way it did when these steps were written. So don't let that stop you from trying it out!

1 Search the App Store for Epicurious Recipes and Shopping list. Tap Get, and then tap Install to download the app. Tap the Epi icon on your Home screen to open the app.

2 The opening page includes scrollable images of the topics available in the Epicurious app. These topics will change depending on the season.

3 We tapped What's In Season.

4 On the next page, tap Continue and then OK when asked permission to use your location.

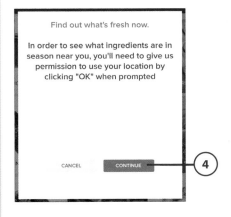

Find out what's fresh now.

In order to see what ingredients are in season near you, you'll need to give us permission to use your location by clicking "OK" when prompted

CANCEL   CONTINUE

(5) The alphabetized list of What's In Season is huge, including some items I hadn't considered. Scroll up to see the entire list.

(6) Tap the arrow in the upper-left corner to return to the main screen.

(7) On the main screen, we tapped Main-Course Salads to explore that.

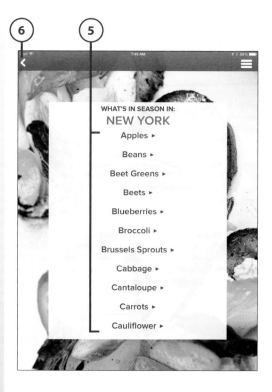

8 Main-Course Salads opened with a tasty sliced steak with arugula salad; to see this recipe, tap View Recipe.

9 On the recipe page, tap Cook View.

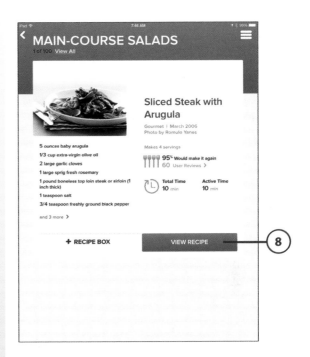

10 In addition to ingredients, preparation, and reviews for this recipe, you can also access one of the coolest recipe features on Epicurious—voice control. Tap Voice Control.

11 The voice control page explains commands, how to end voice control, and battery use issues.

12 Tap Continue to try this out.

Voice Control

The Voice Control option on Epicurious allows you to move back and forth through the recipe hands free. This is a great asset, especially when your hands are busy chopping or mixing.

13 After trying out the voice activation, we tapped the arrow in the upper-left corner twice to move back through the app.

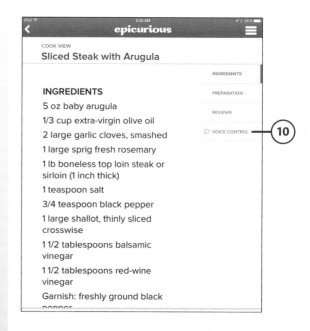

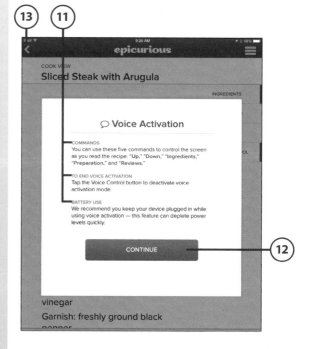

14 Tap View All in the upper-left corner to see all the Main-Course Salads recipes.

15 The list of salads contains a scrollable list of 100 options for great salad meals.

16 Tap the lines in the upper-right corner to access Home, Search, Recipe Box, and Shopping list. You will need to sign in to access some of these options.

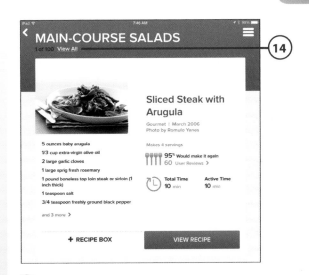

Try It—You'll Like It

Epicurious is a great app with a huge number of interesting options to enhance your experience in the kitchen. Take some time to explore and try this out!

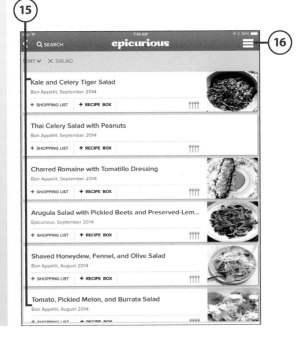

Helpful Tools for Cooking

Have you ever been cooking and wondered just how many tablespoons are in a cup? You can find many apps that address cooking measurements and equivalents, such as Cooking Measures/Easy Weight, Volume and Temperature Unit Convertor for the iPhone Chef. I chose to take a closer look at one app, the Escoffier Cook's Companion.

(1) Search the App Store for Escoffier Cook's Companion. Tap Free, and then tap Install to download the app. Tap the app's icon on your home page to open it.

(2) The opening page provides access to the site content simply by tapping one of the categories encircling Chef Escoffier's head. For this task, tap Ingredients.

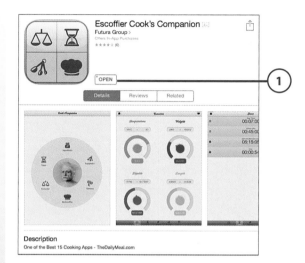

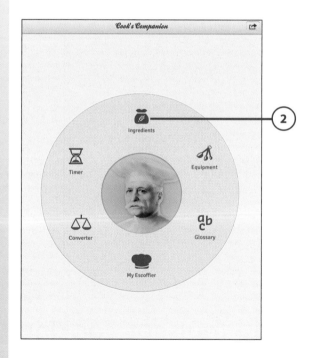

3 This page lists and defines hundreds of ingredients in alphabetical order. I chose Armagnac and tapped it to see the definition.

4 On the right side of the screen, a fairly extensive definition of the French Brandy Armagnac emerges, including sections on Overview, Menu Uses, Quality Signs, and Purchase Specs.

5 Tap the Home button at the top left of the screen to return to the home page and check out another category.

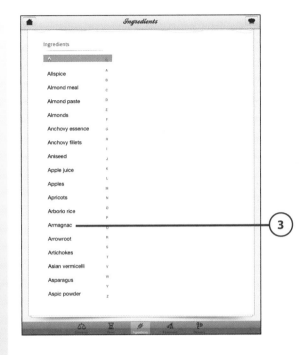

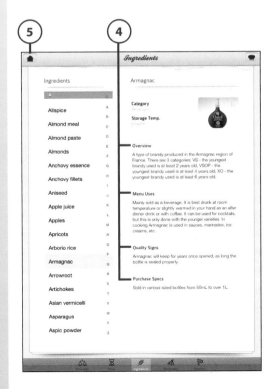

(6) Tap Equipment to see the long list of interesting types of cooking equipment. I tapped one I had never heard of, Dariole Moulds. This created not only an excellent description of what a Dariole Mould is and does, but also a photo and information on how to use such a thing.

(7) Back again at the home page, check out the Converter by tapping on that symbol. The Converter offers several conversions, including temperature, weight, liquids, and length— very handy in the kitchen.

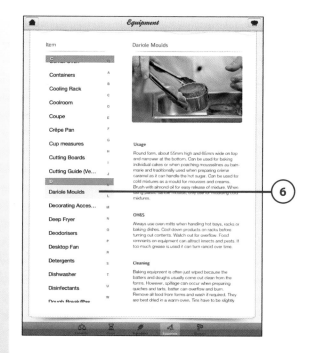

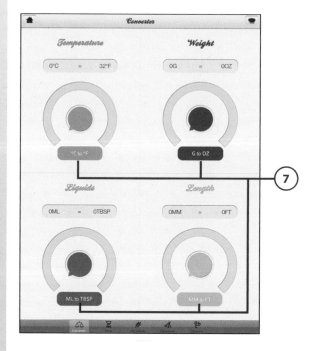

8 Tap the Timer button at the bottom of the screen or on the home screen. Tap the + sign to add a new timer, and then use the scroll wheel to set the amount of time. Hours are set on the left side and minutes on the right. Type a name for the timer in the Name field, and choose the type of alert you want in the Alerts list. Tap Start timer to begin the countdown. Tap the + sign again, and another timer pops up for you to again set the duration of time, type the name, and choose the type of alerts.

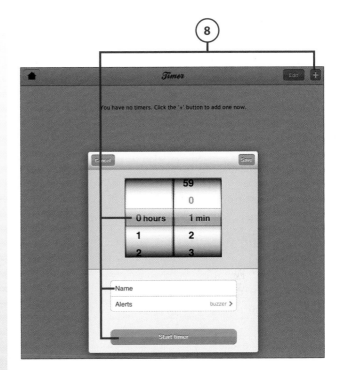

The iPad's Clock App Has a Timer

Your iPad's Clock app has built-in world clock, alarm, stopwatch, and timer functions. Simply tap the Clock app's icon on your iPad's home screen. Then, tap the icon at the bottom for the function you want to access. The advantage to the Escoffier app's timer is that you can set multiple timers at once. The iPad's Clock app allows for only one timer, although you can set up multiple alarms and world clocks.

9 The next screen shows the progress of both timers. If you need to temporarily pause the countdown, tap the little Pause button on the left side of the timer.

10 Tap Edit in the upper-right corner to change the amount of time a timer is set for or to delete a timer completely.

Using the Internet to Search for Recipes

One of the great things about your iPad is that it provides easy access to the Internet. As you know, there is a huge amount of information on the Internet on just about any topic. Very often, you can find recipes for items you have tasted in a restaurant and wanted to try to make at home.

I recently had lunch at the Hog Island Oyster Bar at the Ferry Building in San Francisco. We were not given the best seats in the house. Our view was of the chef and his range rather than the Bay Bridge. We love to cook, so this happened to be the perfect view for us. Throughout our meal, we watched as he often created Hog Island's famous clam chowder. It looked amazing, and I decided I was going to learn that recipe. Here is how I tracked it down.

(1) I tapped Safari to access the Internet on my iPad.

(2) After the Safari page opened, I typed the words **Hog Island Clam Chowder** in the search line.

(3) As I typed, the search engine filled in the words below, anticipating my search terms.

(4) Many options containing my search terms appeared, and as luck would have it, the recipe I was searching for was the first. I tapped it.

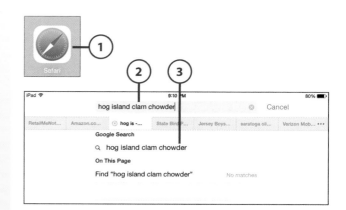

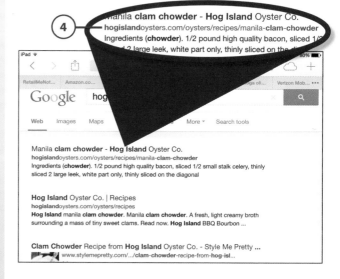

5 A very detailed recipe, as well as a photograph of Hog Island Clam Chowder, was now on my iPad screen. I immediately headed to the kitchen to make this beauty.

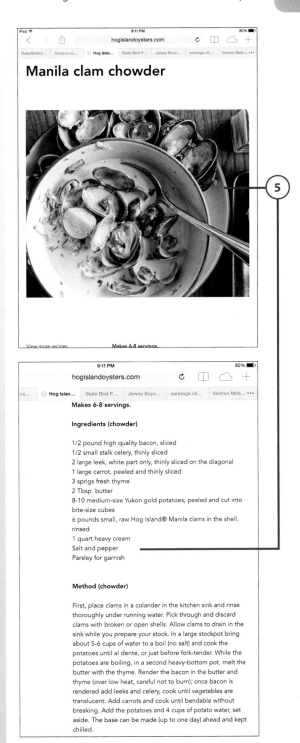

6 One of the great things about using Safari for an Internet search on your iPad is that you can often find several photos of your search term as well as many other items that may further pique your interest.

Using Open Table for iPad to Make Dining Reservations

Open Table is an app that enables you to make dining reservations from anywhere.

1 Type **Open Table for iPad** in the App Store's Search field. Tap the Get button to download and install this app to your iPad. When the Get button becomes Open, tap it to open the app.

Apps in the Cloud

Sometimes when you search for an app in the App Store, instead of the Free button or a price for the app, you see a cloud button with a down arrow. That icon means you've already downloaded this app.

(2) After the app loads, you are asked if Open Table can use your present location. We suggest you allow this to make it easier to locate a restaurant in your current area. In the example, we are located in Berkeley, California, and the results show the restaurant options we have to choose from.

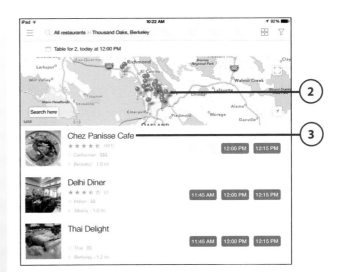

Choose Your Location

If you prefer not to use the GPS on the iPad to allow Open Table to know your exact location, you can still choose a location on the map by swiping and pinching/unpinching to zoom in on the exact location you want to search, and then tap Search here. Search results in the chosen area will appear on the map as pins. Tap the pin to view the name of the restaurant and its rating. Tap the name of the restaurant on the pin, and then find out more about it as described in steps 4-7.

(3) We chose to tap the listing for Chez Panisse Cafe in Berkeley.

(4) The Chez Panisse Open Table page comes up with options to see the menu, read reviews, read a description of the restaurant, view a map to the place, check out the hours of operation and the price ranges, as well as other relevant information.

(5) Prior to making a decision to reserve a table, it is always a good idea to read the reviews. Tap Reviews to take a look.

6 Chez Panisse has 3118 reviews; the vast majority are excellent. Nonetheless, we read through several to be sure that we were making a good choice.

7 To make your reservation, tap the back arrow to return to the previous page.

8 You can make a reservation by tapping the time you would like to dine. We tapped 2:30 PM.

9 You have the option to sign in to Open Table by creating an account, sign in with Facebook, or make a reservation as a guest. We chose to sign in as a guest for our first Open Table experience. It turned out so positively, we created an account soon after.

10 In order to complete a reservation, you need to add your name, email, and phone number on the Reserve as a Guest page. To continue with the reservation, tap Next in the upper-right corner. The reservation will be confirmed via email. Should you modify or cancel your reservation, Open Table will send you an email to confirm. After you have dined, you will be asked to rate the restaurant.

Using Open Table is easy and extremely convenient. Once again, using your iPad can make your life more interesting—and tasty.

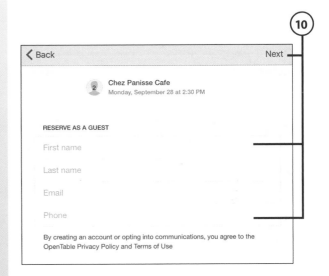

Other Apps Link to Open Table

Other apps, such as Trip Advisor and Urban Spoon, have a direct link to Open Table. If you search for a restaurant in another app and tap the link for reservations, you most likely will be taken to Open Table.

Choosing a Restaurant Using Yelp

With Yelp, you can look at the restaurants (and many other things for that matter) in an area, see what others have to say about them, and many times link to their websites and menus on line. Each business included in Yelp is given a rating based upon the reviews it has received. You can use Yelp when choosing a place for lunch or dinner, particularly when you are in a place where you have limited familiarity. In addition to finding restaurants, you can use Yelp for any number of purposes because thousands of different businesses are referenced and rated through this app. This is one of the most useful iPad apps.

(1) Search for Yelp in the App Store. Tap Get, and then tap Install to download the app. Tap the Yelp icon on your Home screen to open the app.

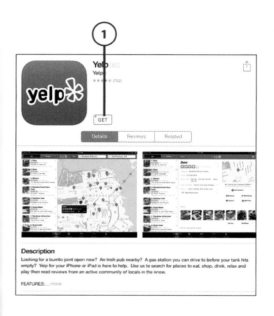

Allow Location

When asked to allow Yelp to use your present location, tap Allow. You are also asked to sign up or use Facebook to access Yelp. I tapped Skip in the upper-right corner to move on to the app.

2 Tap the list view shown for your current location, which includes all sorts of different businesses. To narrow the list of possibilities, you must search for something specific—in this case, restaurants.

Different Ways to Search

Depending on your search preference, you can check out Yelp by either using the list, map, or photos feature. You may also filter your choice by distance, rating, cost, or even Open Now.

3 In the upper-right corner, tap in the find box. Popular categories come up automatically, including restaurants. If you have an interest in something more specific, simply type in your topic and Yelp automatically searches for listings that match it.

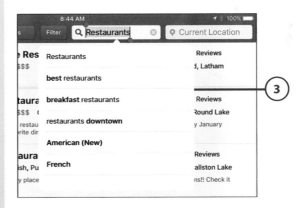

(4) Our search yielded eight restaurants on the first Yelp page with their locations. You may have more results than can fit on one page. To see the rest, swipe the screen with your finger from bottom to top.

(5) The results include details about the individual restaurants, including a photo, the type of food offered, the address, the received customer ratings, and how expensive they are (the more dollar signs, the more expensive).

Reading Ratings

When considering what restaurant to choose, check out the rating and also the number of reviews. If a place has only five reviews, the results might be considered less accurate than the one with 500.

(6) For this example take a closer look at Rivoli, the 4th restaurant in the search—it has 628 reviews and a rating of 4/5 stars. To do this, simply tap Rivoli on the list.

(7) The expanded version for Rivoli provides more information, including a map, phone number, and hours of operation. In addition, you can scroll down to read all 628 reviews.

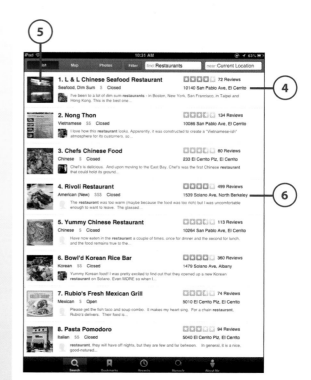

(8) With each review, you have the opportunity to provide feedback at the bottom by tapping useful, funny, cool, or compliment.

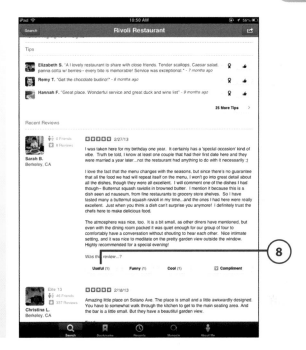

>>>Go Further
MORE USEFUL FOOD-RELATED APPS

We don't have room in this book to cover all the apps out there that can help you find recipes or locate restaurants of interest to you, but this list highlights some additional apps that you might want to check out.

- **All Recipes**—This app is a video cookbook that offers step-by-step video directions for some delicious recipes.

- **Big Oven**—Take 350,000 recipes, your grocery list, and menu planner anywhere.

- **Food Network in the Kitchen**—Access the culinary gems found on the Food Network while at home.

- **Foodgawker**—This offers a huge number of recipes with photos and directions.

- **Harvest to Hand**—The main thing we love about this app is that it has catalogued the location and times for all farmer's markets in an area.

- **Urban Spoon**—This is a restaurant review app that allows you to search by price and by the type of food served. In many cases, you can also make reservations through Urban Spoon.

- **Zest**—Searching the web for a recipe is quickly replacing looking through a cookbook. Zest is an app that allows you to store all your recipes from wherever you may find them on the web

- **8500+ Drink and Cocktail Recipes**—This app is exactly what it sounds like—a whole pile of recipes for drinks. It appears that this app might have drinks that challenge your favorite mixologist.

Find videos of friends and family, as well as how-to videos and much more.

Keep up with the daily lives of friends and family through Facebook.

Share and view photos and short videos.

Use these apps to talk with friends and family just like you are in the room with them.

Share your photos and even add effects.

In this chapter, you learn to use iPad apps to stay in touch with family and friends, as well as share photos and videos.

- → Use email to correspond—no stamp required.
- → Share and view photos quickly and easily using Shutterfly and Flickr.
- → Get on Facebook to stay up to date with friends and family.
- → Keep up with the younger generation through Instagram.
- → Converse face-to-face with those you can't be with using FaceTime and Skype.
- → Post or view videos on YouTube for an easy way to share life's moments.

Communicating with Your Loved Ones Using Your iPad

There may be no more important activity than communicating with those you love. Sharing your lives with the lives of your children and grandchildren is a source of incredible happiness. You no longer have to wait to receive the photograph of some great event through the mail. You can now receive that communication almost as fast as it happens. Thanks to your amazing iPad, you have the opportunity to become much more involved in your loved ones' lives, even if they live thousands of miles away. This chapter explores some of the ways to make this happen.

Using Email to Stay in Touch

Unfortunately, the handwritten letter and the postcard—that personal touch in communication—though not dead, are certainly on life support thanks to email. Email is free and easy to use, and there is absolutely no excuse not to have your own email account. Everyone who has an iPad has access to an email account. Even if you do not have one with an outside service, you have access to an iCloud email account.

Email is often your first line of communication with the outside world. Your children, grandchildren, and friends can easily communicate with you via your email account, no matter where you (or they) are. They can send you photographs, video, and updates on their current activities using mail. Additional options for instant communication are texting and iMessage, discussed in detail in Chapter 8, "Communicating with Email and Messaging."

If you've not already done so, create an email account. If you aren't sure how to set up email accounts on your iPad, return to Chapter 8 for the information. Email is a lifeline that you can't do without in this day and age.

Sharing Photos, Videos, and Other Information

Facebook is one of the most widely used apps to keep in touch with friends and family. It is also integrated into many of your iPad's default apps, such as the camera, Safari, and even Siri. With the tap of a button on your iPad, you can share a comment, photo, or video with your Facebook friends. When your children or grandchildren do something that is just too cute, you can capture it with your iPad camera and share it within seconds. It is a great way to stay connected with those you care about. Other apps that your grandchildren (or even your older children or other family members) are most likely using to share their daily lives with others are Instagram, Vine, and YouTube. The following tasks explore some of the ways to use these apps to stay in touch.

Facebook

Many people now spend more time on Facebook than the rest of the Internet combined. If you are one of those people, the official Facebook app is probably the first third-party app you should put on your iPad.

With it you can browse your wall, post status updates, send messages, post photos, and do most things that you can do on the Facebook website, but inside an environment designed for iPad users.

(1) Search the App Store for the Facebook app. Tap Get to download and install it.

(2) Enter the email address and password you use to log into Facebook.

(3) Tap Log In.

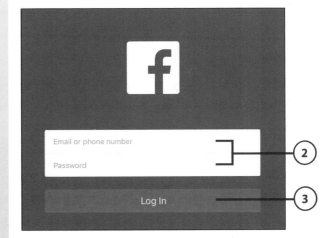

(4) Scroll up and down to view your News Feed.

(5) You can Like posts just as you would on the Facebook website.

(6) You can also tap Comment to add a comment to a post.

(7) View and handle friend requests.

(8) View direct messages and send messages to friends.

(9) See your list of Facebook notifications.

(10) Tap the More button to get further options.

(11) Tap your name to examine your own wall and edit your profile.

(12) Search for people, places, or things by typing in the Search bar.

(13) See a list of your friends and view their information and their wall.

(14) You can also post to walls of Facebook pages that you manage.

(15) Tap your image in the upper-right corner to update your status and add a post to your wall.

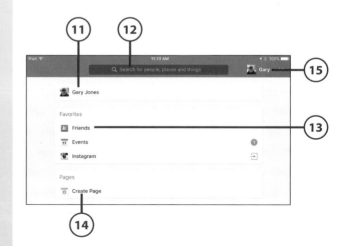

(16) Tap Write Post to update your Facebook page.

(17) Type the text of your update.

(18) Add friends who are with you to the update.

(19) Add a photo from your Photos library, or take a new photo using your iPad's cameras.

(20) Choose people and groups you want to allow to see your update.

(21) Post the update to Facebook.

It All Looks Different

If there is one consistent thing about Facebook, it is change. Facebook loves to change how its website and apps look. So if the Facebook app looks different from what you see here, it could simply be that Facebook has, once again, decided to redesign the interface.

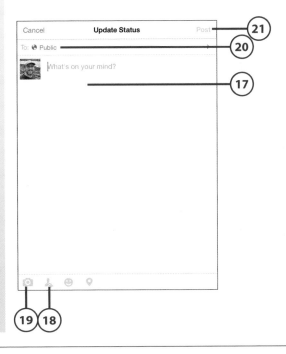

Post from Outside

You don't need to use the Facebook app to post pictures. You can do it right from the Photos app and other image-handling apps. But you first need to go to the Settings app, then the Facebook section, and enter your email and password again. This gives iOS permission to use your Facebook account for posting. Then you can do things like post pictures from the Photos app, post links from Safari, and ask Siri to "update my Facebook status."

Instagram

Another social media app that your children or grandchildren are apt to tell you about is Instagram. It is a photo-sharing site that is popular among the younger segments of the population. Learn how to use apps like this one to effectively communicate with them.

1. Search the App Store for Instagram. Instagram is an iPhone app that works fine on your iPad. Tap Get, and then Install App to install it. Tap Open to open it.

2. You have the option to sign up or log in. If you do not have an Instagram account, tap Sign Up.

3. An easy way to register is to use your Facebook profile.

Forget Facebook

You can also just create an account with Instagram if you prefer not to use your Facebook account to sign in. However, you need to go to your Instagram profile settings and manually choose to have your Instagram photos posted on Facebook. It will not happen automatically if you go this route.

4. Tap Log In and enter your username and password if you already have an Instagram account.

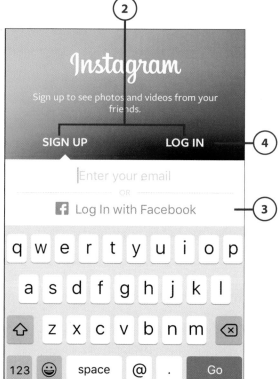

5 I signed in using my Facebook profile, so I was able to find my Facebook friends that also use Instagram. (Personal contact information is blurred intentionally in the image.) Tap the Follow button for any friends that you want to follow on Instagram. I tapped Follow on one friend to see photos of my nephew.

6 I can now see a photo of my beautiful daughter and granddaughter. I can choose to tap the Heart button to like it or the Comment button to comment.

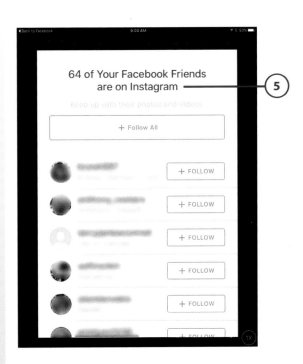

Hashtags

If you use Twitter, you already know what a hashtag is. A hashtag always starts with a hash (#) character and can consist of any word, series of letters, or phrase that you want to use to describe a photo (or a tweet, in Twitter). If it is a phrase, you type the words all together without punctuation or spaces. A hashtag can then be used to search for similar photos (or topics, in Twitter). The photo shown with step 6 might have a hashtag of #baseball. If someone searches Instagram for #baseball, this photo will appear (unless the owner has marked it as private).

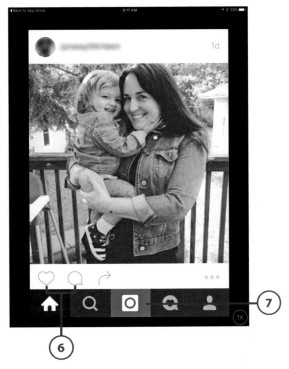

7 To post a photo of my own, I tapped the camera icon in the row of icons at the bottom.

8 You have three options: Tap Library to choose an existing photo, tap the Photo circle to take a photo, or tap Video to take a short video. For this task, I selected a photo from my iPad's camera roll to post.

Editing Photos

If you choose to take a new photo within Instagram, you then have the option of making a variety of edits to the photo before you post it. You can add filters to give it a different look, such as turning it into a black-and-white photo. You can adjust the brightness and contrast, and can even add a frame. There are other apps out there as well, such as InstaFrame, that give you the ability to make even more edits to your photos before you post them.

9 I searched my photos along the bottom of the screen and chose a photo of my grandson. After the photo is posted, my Instagram friends can see it and choose to like or comment on it. Instagram is a great way to stay connected.

It's Not All Good

No Privacy

Vine presently has NO privacy options; anyone can see whatever you post. You have the ability to block others from following you, but that's it.

Communicating (Almost) Face to Face with FaceTime and Skype

You may remember, as a kid, hearing futurists speak of the video phone—a telephone where you could actually see the person you were speaking with! Do you remember the comments? First, "That would be so cool," and then right after, "Oh my, I'll have to comb my hair, put on my makeup, and make sure I'm dressed before answering the phone." Well folks, it's here! Thanks to your amazing iPad and the FaceTime and Skype apps, you can make calls and see the person you are talking to up close and in living color.

Think about all the great opportunities you could avoid missing out on by using just these two apps. Can't attend the family reunion? Have someone take her iPad and open up a Skype call or FaceTime connection with you. Spend the winters in Florida while the rest of your family is back in the cold? Skype and FaceTime can help you feel like you are there, while you are still enjoying the warm weather.

FaceTime

On his 90th birthday, I handed my dad my iPad so that he could see *and* talk to his granddaughter in California. (He was in New York.) He looked at her with amazement and wondered just how that thing worked with no wires or anything. Your iPad and FaceTime can open up a whole new world of communicating with family and friends.

(1) Prior to using FaceTime, a bit of setup is required. Tap your Settings app to open it, and then tap FaceTime on the left.

(2) Enter your Apple ID and Password if it isn't already entered.

(3) In the list of phone numbers and addresses that can be used to reach you using FaceTime, tap to check the ones you prefer to use. (My personal contact information is blurred out in the associated image intentionally.) Your list will contain any contact information you have previously entered into your iPad. Tap Add Another Email to enter new contact information that you want to use with FaceTime.

(4) The last piece is the caller ID; just like the caller ID on a phone, it lets the person you are contacting with FaceTime know who is calling. You can now close the Settings app by pressing the Home button.

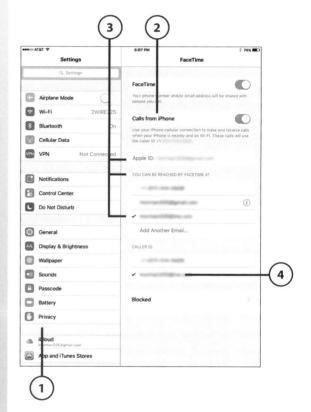

FaceTime Is Limited

FaceTime is an Apple product that works only with other Apple products (iPhones, iPads, and so on). You can have a video conversation using Skype on your iPad with anyone else who has Skype on any device or computer.

(5) Tap the icon for the FaceTime app on your iPad to start it.

FaceTime

(6) The FaceTime app opens, and you see yourself via the front-facing camera on your iPad. At the top left, type the name, email, or phone number of the contact you want to FaceTime with. Or, you can tap one of the people you have recently contacted. My contacts have been blurred to protect privacy.

(7) In this example, I chose to FaceTime my wife, Susan. I tapped her name in my Contact list, and her information came up opposite my image.

(8) I tapped her phone number to activate the FaceTime call to her iPhone.

(9) After the contact number or email is tapped, FaceTime responds with a message, such as FaceTime with Susan Jones. If the person you are trying to FaceTime with accepts your "call," FaceTime shows a Connecting message.

(10) Either party can end the call at any time by tapping End at the bottom of the screen.

(11) After the connection is made, the person you are calling can be seen on your iPad.

(12) Your image appears at the upper-right corner of your screen, and the person you are calling sees you on their full screen with their own image in the upper right. (You can drag that image to other locations on your screen if you want.)

(13) By tapping the rotate camera symbol, you can see what the rear-facing camera sees. This is a great feature if you are trying to show your surroundings to the person you are talking with. To end the call, tap the red phone in the middle.

(13)

Muting a Call

There may be times when you don't want to end the call, but you also do not want the person on the other end to hear what is going on around you. To mute the call, tap the Mute button (the microphone with the slash through it). To turn mute off, just tap the Mute button again.

>>>Go Further
UNIQUE USES FOR FACETIME

It was a Saturday afternoon, and all was well. Then my cell phone rang. It was my daughter from her apartment in New Jersey asking the question, "Dad, what can I do? I have no hot water." I tried to solve this problem via the telephone, asking questions about the hot water heater: "Is it gas or electric? Who pays the gas bill? Are you sure it's turned on? Did a circuit breaker trip?" I appeared to be asking these questions in some language that my beautiful child couldn't understand. Somehow, while she was growing up at my house, she missed the course in hot water heaters!

Finally, it occurred to me that I might be able to facilitate the solution to this problem with my iPad. Could FaceTime actually allow me to see and diagnose the problem? I suggested, "Go to the hot water heater and call me back on your iPad using FaceTime."

I noticed that the control was set to pilot, not to the on position. I asked if she had been doing anything around the water heater. She said that they were cleaning in the area of the water heater. "Oh. Maybe we did bump the heater...."

"Turn the knob from pilot to on," I told her. "Will it explode?" she responded. Finally, she turned the knob and swoosh, the heater lit. There was a scream in the background, but the water was now heating.

My girl was happy once again. Thank you, iPad and FaceTime! Another mystery solved!

Since the hot water heater incident, we have had several instances where we could solve problems using FaceTime. This app and my iPad have become an invaluable tool.

Skype for iPad

Skype and FaceTime do some similar things. With either one you can make video calls with your friends and loved ones far away. One advantage with Skype is that anyone with a computer, laptop, other Internet device and a web camera can use it. FaceTime, on the other hand, is only available to Apple products, like your iPad, iPhone, Mac computer, and so on.

One other great aspect of Skype is the ability to make phone calls using Skype. It's a free call to any other Skype users' computer, and for a small fee you can make calls worldwide using your iPad. Whenever you are traveling to a foreign country that might not be compatible with your cell phones, you can add the extra Skype service to your account so that you can contact your family in the United States. As long as there's a good wireless signal, it works just great.

(1) Search for Skype in the App Store. Make sure you look for the iPad app, not the iPhone/iPod touch app of the same name. Tap Get to download and install it.

(2) When you run the Skype app, you need to enter your ID and password and then sign in. After you do this the first time, you can skip this screen.

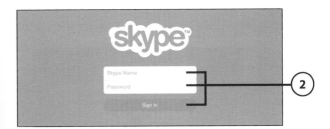

Get a Skype Account

You need a Skype account to use the Skype app. You can get a free one at www.skype.com. If you find the service useful, you might want to upgrade to a paid account, which lets you call land lines and other phones. The free account lets you call only other Skype users.

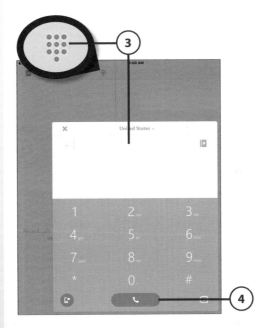

(3) Use the on-screen keypad to enter a phone number. You need a country code, too, which means using a 1 for U.S. calls. It should be there by default.

(4) Tap Call.

(5) While placing a call, you see the status, and eventually the elapsed time.

(6) Along the bottom of the screen are additional buttons to mute the sound and add a contact to the call.

(7) Tap the end call button to hang up.

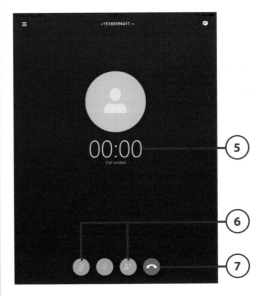

How Do You Hold Your iPad to Talk?

The microphone is at the top of your iPad. The speaker is at the bottom on the back. The best way may be to just put the iPad in front of you and ignore the locations of both. Or, you can get a set of iPhone EarPods, which include the speakers and the microphone.

How About Skype Video?

In addition to making phone calls using your iPad and Skype, you can also make video calls. To make a video call, both caller and receiver must be Skype users and have video capability on their iPad or computer.

Using Photo Sharing, Storage, and Management Apps

Posting pictures on Facebook or Instagram is great because they are immediately viewable by anyone you are friends with. However, you cannot order prints or other photo products, so your pictures just stay in the virtual world. You cannot put one in a frame or create a photo calendar to hang on the wall. Sites like Shutterfly.com and Snapfish offer the ability to not only share and organize your photos, but also to order products or prints of those photos—or of photos someone shares with you. Shutterfly and Snapfish also offer an iPad app so that you can easily post the pictures you take on your iPad (or iPhone) to an existing album, or create a new one. In this section, we take a look at Shutterfly.

Flickr gives you an opportunity to upload and share your photos as well as the opportunity to see the photos of others. One of the activities you might enjoy with Flickr is searching others' photos for travel destinations. The results are inspiring, and can give you an opportunity to see a location through the eyes of others.

Sharing with Shutterfly for iPad

Shutterfly is a free photo storing and sharing site and is connected to the Shutterfly app. After you upload your photos to Shutterfly, it's easy to share them with family and friends. The days of film developing are clearly over.

1. Search the App store for the Shutterfly app. Tap Get, and then tap Install to download. Depending on how you have your security set up, you might also have to enter your Apple ID and /or password.

2. The first Shutterfly screen is an advertisement for several products they offer. Tap the Account button, and then tap Sign In to Shutterfly on the next screen to either sign in with an existing account, or to create an account.

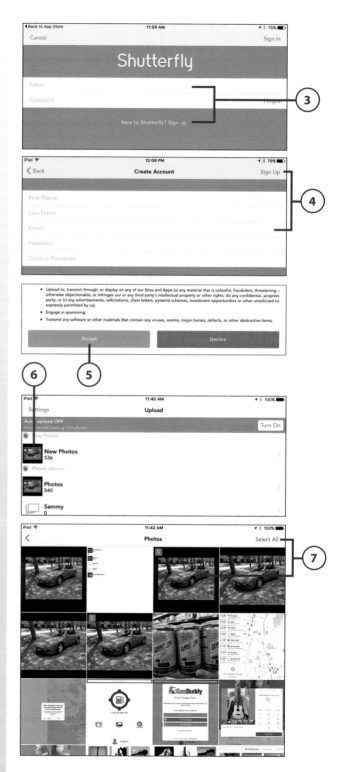

(3) The next screen asks for your email and password if you are a member; if you aren't, tap New to Shutterfly? Sign up to create an account.

(4) Creating a Shutterfly account is easy. Simply enter your name and email address in the appropriate fields, create a password, and tap Sign Up at the top-right corner.

(5) You need to accept the Terms of Use for Shutterfly to create your account. Tap Accept to continue creating your account. Tap Decline if you prefer not to create an account.

(6) Shutterfly asks you to Allow Photo Access. After you agree to allow access to your photos, you see your iPad photos on the next screen. Tap an album that contains the photos you want to upload to Shutterfly. For this task, I chose New Album, and the entire album of photos came up on the next screen.

(7) Choose the photos you want to upload, or tap Select All in the upper-right corner to upload the entire album. After you select the photos, the word Upload appears in the upper-right corner of the screen. Tap Upload to send the photos to Shutterfly.

8 The next screen asks you to choose an album to upload to. You can choose an album that you created previously on Shutterfly, or you can tap the + sign in the upper-right corner to create a new album to upload to.

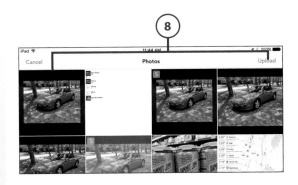

9 After the photos begin to upload, tap the Photos button at the bottom of the screen to return to your Shutterfly albums.

10 Tap the album from which you want to create prints, and then tap Create Prints.

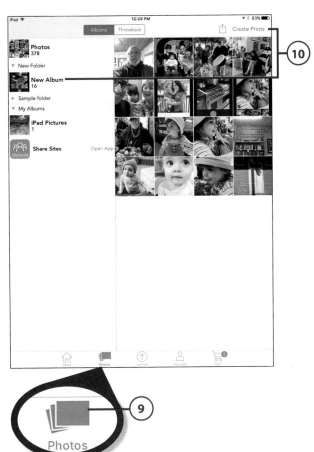

Auto Upload

Shutterfly asks if you want to turn on Auto Upload. This works similarly to your iCloud Photo Library in that it automatically uploads new photos to your Shutterfly account and stores them there for you. This is a nice backup option, especially if you don't use iCloud Photo Stream or iCloud Photo Library.

(11) Tap the size prints you are interested in ordering; I chose 4x6.

(12) Tap the photos to be printed; they will be collected at the bottom right of your screen.

(13) If you do a "long press" on the photo you have chosen, you can edit that photo. When you are finished, tap Done in the upper-right corner.

(14) When you reach your cart, add your shipping information and tap Next.

(15) Tap Checkout and follow the directions from there.

Much More to Do

There is a lot more you can do with the Shutterfly app, including accessing social media sites like Facebook and sharing your photos there. Shutterfly can also store a large number of photos for you to access, share with loved ones, and print at your leisure.

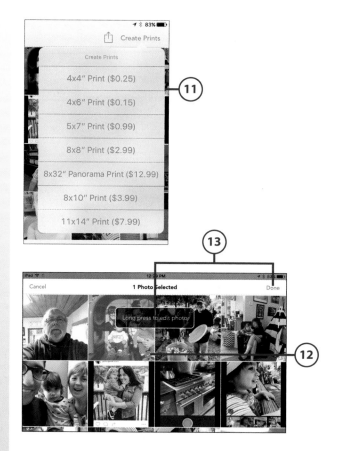

Flickr by Yahoo

Flickr is an app designed for the iPhone that works just fine on your iPad with no ill effects, other than that the image size will be a bit reduced.

1. Search the App Store for Flickr by Yahoo. (Be sure you tap the iPhone Apps button at the top of the screen.) Tap Get, and then Install to download the app. Tap the Flickr icon on your Home screen to open it.

2. Tap Get Started.

Signing In

To access Flickr, you must sign in using your Facebook or Google account, or create a Yahoo! ID and password. Doing so is easy and free from the Yahoo.com website.

3. For this task, I am signing in using an existing Yahoo! ID and password. Tap your Yahoo account ID to sign in.

4 The next screen offers the option to store your photos on Flickr. For the purpose of this task, tap I'll decide later.

5 There are two ways to add photos or videos to Flickr. The first way is to tap on the camera button. Doing so turns on your iPad's camera. You can now take a photo of whatever you are looking at and load that to Flickr.

Sharing Privacy

Through the Flickr settings, you can add layers of privacy to your photos ranging from Public, to Friends and/or Family, to totally private (only you). Security settings are something to be considered if you are at all sensitive about who sees your photos.

6 Another option is to tap Camera Roll in the upper-left corner to see all photos on your iPad.

7 For this task, I selected a photo of a car I like. When you tap the photo, a larger photo shows on the next screen.

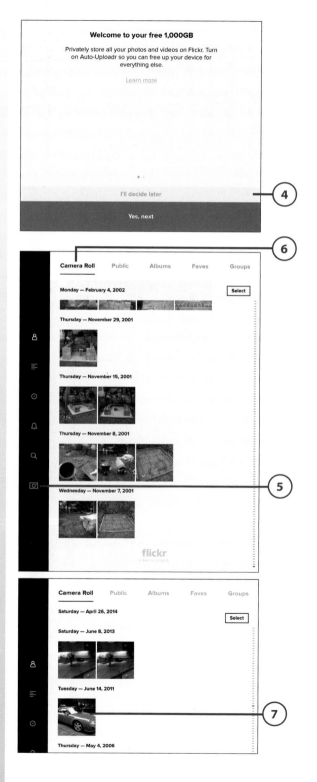

8 Along the bottom of the selected photo are options to add a comment, see technical information on the photo, or share the photo.

9 Tap the pencil at the bottom left to load the photo.

10 After you choose your photo, Flickr gives you several filter options along the bottom to improve the photo. Tap a filter to see how it changes your photo. You can always go back to the original.

11 Tap Save in the upper-right corner to save your photo.

(12) In addition to uploading your masterpieces, you have an opportunity to make contacts and join groups that have similar interests. I joined a group that includes nearly a thousand photos of wood-fired ovens.

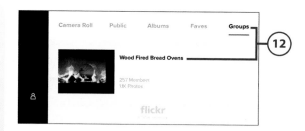

>>>Go Further
OTHER FLICKR OPTIONS

There are many other options and ways to enjoy and use Flickr. If you are planning a trip, you can search for photos of your destination to see all the photos others have taken. This is a great way to get your creative juices flowing and prepare for a great adventure. Other options available in Flickr include

- Create favorites.

- Separate out photos of yourself.

- Join others whose photos you admire by making them contacts.

- Join any number of groups taking photos that interest you.

- Search all Flickr photos, all people, or groups. You can also do a search specific to your photos or groups.

There is a great deal of flexibility using Flickr, and it's fun to see what others are photographing. Flickr is filled with photographs posted by talented people.

YouTube

YouTube is an app that enables you to save and share video moments that are meaningful to you. In addition, you can view the videos of family and friends and keep in touch with those you love. YouTube provides a nearly endless supply of entertainment viewing the videos of others, as well as those of friends and family. In addition to many entertainment videos, there is a plethora of do-it-yourself videos to help you with some of those home projects.

Often you see a YouTube video linked to a friend's Facebook page, indicating something that they would like to share. YouTube is great fun and a must for any iPad user.

(1) Search for the YouTube app in the App Store. Tap Get, and then tap Install to install the app.

(2) Tap Open to open the app.

3 Tap the Sign in arrow; or if you have a YouTube account, tap the blue Continue as... bar at the bottom.

4 Tap the Sign In button.

5 Setting up your YouTube account is easy! After you tap the Sign In button, you see two options. Enter your login information and tap Sign In if you already have an account, or tap Sign Up to create an account. For this task, I am going to tap Sign Up.

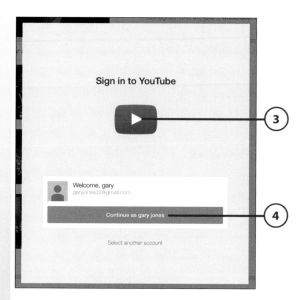

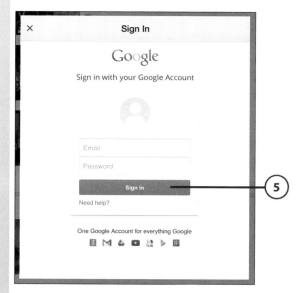

6 You will be asked to create a Google account. (Hint: Google owns YouTube.) This is not a big deal, but you will be required to provide your name, create a username and password, and give some personal information. You then enter the letters shown in the captcha (they ask you to interpret some misshapen text to prove you are not a robot), give your location, and then agree to Google's terms.

Information Overload

Providing all this information can be annoying and might even make you feel uneasy. It is all worthwhile when you can see videos of your children or grandchildren performing in plays and dance classes, or playing soccer. In addition, you can share your own videos with family and friends.

7 Now that you have your official YouTube account, it's time to upload a video. First, choose the video you would like to share with your loved ones. For this task, I searched the albums in the Photos app on my iPad and tapped the video I wanted to share on YouTube. I chose a video of my wife and granddaughter. Tap the symbol in the upper-right corner (the box with an arrow pointing up).

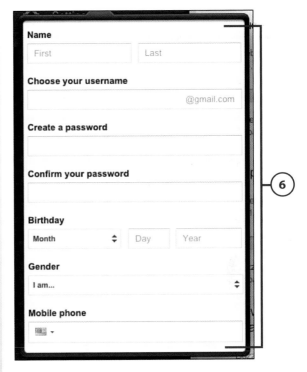

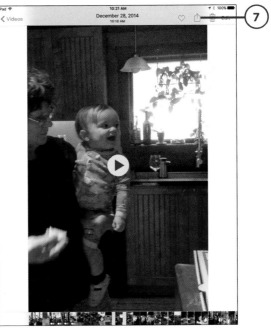

8 As you can see, I now have several options, including sending the video as part of a message or email. For this task, I am tapping the YouTube button.

9 You are required to complete several boxes that describe your video for others. Options that need to be entered include title, description, tags, category, and privacy determinations. (These settings determine how public or private your video is.)

10 Tap the blue Publish button in the upper-right corner, and off it goes!

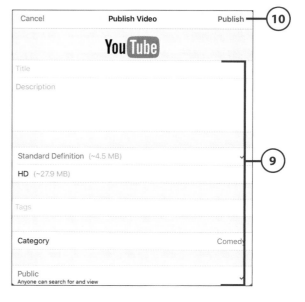

(11) The example video was named "Happy Yaya and Skyler" Published. After a video is published to YouTube, you have a couple of final options. You can view it on YouTube, tell a friend, or close the notice.

Searching YouTube

At any time while viewing videos in YouTube, you can type keywords in the search box and find the YouTube videos related to the words. I use YouTube to search for everything from learning how to install a dishwasher to finding my favorite Paul Simon videos.

>>>Go Further

MORE USEFUL APPS FOR COMMUNICATING

Due to the vast number of apps that exist, this book is not able to cover all of them. There are many different types of apps available for helping you communicate. This list highlights a few others that you might find helpful.

- **AIM**—This is an instant messaging app that makes it easy to "speak" with your loved ones, ask a simple question, or just touch base when a phone call is unnecessary.

- **Dragon Dictation**—This is an amazing app that translates your spoken words into text. This app can speed up your emails or letters.

- **Hangouts**—This is a video chat app that allows you to speak to more than one person at a time.

- **Twitter**—This app allows you to "tweet" (post a short comment) about what's happening in your life, comment on any topic, and and follow the "tweets" of your friends and other interesting folks.

Check out the latest movies and buy your tickets using the Fandango app.

Find great seats to most any sports or music venue using Seat Geek.

Create your own radio station using the Pandora app.

The NPR app is a great source of information and entertainment.

Experience a world filled with great ideas through Podcasts and the TED app.

Purchase music, movies and more at the iTunes Store.

Buy a best-seller and read it on your iPad.

Use your iPad to play some great games.

In this chapter, you learn some other wonderful ways your iPad can enhance your entertainment options:

→ Check out movies in your area and buying tickets using Fandango.
→ Pass the time playing fun games with Solitaire and Words with Friends.
→ Watch movies with iTunes Movies and Netflix.
→ Listen to music Pandora Radio.
→ Listen to new and stimulating ideas using Podcasts, the NPR app, and TED Talks.
→ Purchase event tickets using Seat Geek.

Finding and Using Apps for Entertainment

Finding a great radio station to listen to "your music" as you sip coffee on a Saturday morning might be one of your quests in life. Watching a great movie that stays with you long after the final credits have run; listening to a song that transports you to a wonderful memory; reading a great book; listening to international or local news and ideas/discussions; or simply playing a game of solitaire are all activities that you can experience using your iPad. The tasks in this chapter give you clear, easy-to-follow steps to accomplish all of this—and more!

Getting Times and Tickets Using the Fandango Movies App

Your iPad not only gives you access to the movies playing at a "theater near you," but using the Fandango app, you can also see trailers, read reviews, find out where and when your favorite movie will be playing—and even buy your tickets! Not quite the same as standing in line in the rain to get into the latest blockbuster.

(1) Search the App Store for the Fandango app. Tap Get, and then tap Install to download it. Tap the icon on your iPad's screen to open it, or tap Open on the App Store page.

(2) The opening page spotlights some of the movies now playing in theaters. To view movies in your specific area, you must allow Fandango to access your location. Open the Settings app, and then tap Privacy. Find the Fandango app in the list, and slide the Location button to the right. This turns on Location Services for this app.

(3) Tap Movies to see all the movies in your area.

Location

Fandango uses your location to help give you the most appropriate results to your searches. To allow this, click OK when asked if you want Fandango to know your location. If you click Don't Allow, you will have to provide details about your location later to get accurate search results.

4 Along the top, you can tap options such as In Theaters, Top Box Office, Coming Soon, and My Movies to search in those categories.

5 Tap Filters.

6 The Filters option allows you to search by genre and MPAA rating. If you want to search for a movie that would be appropriate for your young children, you might tap the G for general rating to see only those G-rated movies.

7 I tapped Pawn Sacrifice to check out that movie.

8 The resulting page gives access to the movie's trailer and clips.

9 If you have manually set a location, or given Fandango permission to access your location, you can also find show times and tickets at your local theater. If no theaters show up here, you have not yet set the location.

10 Tap a time to find ticket availability. To change to another day, tap the orange arrow, and then select the day and time you want.

11 Tap the number of tickets you want. I tapped 1 Senior ticket. I then tapped Checkout as Guest.

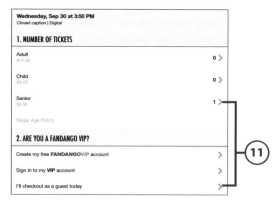

(12) To receive your receipt, type your email address in the space provided. Tap Continue.

(13) Tap your choice of payment options. Most major credit cards and PayPal are accepted. On the next screen, fill in your credit card or PayPal information to purchase your tickets.

(14) Note that there is a $1.35 "convenience fee" for using this service.

Playing Games on the iPad

Many of you enjoy playing games; card games, board games, and games of chance are some of the favorites. There are apps that re-create the game environment and enable you to have similar, if not the same, experience as you did playing the games at home. Games is a huge segment of the iPad App Store and worth exploring further than the ones reviewed here. Take a look; chances are that you will find a digital version of a game you have always loved.

Playing Solitaire

This section discusses the iPad version of two classic games: Solitaire and Words with Friends. Playing these games on your iPad is a fine way to spend some time, and in at least one case, have a little friendly competition with friends and family.

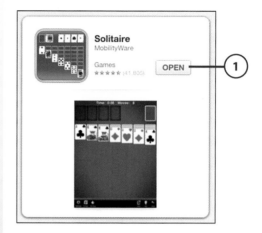

1. Search the App Store for Solitaire. (I chose the Mobilityware version.) Tap Get, and then tap Install to download it. Tap Open (or tap the app's icon on your iPad's screen).

2. Using the free version of this app, you do have to deal with some annoying ads that pop up between games. You have to watch them, at least briefly, and then tap an X or cancel to close.

3 After you get past the ads, you have access to the game. Tap Play to start.

4 I tapped Random Shuffle for this task.

5 The solitaire card game we all played as kids appears on the screen. To play the cards, simply tap them. In this example, I have no plays on the board, so I tapped the deck to see the next card. I chose to play draw 3 solitaire, (See step 10 for choosing the game type.)

6 As the game progresses, make plays by tapping cards that reflect the next play. You can either tap a card and it automatically moves to the correct place, or you can tap, hold, and drag the card to where you want it placed.

7 If you are stumped, tap Hint and the cards automatically move to show what you missed, or you see a "No useful moves detected" message.

8 Tap Undo to go back to the previous play.

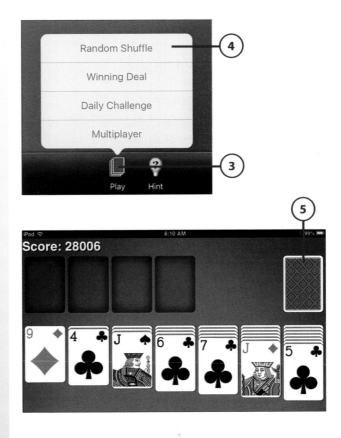

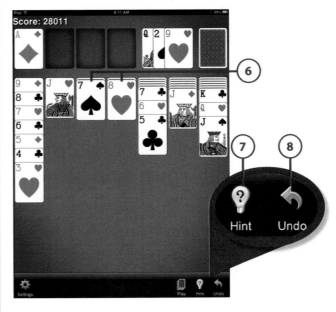

9 After you have made all the moves required to win the game, a sign emerges: Auto Complete to Win. You can tap that and your iPad finishes the game for you, or you can ignore it and finish the game yourself.

Finishing the Game

There is some on-screen "celebration" when you win, and then a screen displays that calculates how well you did compared to your other games. You are also given an opportunity to tell your friends via Facebook or email.

10 Tap Settings to access other ways to adjust the game to your liking.

11 You can also choose to tap the Hate ads banner at the top to buy the gold edition and avoid the annoyance. Tap Done to close the Settings window.

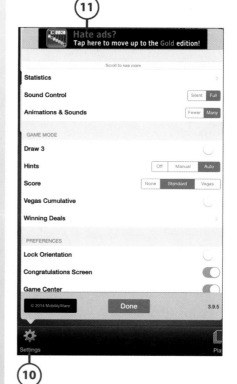

Words with Friends

Words with Friends is a wildly popular Scrabble-like game. You can play games with any number of people, and you can play any number of games at one time. The "board" is set up like a Scrabble board, with each letter assigned a value and certain spots on the board earning bonus points. Playing Words with Friends keeps your competitive spirit alive; it's a great game.

1. Search the App Store for Words with Friends HD Free. Tap Get, and then tap Install to download it. After it downloads, tap Open in the App Store to open it.

Additional Screens

Before arriving at the game, three screens appear asking to enable push notifications, add an additional language, and introduce fast play. I passed on all those screens.

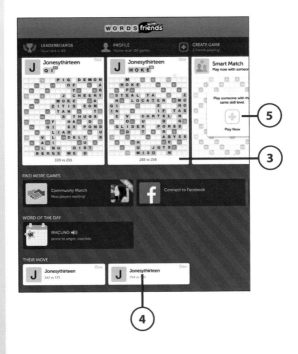

2. After tapping Not Now to the previous three screens, you can see that I have several games going simultaneously.

3. I have several games underway with my daughter. This tile represents the games where it is my move.

4. I can tap on any of the games to view our progress.

5. Tap this option to allow Words with Friends to pair you with a competitor of your skill level.

6 This example represents a new game where I have made the first move, playing the word "BRAID."

7 For the word, "BRAID," I earned 16 points. From here we go back and forth, playing our words and getting new letters, just as one would in the Scrabble board game.

8 The number at the bottom left represents the number of letters remaining.

9 The box in the upper-right corner enables you to chat with your competitor. Just tap it, and then type your comment. A green bubble with a number that represents the number of unread chats you have appears when someone else has left you a comment.

10 In this case, Jonesythirteen is my daughter, and I trash talk her all the time. She consistently beats me.

11 Tap Create Game in the upper-right corner of the app, and then tap an option to choose an opponent. Tap Play Now to begin the game.

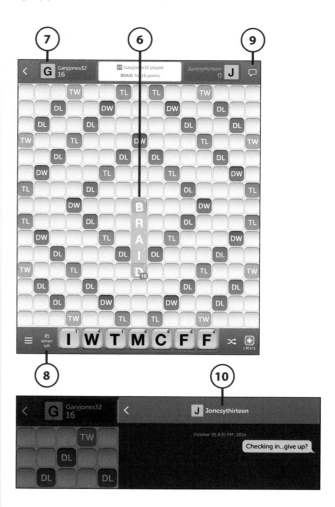

Finding and Reading Books in iBooks

iBooks offers a great reading experience. Many people are fond of having an actual book in their hands, turning the pages, and enjoying all that reading a book entails. Your iPad and the iBooks app represent a new frontier in reading that I encourage you to try. With the iPad, you can download and read almost any title you can think of. You can also browse best sellers, read a sample of your favorite author's most recent book, and if you choose, purchase it on the spot. Your iPad is, in reality, a library and bookstore at your fingertips! See Chapter 5, "Reading Books," for details.

iTunes Movies

Using your iPad, you have the ability to buy and download movies. You can find a movie you loved as a child, or browse through recently released movies. You should never have another, "There's nothing on TV I want to watch" evening.

1. Tap the iTunes icon on your iPad.

iTunes Store

2. The iTunes screen opens to whatever category of content you were viewing the last time it was opened. Tap Movies along the bottom to go to the movie category.

3 Recently added movies scroll across the top of the page. You can tap one to go directly to its information page, or you can type the name of a movie into the search field.

4 In addition, you can select from a number of movie categories by tapping the Genres button. A list of many different genres of movies appears.

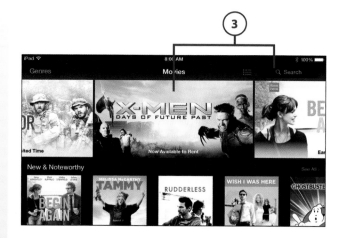

Rules for Renting Movies in iTunes

- You have 30 days to start watching after download.
- The movie must be watched within 24 hours after you start it.
- The movie expires 24 hours after you start watching, or 30 days after download.
- You can move the rental between devices but watch on only one device at a time.

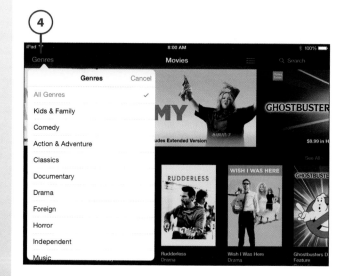

5 For this task. I searched for one of my all-time favorites—*Butch Cassidy and the Sundance Kid*.

My search produced several options in addition to the movie: songs, albums, ringtones, books, audio books, and podcasts.

6 I selected *Butch Cassidy and the Sundance Kid*, the movie.

7 The page for *Butch Cassidy and the Sundance Kid* includes a trailer, plot summary, cast and crew, as well as other information.

8 Tap $14.99 BUY to buy the movie.

9 Tap $3.99 RENT to rent the movie.

10 After you tap Buy, you have the option to download the movie now, or download it later. If you rent, you must start watching within 30 days, and the movie expires 24 hours after you start watching.

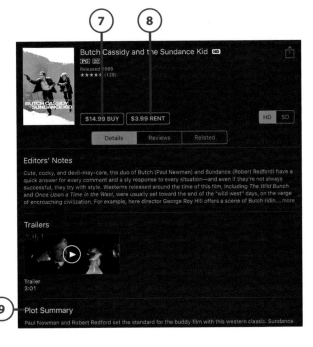

Accessing Music Through iTunes

Apple has changed the music world in remarkable ways. You can quickly and easily search for, purchase, and download your favorite songs and albums using only your iPad. Within seconds after purchasing, you can have that favorite song loaded on your iPad and listen to it.

You can use the iTunes app to purchase and download music. You can simply add more music to your iTunes collection on your computer, and then sync those songs to your iPad. You can also use iTunes Radio to listen to streaming music. See Chapter 4, "Playing Music and Video," for instructions on how to use iTunes and iTunes Radio to access your favorite music.

National Public Radio (NPR) for iPad

NPR for iPad offers any number of interesting articles, both written and broadcast, on a variety of topics. In addition, you can listen to updated Hourly News any time you feel the need to catch up. You can search for your favorite station to listen to, whether it is one from far away or the NPR station in your hometown, and listen anytime you want on your iPad!

(1) In the App Store, search for the NPR for iPad app. Tap Get, and then tap Install to download it. Tap its icon on your screen to open it.

2 The opening page shows many topics that you can choose to listen to. The topics are organized in three main categories: News, Arts and Life, and Music.

3 You can swipe each category from right to left to see more offerings.

4 For this task, swipe the music column to find a show involving the violin virtuosos, Joshua Bell and Jeremy Denk, discussing a topic they call "Song Travels."

5 You have two options. You can listen to the program right now by tapping the speaker symbol, or you can tap the + Playlist to save it for later.

6 Also along the bottom of the screen are a number of options to further diversify your listening experience.

7 You can find your Playlist by tapping the menu button.

8 Tap on Hourly News to get a news update any time you want.

9 Tap programs. A page consisting of many NPR offerings displays.

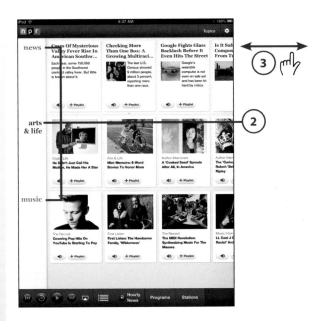

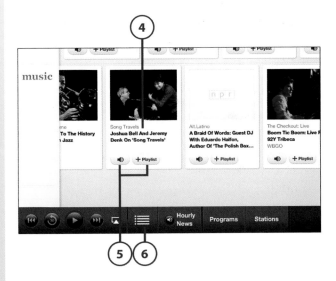

10 Tap Stations at the bottom. You can choose to listen to any of the NPR stations across the country. For this task, I chose to find my local station by tapping Find Nearest. You could also choose to type a ZIP code, city name, state, or a station's call letters in the search field to find a specific station.

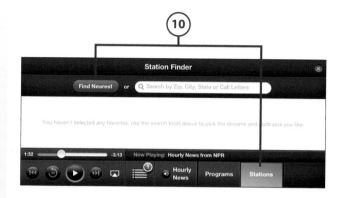

Watching Movies and TV Shows Using Netflix

The Netflix App allows Netflix consumers to stream TV shows and movies on their iPads. Streaming enables you to see video wirelessly on your iPad. This is a convenient way to experience some of the best in television and film from your easy chair.

1 Tap the App Store icon on your iPad. When the App Store opens, type **Netflix** in the Search field. Tap Get to download and install the app. When the Get button becomes the Open button, tap it to open the app (not shown).

Apps in the Cloud

If you have already downloaded the Netflix app on a device using your Apple ID, you see the download icon instead of the word Free. Tap the download icon shown in the image to the right (cloud with arrow) to download the app to the iPad. If the app is already on your iPad, you see the word Open.

2 If you have a Netflix account, click Sign In and proceed to sign into your account. If you do not have a Netflix account, tap Start Your Free Month. The first month is free, and after that Netflix charges for the service.

3 Choose the plan for your free trial. This is also the plan you will be charged for after your 30 days is up.

4 Tap Continue.

More Movie/TV Apps

In addition to Netflix, Snag Films, Hulu, and Amazon Prime have a great selection of movies and TV shows that are included in their membership. Amazon Prime membership is $99 per year which, in addition to the video options, includes free shipping on many items and a large music streaming service. Go to www.amazon.com for a free trial. Hulu starts at $7.99/ month and Snag Films is free.

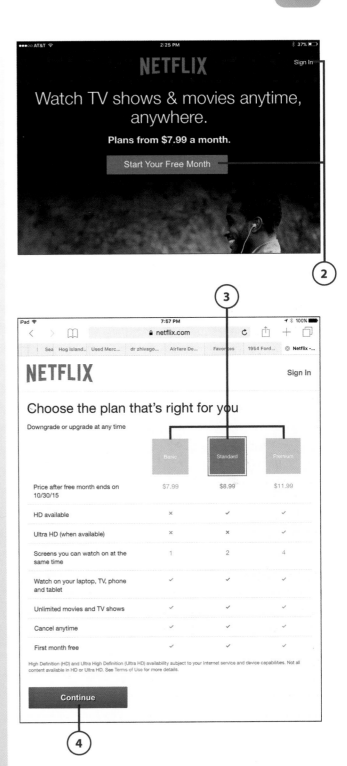

(5) To register, type your email address, create a password, and then tap Register. You also need to provide your credit card information so that Netflix can bill you after your free trial is over. Complete the payment information as necessary, following the onscreen instructions.

(6) If you already have a Netflix account, the opening page shows items you have watched and makes recommendations for others you might like.

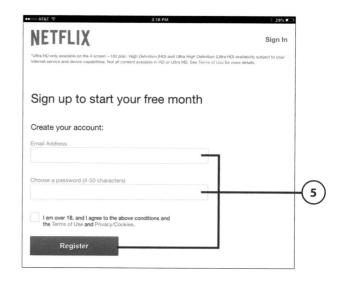

7 You can also type in a search term to search all Netflix options for something you might want to watch.

8 I typed **bott** in the search box to find the movie *Bottle Shock*.

9 *Bottle Shock* was the first movie listed. I tapped it to get that movie.

10 Tap the Play button to begin watching.

11 Netflix also lists a variety of other options to *Bottle Shock* that I might want to consider.

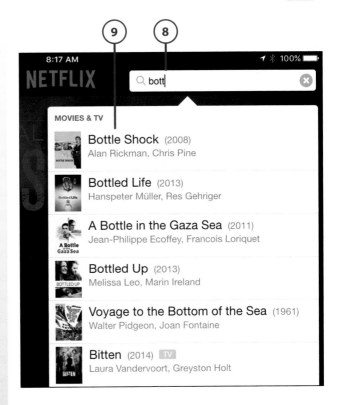

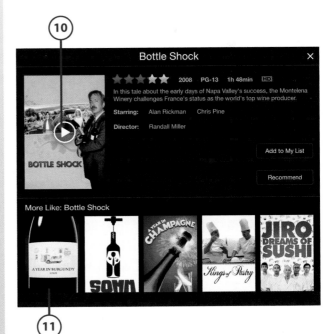

(12) Tap the lines in the upper-left corner to access a list of the many different genres available on Netflix. Scroll down to see the entire list. Tap any item in the list to see videos in that category.

There are many movies and TV shows to choose from, so be sure to use the search tool or category listing to locate programs of interest to you. There is no limit to the number of programs you can watch or any time restriction on how soon you need to finish a program you start viewing.

Listening to Music Through Pandora Radio

Pandora Radio is a popular app that enables you to choose your favorite musical artist, and then creates a radio station that plays only music similar to that of your favorite artist. One of the nice things about Pandora is that you can hear and learn about artists you might never have known. It provides a biography and other interesting information about artists while their songs play.

1. In the App Store, type **Pandora Radio** in the search field. Tap the Get button, and then tap Install to download it. Tap the Pandora icon on your Home screen to open it.

2. When Pandora opens for the first time, the sign in screen is shown. Type your email address and password for your Pandora account. If you do not have one yet, tap Register for Free and sign up for one.

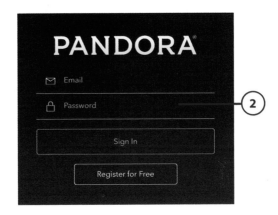

3. The opening page shows all the Pandora radio stations that I have already created.

4. One nice thing is that you can create a station for almost anything, including a special event. For example, we were having a pizza party and someone asked for some traditional Italian music. Simple! Create a Pandora station, and you are transported musically to Italy.

5. Each time a song plays, biographical information on the artist shows on the right side of your screen, often enhancing your knowledge of the artist or group.

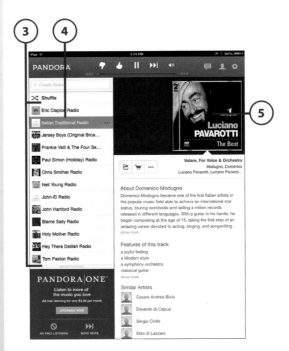

Opening Apps

If you have already downloaded an app, you no longer see the Free or Buy button when you search for that app in the App Store. Instead, you see an Open button that enables you to open the app on your iPad from within the App Store. If you downloaded the app on another device, you might see a cloud button with an arrow in it. This means the app is in iCloud, but not on your device. Tap the cloud button to download and install the app. You can always open an installed app by tapping its icon on your iPad's screen.

(6) Tap the gear symbol to access the settings for Pandora.

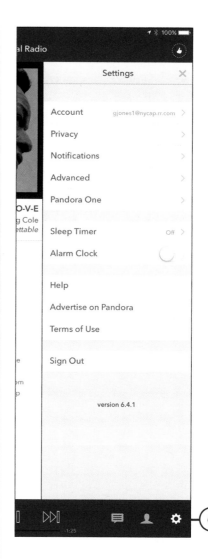

7) On occasion, Pandora asks if you would like to upgrade to Pandora One for $4.99/month to receive your music ad-free.

8) To create a new station, simply type your favorite artist, song, or genre's name in the search box at the upper left. As you can see, Pandora makes suggestions based upon what you type. Tap Return on the keyboard to keep what you typed, or tap one of the listed suggestions, and poof, you have a new radio station!

Continue to Use Pandora for Free

You do not have to pay anything to continue using the version that includes ads. Just ignore that "Upgrade to Pandora One" ad, and it will go away and return to playing your station. That goes for any other ad that is played. Just wait a few seconds, and the music returns.

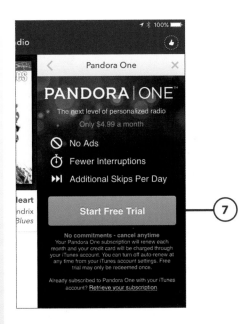

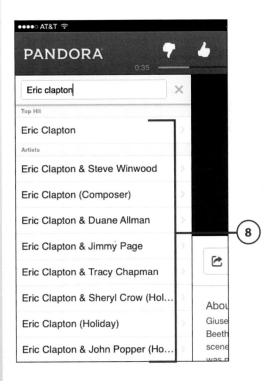

(9) Tap ... to bookmark the song or the artist track you are listening to.

(10) At any point during a song, you can tap thumbs up or thumbs down to communicate to Pandora your approval or disapproval of its choice. Tapping thumbs down doesn't necessarily mean you won't hear that song again.

(11) To skip to the next song, tap the fast forward button. You can tap this only a certain number of times before Pandora tells you it can't skip the current song. After a period of time, you can again tap to skip the current song. In the Pandora One version, you can skip as many songs as you like.

(12) Tap Shuffle to have Pandora play randomly from all your saved stations. Tap again to remove the Shuffle option and return to playing just the selected station.

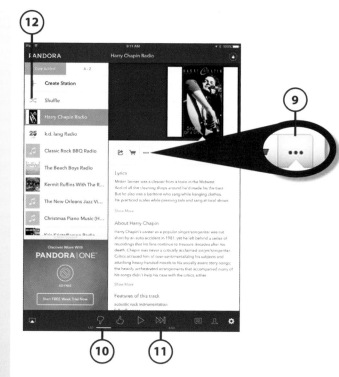

Finding and Listening to Podcasts

By listening to Podcasts on your iPad, you can learn new things and experience many delightfully entertaining and stimulating hours learning about subjects that you find appealing. Simply put, it is just one more remarkable way to use this device.

That said, this whole podcast business can be a bit overwhelming (but worth it). There are hundreds of thousands of podcasts. That alone can be a bit daunting. This task gets you started and encourages you to explore further and experience this remarkable world of information.

1. The Podcast app comes preloaded on your iPad with the iOS 9 operating system. Tap its icon on your iPad screen to open it.

Apps Change Frequently

The images you see here are how these apps appeared at the time this book was written. App developers do occasionally update their apps by changing the way they look, moving buttons around, or adding new features. You might find that an app looks slightly different from what you see here; but unless the developer has given it a total overhaul, it should function basically the same way it did when these steps were written. So, don't let that stop you from trying it out!

2. You are asked if you would like to "Turn on Auto Downloads" and if you would like to "Sync your Podcasts between Devices." Answer no to each in this example, and you come to the main Podcasts page where you can tap Featured. This page shows a large number of featured apps that can be swiped from right to left.

3. Tap Categories to see a list of Podcast categories you might be interested in.

4. The Top Charts page lists the most downloaded podcasts in the audio and video categories.

(5) The Top Podcasts are divided into two columns: Top Audio Podcasts and Top Video Podcasts.

(6) Tap This American Life to open. Tap Subscribe to see all the podcasts available from that show.

(7) You can also tap an episode at the bottom to hear a podcast before subscribing—just tap on any of the shows listed that you find interesting. For this task, I chose #379: Return To The Scene Of The Crime.

Storytelling Podcast
If you like This American Life, take a look at The Moth. It is live storytelling in front of an audience and an entertaining podcast.

8 Tap the play arrow to move back to the Podcast app screen and listen to the podcast.

9 Tap the sleep timer to turn the podcast off after a certain amount of time.

10 To make the podcast play faster or slower, tap the 1x button at the top. If you keep tapping the button, the speed increases to 1.5x, and then to 2x. If you tap again, it goes to .5x, which is the slowest speed. Continue tapping to return to 1x.

11 After you finish listening to the podcast, tap the arrow at the upper left to return to the main This American Life page in the Top Charts category of the store.

12 At this point, you have experienced a podcast. To find other podcasts that you might enjoy listening to or watching, tap Categories or Search.

13 You can also choose to revisit Top Charts or Featured by tapping the buttons along the bottom of the page. These are all ways to explore the voluminous world of podcasts.

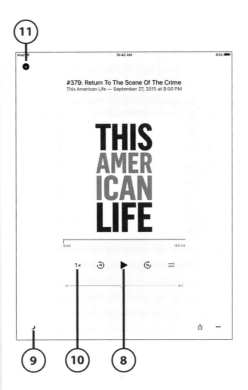

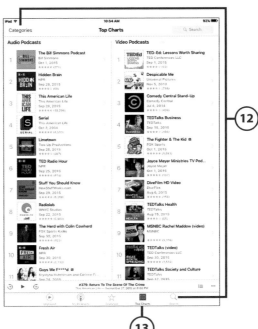

Viewing TED Talks

The TED app can provide hours of stimulating discussion and interesting viewing. Periodically, the TED organization gathers many great thinkers and creative people and puts them on stage to talk about topics that they find of interest. These recordings are available through the TED app.

1. Search the App Store for TED (TED Conferences). Tap Get, and then tap Install to download the app. Tap its icon on your iPad's screen to open it, or tap the Open button on the App Store page.

2. The opening TED page shows links to the TED Talks that are trending currently.

3. For this task, I chose to tap Surprise Me from the options along the bottom.

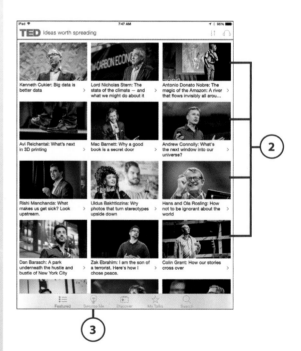

4 The Surprise Me tab takes you to another page. Tap Surprise Me again, and then choose a topic to be surprised by. I chose Beautiful.

5 A part of becoming surprised is just how much time you have available. I chose the default time of 20 minutes, and then tapped Continue.

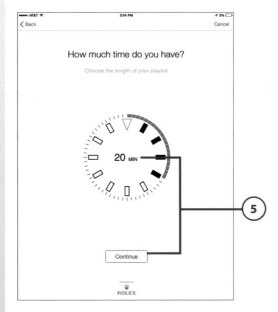

(6) TED chose to inspire me with a 19-minute piece on mistakes doctors make, and encourages doctors to talk about being wrong.

(7) You have the option to Watch Now or Watch Later. I chose to Watch Later so that I could find another talk to watch.

(8) Tap Cancel.

(9) Tap the Search button.

(10) Type **Virtual Choir** in the search box, and tap Search. (Your keyboard's Return button now says Search.)

(11) Two choices come up; tap Eric Whitacre: A Virtual Choir 2,000 Voices Strong and prepare to be blown away!

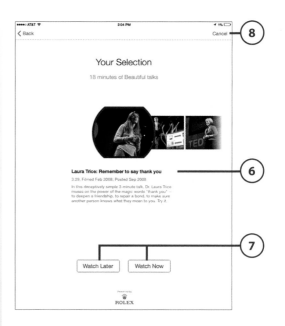

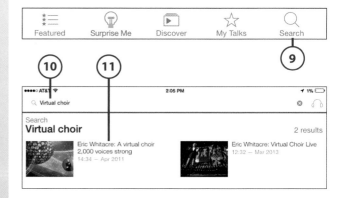

(12) A description of the TED Talk, and a photo of Mr. Whitacre, appear. Tap the play button to watch the video. This video shows you how, with the power of the Internet, Eric Whitacre incorporated 2,000 voices to sing one of his compositions– a beautiful experience to be sure.

Finding and Purchasing Event Tickets

Seat Geek is one app that makes it easy to buy tickets to concerts, and most any other venue, thanks to your iPad. Using this app is a great way to keep current on what events are happening in your area, as well as keep tabs on where your favorite artists may be playing. You will never miss finding out about another concert with this awesome app.

(1) Tap the App Store icon on your
iPad. When the App Store opens,
type **Seat Geek** in the Search
field. Tap Get to download and
install the app. When the Get
button becomes the Open button, tap it to open the app.

(2) The first few slides provide an
overview of Seat Geek. This one
explains that Seat Geek searches
numerous ticket services to
determine just what is available
for any given venue.

(3) Tap Next.

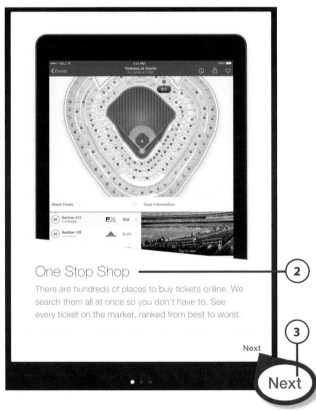

(4) The next slide indicates that in addition to providing options to buy tickets, Seat Geek also tracks concerts worldwide and will inform you of when your favorite artist is playing nearby.

(5) Tap Next.

(6) The next slide asks if you want to know what's happening nearby. Tap Allow if you want Seat Geek to use your current location when searching for nearby events.

You will also note there are two options at the bottom: Skip and Connect. If you tap Connect, this allows Seat Geek to access your Facebook account (if you have one), as well as your iTunes Library or last.fm, to determine artists you listen to. I chose to tap Skip.

(7) Tap Tracking or Announced to see a list of your favorite acts, and receive announcements of when they will be playing in your area.

(8) Along the bottom of the screen are several other options to tap and further expand your Seat Geek experience: Explore, My Events, My Performers, and Search. Tap Settings to further customize your experience with this app.

(9) This screen shows several events taking place in my immediate area. I chose to tap The Josh Groban concert to check on tickets.

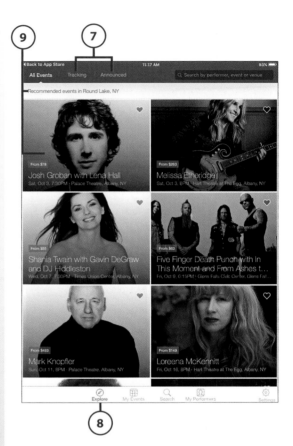

(10) I see the seating chart at the venue indicating where there are seats available. I tapped the seat at the right center, and the price for that seat was shown ($72).

(11) Additionally, Seat Geek provides information on extra charges and lets you know if they are included. Tap BUY NOW to make the purchase.

(12) After choosing to purchase the tickets, you are asked to provide your credit card information. Also notice that you are buying this from Uberseat through Seat Geek. Fill in your billing informa- tion and delivery preferences to complete the purchase.

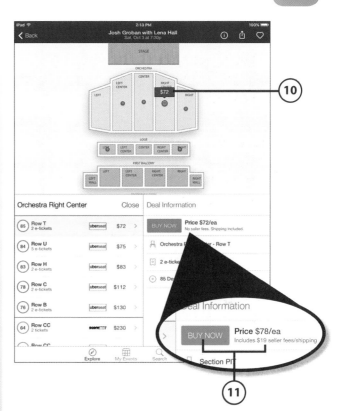

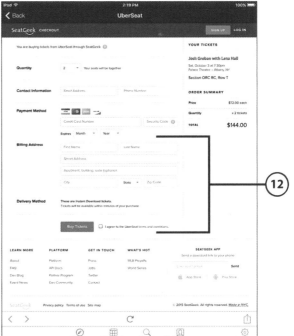

>>>*Go Further*

MORE USEFUL APPS FOR FUN AND ENTERTAINMENT

There are many hours we can spend with games, music, and other forms of entertainment on an iPad. In addition to those already covered in this chapter, this list points out a few others that you might want to consider.

- **Blackjack**—This is a digital card game that can provide hours of entertainment.

- **IMDb**—This app is your source for all things related to movies, TV, and celebrity content.

- **Pinterest**—This is an app where artists and craftspeople can show and sell their wares—a very interesting place to tour.

- **Stitcher**—This offers a single point of contact to more than 25,000 podcasts and radio shows. It's a great way to streamline your listening experience.

- **Yesterday USA**—This app features old-time radio shows from the 1920s to the 1950s.

Stay current on business trends with the CNBC app.

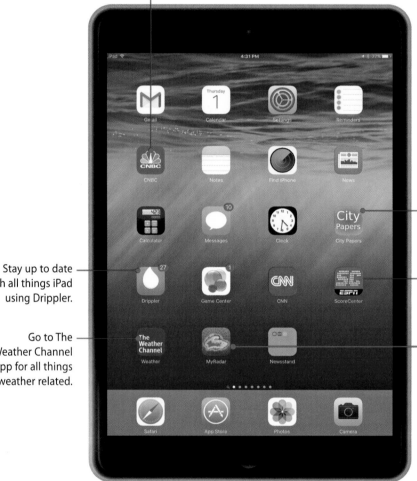

Check out City Papers, a world-wide newspaper source.

Find your sports-related news provided by ESPN here.

Stay up to date with all things iPad using Drippler.

Go to The Weather Channel app for all things weather related.

Use My Radar to track current weather in your area.

In this chapter, you look at apps that help you keep up with the latest in news, sports, finance, and weather.

→ Use the City Papers app to get local news throughout the world.
→ Stay current with financial news using the CNBC Real-Time for iPad app.
→ Keep up with breaking news around the world with the CNN app for iPad.
→ Stay current on your iPad with Drippler.
→ Follow all your favorite sports news with the ESPN app.
→ Track a storm live with My Radar.
→ Use the Weather Channel app to check the forecast anywhere in the world.
→ Stay informed with all things tech using Yahoo! Tech.

Keeping Informed Using News and Weather Apps

Whether your interests are finding out what is happening in your hometown, following the world and national news, checking out your favorite team or your stock portfolio, or simply finding out the local or international weather forecast, a tap of your iPad screen can meet those needs.

Getting Local and Global News

City Papers is one app that gives you up-to-date access to hundreds of newspapers worldwide. Papers are organized by state, and then by city, in the United States. You can also find international newspapers organized by continent, and then by country. The City Papers app is very easy to navigate. Browse as much as you like for a very reasonable price.

1. Search the App Store for **City Papers**. This app does come with a small price tag ($.99), but it's worth the investment.

2. Tap the price button, and then tap Install to download the app. Tap Open.

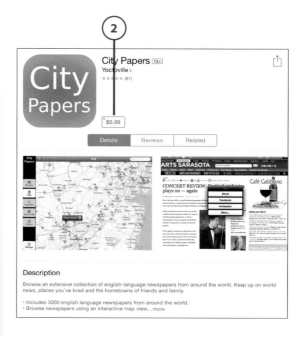

DOWNLOAD TIPS

If you've read other chapters in this book, you'll remember that when you tap the button to download and install an app (the button is sometimes labeled FREE and sometimes shows a price), you might be asked for your Apple ID password. If this occurs, it means you've enabled the setting in the Restrictions that requires your Apple ID password to be entered every time you download an app (whether or not it costs money). This is a good security feature to have enabled, especially if others use your iPad (such as children or grandkids who might not understand in-app purchases). If you prefer not to have to enter the password, or if you want to change the frequency that it has to be entered when down-loading apps or content from iTunes, go to the Settings app and tap General, and then tap Restrictions. If you've already enabled Restrictions, you'll be asked to enter the four-digit password that you would have created when you set up the restrictions. Swipe from bottom to top until you see the Allowed Content section. At the bottom, you should see Require Password. Tap the Require Password setting. You can choose Immediately, which requires your password be entered for every download regardless of how long it's been since the last time you entered the password. Or, you can choose 15 minutes, which allows you to download content or apps for 15 minutes before being asked for the password again. Tap the Restrictions button at the top of the screen to return to the list of settings. You also see In-App Purchases in the list of Restrictions settings. If it is set to Off, you cannot make In-App Purchases without entering a password. This is a useful security feature that prevents someone from accidentally downloading paid content within a game or other app without realizing it. If you set it to On, In-App Purchases will be made immediately without requiring the password.

(3) The opening page shows the regions represented and the newspapers you can browse. For this task, tap the United States.

(4) Another option is to search by Map.

(5) You can save searches by Favorites, Quick Lists, or History.

(6) Searching in the United States yields a scrollable list of all the states. Scroll down and tap California.

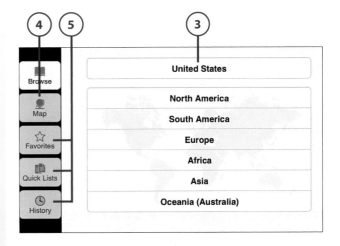

(7) The California search lists literally hundreds of newspapers throughout the state of California. One of my favorite newspapers, in one of my favorite cities, is the *San Francisco Chronicle*. Scroll down and tap the Chronicle.

(8) Today's issue appears, live and in living color.

(9) Tap Sections to see the options available in this paper.

(10) Tap Food to see the Food section of the *Chronicle*. Sure enough, the Food section of the *San Francisco Chronicle* emerges. It is so exciting to get a look at this from another state.

(11) When you finish reading, tap Done in the upper-right corner to return to the states list to browse further.

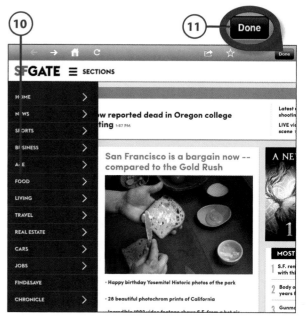

(12) You can look at local papers to get a sense of how thorough the City Papers app is. To do so, tap New York. Albany is the first listing. Included in the Albany listing is the largest local paper, *The Times Union*, and a weekly, *Metroland*.

(13) Tap *Metroland* to view the latest issue of this weekly in its entirety. City Papers may just be the best $.99 you will spend this year. Not only can you find local news, but also local news throughout the world.

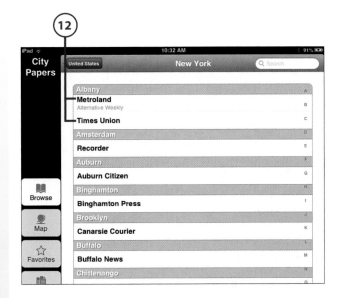

Getting Financial News

Whether you're working, near retirement, or retired, it's always helpful to stay current with the changing financial times. CNBC Real-Time for iPad is one app that provides the tools to help you make wise financial decisions. In addition to finding up-to-date information on stocks that you might follow, CNBC has a huge amount of information on currencies, bonds, and a number of other financially related items. This is a key app for anyone who dabbles in the stock market; however, there are many other finance-related apps in the App Store, such as Bloomberg for iPad and Yahoo! Finance.

1 Open the App Store and type **CNBC** in the Search field. Tap Get, and then tap Install to download the app. Tap Open.

2 On the opening page, identify your region by tapping International or United States.

3 On the next screen, choose whether the app is allowed to send you notifications. Then, tap Get Started.

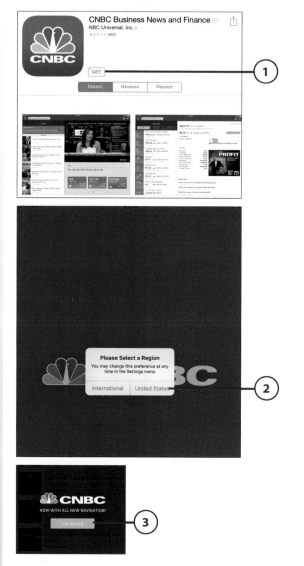

4 The home page shows a scrollable list of the top financial news stories for the day.

5 The opening page also shows the U.S. pre-market trends. (This image shows what you see before the markets open. After they open, the actual numbers appear here.) Scroll to the left to see other markets worldwide.

6 Along the bottom left is a summary of options available at CNBC, including Home, Markets, Watchlist, Videos, and more.

7 Tap Top News to see a list of options available. Tap any of the options to see further information.

8 The News Stories available on this app are numerous. You can find information on technology, finance, health care, and many other topics.

9 To check out a stock, type the name of the stock, or its symbol, in the search field above the news column.

10 For example, I typed the symbol for Facebook, which is FB. A number of options came up. I tapped Facebook.

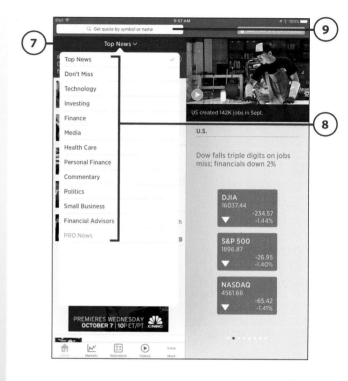

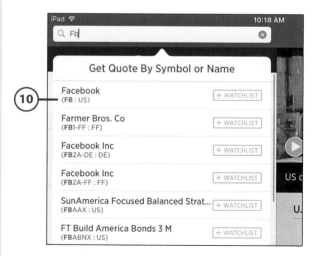

11 The Facebook financial page offers an up-to-the-minute overview of the stock and other relevant information.

12 Tap +Watchlist in the upper-right corner to create a list of stocks you want to follow. Add to that list any stocks you want to track.

As with most of these content-rich applications, there is more to explore than covered here. Tap different buttons to find more information, or to narrow the type of content shown.

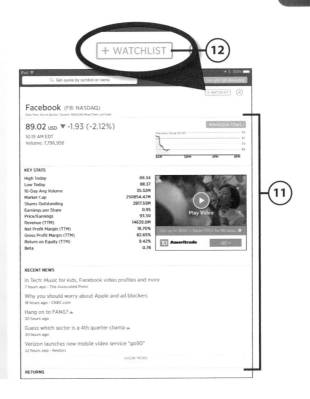

Staying Informed

It seems that anytime there is a breaking national or international news story, the place I end up watching it on television is CNN. The Cable News Network is a 24-hour news program that is often right smack in the middle of the action. Now, you can join it using your iPad.

1 Open the App Store and type **CNN App for iPad** in the Search field. Tap Get, and then tap Install to download the app. Tap Open.

(2) After tapping no to location, notifications requests, the opening page asks if you want to listen to the "This is CNN" voice each time you open the app. Slide the switch to the right to turn it on. Otherwise, tap Done.

(3) The Home page has a lined symbol at the top left. Tap it to get a list of news topics you might be interested in viewing.

(4) Tap any article on the home page to go to the newscast or written story.

(5) If you have the live TV option, tap Watch Live TV to see the available options.

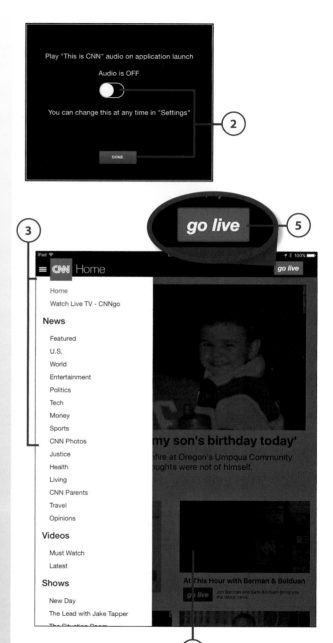

6 Tap a story of interest and move through the list of photos by swiping from right to left. It displays as either a photograph or a video.

7 For a video, tap the play button.

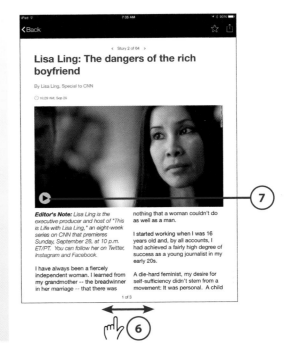

Staying Current on Your iPad with Drippler

Drippler is an app that encourages you to stay current with all that's happening in the world of iPads. Almost on a daily basis, you receive a "Drip" from Drippler alerting you of something new to do with your iPad, or telling you about a new app that you might want to check out. Drippler is a great way to keep up with the many changes and innovations that involve your iPad.

1. In the App Store, search for the Drippler-Tips, Apps & Updates for iPhone, iPad, & iPod Touch app. Tap Get, and then tap Install to load the app. When it finishes loading, tap Open to begin working with Drippler.

2. The first time you use it, Drippler asks if it can send you push notifications. Tap OK to hear a "drip" sound whenever Drippler adds content for you to review. Tap Don't Allow if you do not want to receive this notification.

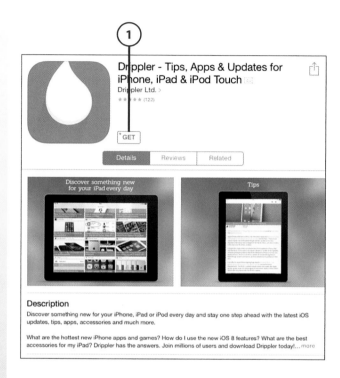

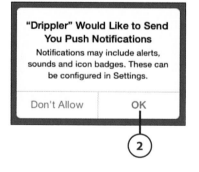

(3) Scroll up and down to see the various types of information that you can find on Drippler, or tap Skip to move to the next step.

4 Drippler completes an analysis of your iPad.

5 Tap Yes or No to the question "Do you like games?"

6 Tap Get Started to try out the Drippler app.

7 The next page shows the Drippler list of interesting topics. Tap on any one to delve further into a topic, or tap the search icon in the upper-right corner to find specific topics. 10 Best Photo Editing Apps for iPad is the topic we'll look at for this task.

More Drips
Swipe left or right on a page to move between more drips on similar topics to the one you chose.

8 Tap through the instructions about liking and swiping until you get to the content of the drip. Scroll down to see descriptions of the recommended apps.

9 Tap the icons in the upper-right corner to bookmark, like, or share the drip.

10 Tap the back arrow to return to the Drippler home page and continue exploring.

My Drips

You'll notice at the top of the Drippler screen there is a My Drips drop-down menu. Tap it to open a menu containing options for filtering the "drips" such as by Apps or News & Tips. You can also sort by Top or Recent.

Following Your Favorite Team

The sports channel ESPN has several apps available in the App Store. Some require a specific Internet provider, whereas others can be viewed on any Internet-connected iPad. Find all the latest scores and recaps of your favorite teams and sports using the free ScoreCenter for iPad app.

1 Open the App Store and type **ESPN** in the Search field. Tap Get, and then tap Install to download it. Tap Open.

Getting the Score

The steps in this task are for getting scores. If you have an ESPN account, you can log in to find even more information.

(2) The opening page provides three options: Sign Up, Log In, or Sign Up Later. If you do not have an ESPN account, tap Sign Up Later. Otherwise, sign in with your ESPN account information.

(3) The next page contains up-to-the-minute scores.

(4) Tap the balls symbol to find other sports scores.

(5) I tapped the Baltimore Pittsburgh NFL game to see more details.

6 The next page has significant details on the game, including videos and statistics.

Staying Alert with Weather Radar

I have found My Radar to be an invaluable addition to weather forecasting in my area. This app enables you to see actual radar images of storms as they pass through. With this information, you are able to prepare for significant weather events as well as get a sense of just how long a weather event will take to pass through. We recently had a serious thunderstorm heading our way at 3 a.m. I was able to check My Radar on my iPad and learn about how long it would last and assess the severity of the storm.

1. Tap the App Store icon on your Home screen. Type **My Radar** in the Search field at the top right of the screen. Tap Get to download and install the app. When the Get button becomes Open, tap it to go to the app.

Apple ID and Password

When you download an app from the App Store, you might be prompted to enter your Apple ID password. This happens if you have set your App Store settings to require a password for any activity in the App Store—even for free apps. See Chapter 10, "The World of Apps," for more information.

2. On the next page, tap Allow, and then tap Skip to see the radar in your current location. This requires that you have Location Services turned on in your Settings app. (Tap Settings on your Home screen. Tap Privacy, and then tap Location Services to turn it on.)

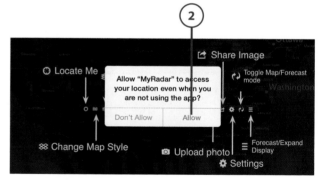

(3) In this example, I checked My Radar as a storm was coming through my home in Round Lake, NY. The My Radar map indicated my location with the blue dot.

(4) The intensity of the storm can be measured by the different colors shown in the radar graphic. The legend at the bottom illustrates what the various colors indicate. The storm I had just experienced was moderate. When the colors get into the red and purple, I will be heading for the basement.

(5) If you unpinch on the screen of your iPad, you can zoom in on your specific area and get an indication of what weather is coming directly at you. My Radar also indicates what direction the storm is heading by showing how it has tracked in the past several minutes.

(4) (3)

(5)

(6) By pinching, you can zoom out on the area to see a larger area and find out what weather may be coming your way in the minutes or hours to come.

(7) You can also use the icons at the bottom of the screen to customize your My Radar experience. You can change the map, update the map, and receive hurricane tracking, temperatures, forecasts, as well as other specific weather events. Some of these options are not available in the free version and require buying the pro version of this app.

(6)

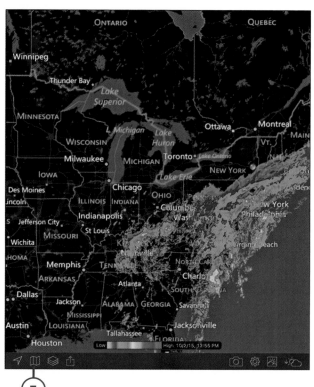

(7)

Using the Weather Channel App for iPad

Paul Simon said it best when he sang, "I get the news I need from the weather report. I can gather all the news I need from the weather report...." Well, you can get all the weather reports you need on your iPad. The Weather Channel is useful for finding out what's currently happening with the weather, and what future weather conditions will be, for just about anywhere.

① Open the App Store and type **The Weather Channel for iPad** in the search field. Tap Get, and then tap Install to download the app. Tap Open.

② After tapping on The Weather Channel home page, you are transported to your own favorites page (if you haven't used the app before, you set a "home" location at this point) containing weather information on the location of your choice.

3 Tap Forecast on the personalized home page, and a more detailed forecast appears. In this page, you can scroll along to see the forecast up to 10 days out.

4 You can change your favorites page by tapping the search symbol at the bottom right.

5 This example shows two favorites: Round Lake, NY and El Cerrito, CA. You can add more favorites by tapping the text box and adding another location. You will instantly be transported to a page that shows the weather in that location. This is a great resource for planning a trip and figuring what clothes to bring.

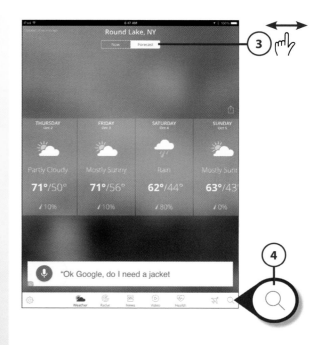

(6) Tap the Health button.

(7) Tap the Flu or Pollen button at the top to get seasonal information concerning things such as pollen count and the spread of the flu.

(8) Tap Radar at the bottom to get a look at the radar showing the weather that is coming your way.

The Weather Channel for iPad is an awesome resource to keep you up to date on the weather at home, wherever your loved ones are, or just a location you are interested in. With this easy-to-use, free app, your iPad is like having your own personal weatherman at your side at all times.

Using the Yahoo! Tech Website

A recent addition to the Yahoo! website, Yahoo! Tech has revolutionized the process of keeping us up to date on all things technology. Yahoo! Tech is a very interesting way to stay informed as technological advances come into our lives at breakneck speed. As a retiree dabbling in this new world, I really enjoy learning about what's happening now in technology, as well as what's on the horizon.

(1) Tap Safari on your iPad's Home screen.

(2) In the Google search box, type **Yahoo Tech** to search for Yahoo! Tech.

(3) Tap Yahoo Tech in the search results.

(4) The Yahoo! Tech home page opens with a huge number of articles on a wide range of topics. Tap on any one to go to an article or video. Additionally, you can scroll down to see many more tech-related items. From reviews of products, to info on games, to a great article on Net Neutrality (something we hear of often on the news), there is something here for everyone.

(5) On this opening page, I particularly enjoyed the article titled "People-rating app sparks firestorm." This was one tech article where I knew exactly what they were talking about.

(6) Another thing I really like about the Yahoo! Tech site, is that they clearly label advertising and sponsored sites. Too often we are tricked into reading an ad. This straightforward approach is appreciated.

(7) The envelope at the upper right will direct you to sign up for Yahoo! Mail if you want to.

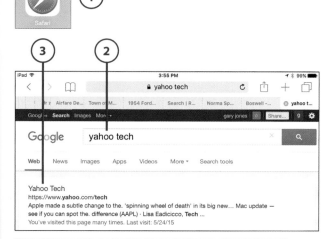

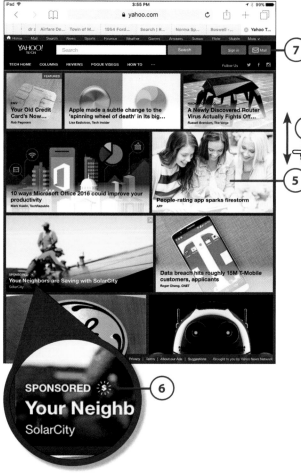

Use MapMyWalk to track fitness and retain records of your daily walks.

Get fit using the FitStar training app.

Learn nutritional facts about the food you eat with Fooducate.

Check symptoms, look up medications, and sort out what may be ailing you using WebMD

Track and order medications using these apps.

Keep your brain in shape using Fit Brains Trainer.

→ Exercise your brain to stay mentally sharp.
→ Get fit and stay fit.
→ Use the Fooducate app to positively affect your food choices.
→ Track your exercise using pedometer apps.
→ Store all your medical and prescription information in one easily accessible place using medication reminder apps.
→ Use a pharmacy app to fill prescriptions and even print photos.
→ Use WebMD to check out bothersome medical symptoms.

16

Using Apps That Help You Stay Healthy and Fit

Be proactive with your health. Several apps are available that help track your physical and mental exercise, track your medications, navigate the pharmacy, and learn to approach your daily life in a healthful way.

Exercising Your Brain

There's a rumor afloat that as we get older, our brains tend to not work as well. Some research shows that brain games can help. I checked out Fit Brains Trainer, an app that operates like a gym for your brain. You can also check out the Flow Free and Luminosity apps for more brain training.

Push Notifications

When you open games and other applications for the first time, such as Fit Brains Trainer, you see a box asking if the app can send you Push Notifications. You have the option to allow this. If you do allow it, the app can send you notifications about different things, such as reminding you to play. If you prefer not to get these notifications, tap Don't Allow. If you accidentally allow those notifications, you can turn them off by opening the Settings app and tapping Notifications. Swipe up until you see the app that is sending notifications. Tap the name of the app, and then slide all the switches from On to Off. You will no longer receive those annoying notifications from that app.

1 Open the App Store, and type **Fit Brains Trainer** in the Search field. Tap Get, and then tap Install to download the app. Tap Open.

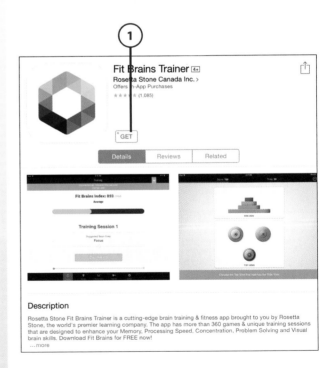

2 Tap New User.

3 The next six pages are a personal Brain Training Calibration that includes areas you are most interested in improving, your education level, age, and so on. Tap Start Calibration. After you complete this basic survey, the training begins. I indicated that I want to improve my memory.

4 Tap Start Training.

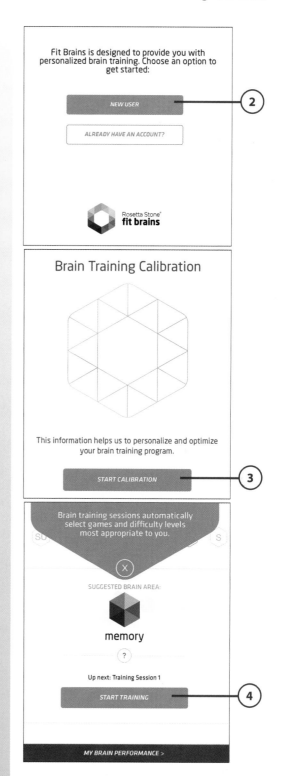

5 This is a timed exercise that requires you to memorize a group of items, and then in the next slide, tap the items that are different. The screen indicates when you get it right, and also indicates when you are in error. This goes on for probably a minute. Tap Start Training.

6 This slide represents the items to memorize. The next slide contains additional items to identify.

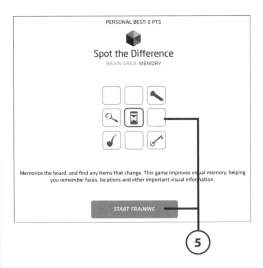

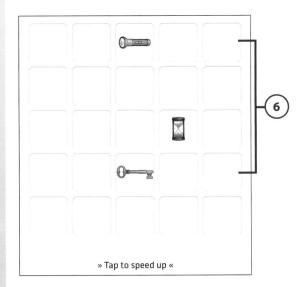

(7) After completing all aspects of the exercise, I was given my score—a depressing 35.8%.

(8) Tap Continue To Next Stage to complete the first exercise. Fit Brain Trainer gives you a summary of your training session. You also have the option to allow the app to remind you of your next session.

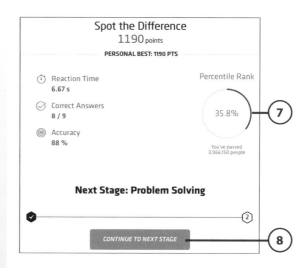

I found the Fit Brain Trainer to be an interesting app that could enhance my brain fitness as I work on the challenges. It's actually fun and enables you to track your progress daily. There are options to upgrade to a paid version that may be of interest as I continue my training. It is clearly worth a look. Remember, it's not where you start that counts—it's where you end up.

Staying in Shape

The App Store has many fitness apps worth looking at, such as Daily Workouts, FitStar, and Sworkit. In this task, I walk through using FitStar. I start at the beginning as an out-of-shape individual in need of training. FitStar analyzes the results of this starter training regimen, and designs future training based on that analysis.

(1) Tap the App Store icon on your Home screen, and type **Fitstar** in the Search field at the top right. Tap Get to download and install it. After it loads, tap Open.

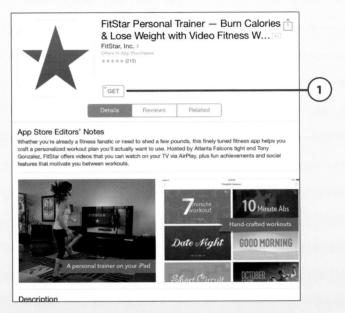

Why the Password?

Depending on your settings for the App Store, you might need to enter your Apple ID password to make this purchase (even though it is free). See Chapter 2, "Customizing Your iPad," for more information on the App Store and purchase settings.

(2) On the opening page, tap Get Started.

3 For this example, I tapped Out of shape.

4 Tap Continue.

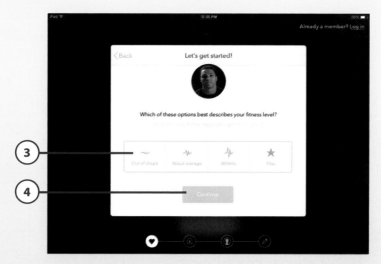

5 Sign up with your email address and password, and then tap Register.

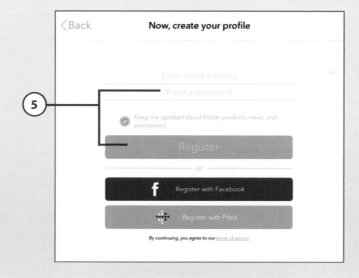

6 The next page asks you to enter your name to personalize your experience. Tap Continue.

7 After tapping Continue, you are asked several personal questions relating to your age, weight, and other pertinent information. Tap Continue.

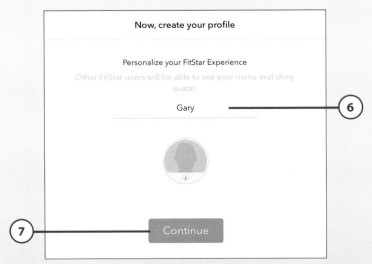

8 The next page summarizes your first set of exercises. Tap Start Session to begin.

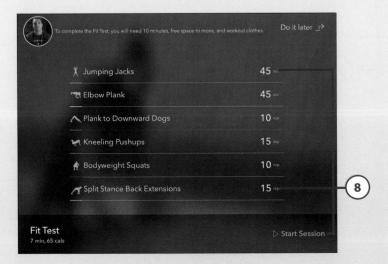

9 The exercise routine begins, and the time counts down until the particular segment of the routine is complete (in this case jumping jacks). There is another timer to indicate the time to complete the entire routine.

10 Each routine has a video, and tips are provided throughout the routine to make it more effective.

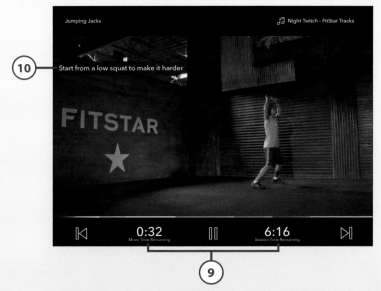

11 After you have completed a task, FitStar asks for feedback on how long you did the task, as well as its level of difficulty. This information helps FitStar individualize your next routine.

(12) The same process is followed through each segment of the fitness routine.

(13) After finishing the routine, FitStar summarizes your results as well as calories burned. Swipe left to see the summary screens. They also give you the opportunity to rate this session.

(14) The final page of the FitStar App shows you several opportunities to upgrade to a paid version of the app.

(15) I suggest you continue with the free basic version until you are confident that FitStar will meet your needs.

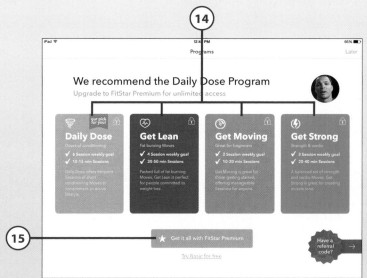

Using Fooducate - Healthy Weight Loss, Food Scanner & Diet Tracker

With the huge variety of food items available at your local grocery store and some, presumably, that would not be so good for you, an app like Fooducate is essential. Using this app, you can determine a great deal of information about what you put in your mouth. Simply point your iPad's camera at the bar code to get nutritional and other information about the product. The Fooducate app is a great way to get up to speed with ways to positively affect your well-being through the food choices you make.

① Open the App Store and type **Fooducate - Healthy Weight Loss, Food Scanner & Diet Tracker**. Make sure you have iPhone apps tapped at the top of the App Store screen because this app does not have an iPad version. Tap Get, and then tap Install to download the app. Tap Open. Tap the 2X button in the lower-right corner to make the app iPad size.

② Next, tap "I agree to the terms of service."

③ Tap Sign up.

Other Food and Nutrition Apps

There are several other related apps you should also check out. HealthyOut is a free app that helps you make healthy choices when eating out. My Diet Diary combines nutrition information and fitness tracking in one, free app. Another popular app is Nutrition Menu. This one comes at a small price, but has been widely recommended by a variety of sources, including *Fitness* magazine and *The Doctors* show on CBS.

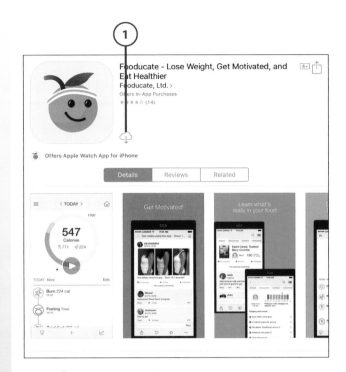

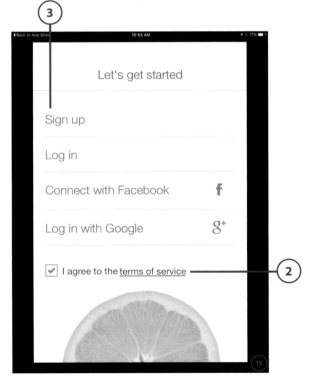

4 There are a number of steps to complete the personal profile. Tap Next at the top right of the screen to proceed to the next step in the process.

5 After you complete your profile and several pages of goals, tap Done. The next screen has several options: Health Tracker, Food Finder, Community, Healthy Recipes, and Daily Tip. I tapped Food Finder to try the scanner.

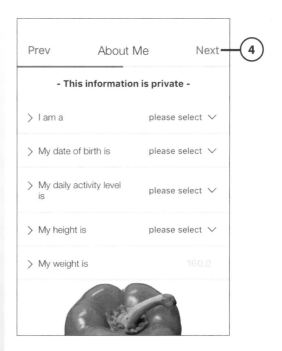

6 The first time you try to scan an item, Fooducate asks you if it's okay to access your camera. Tap OK.

7 I took a jar of peanut butter out of my cupboard. I found the bar code and pointed the Fooducate scanner at it. Without further ado, it was scanned.

8 My peanut butter rated a C+.

9 Tap Why? to find out more.

10 Tap Explanations, Nutrition, and Alternatives to find further information.

The app goes on to track several different forms of exercise and calculates the calorie burn of each, subtracting that from your accumulated calories for each day. This enables you to be far more involved with what you put in your body and how it affects your goals for better health.

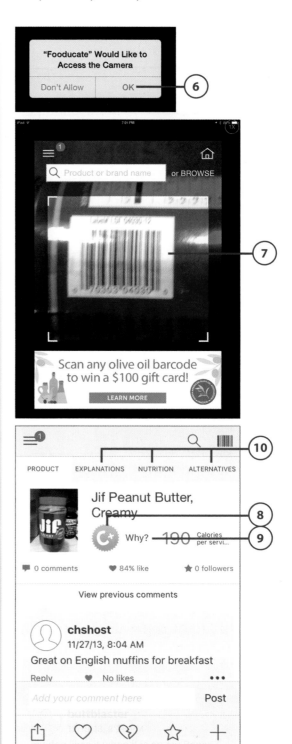

Walking or Jogging with Pedometers

I've always enjoyed the thought of taking a leisurely stroll through a wooded park with my favorite book in hand, stopping at a park bench to relax, read a few pages, and listen to the birds chirping. Through the magic of your iPad, you not only can carry your book, but you also can track your walk and calculate the distance, the time, and the positive effects on your health. In addition, you can load "walk-specific" music via this app. One health app I tried was Map My Walk.

(1) Open the App Store and type **Walk with Map My Walk-GPS Pedometer for Walking, Jogging** into the Search Store field. This one is also an iPhone app, so be sure you have tapped iPhone apps at the top of the Store screen, or you won't find the app. Tap Get, and then tap Install to download the app. Tap Open.

Free Versus Paid

Some apps, such as this one, offer both a free version and one that costs money. This is a common practice among app developers. They offer you some basic features of their app with the hope that you will like it so much, you will be willing to pay later for additional features as an "upgrade" to a plus or pro version of the app. Be sure you choose the free version for any apps you aren't sure you want to keep. It's a great way to test an app before paying for it.

2 The opening screen asks if you want to receive notifications from the app. I tapped Don't Allow. On the next screen, tap Join Now. The sign-up is easy, asking only for an email address, a name and birthday, a gender, and a password that you create.

3 After signing up, you are asked to allow MapMyWalk to access your location, even when you are not using the app. Also, you are taken to a tour of the app. This tour helps you learn all aspects of the app.

4 If you are not interested in going through the tour, tap Skip Tutorial.

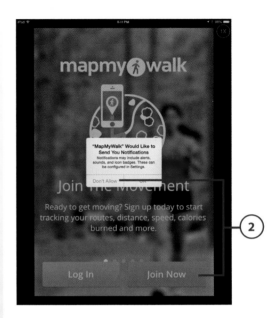

Walkmeter GPS Pedometer

Another app worth checking out is Walkmeter GPS Pedometer. Recently updated for iOS 8, this app provides you with maps, graphs, splits, intervals, laps, and other features that appeal to anyone at any fitness level who walks, runs, or hikes.

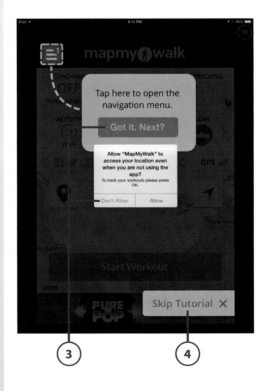

5 I chose to go directly to the app after reviewing the tutorial by tapping Start Workout at the bottom of the last page of the tour. The other option, Go MVP, takes you to an ad page for other, more advanced apps.

6 After establishing a profile, the app saves your routes and workouts.

7 You can also add Coaching, Music, and Live Tracking.

8 I chose to simply start the workout.

9 MapMyWalk tracked my walk around the block.

10 Throughout the walk, I was given feedback about my pace and calories burned.

11 At any point, tap Pause Workout to stop the tracking.

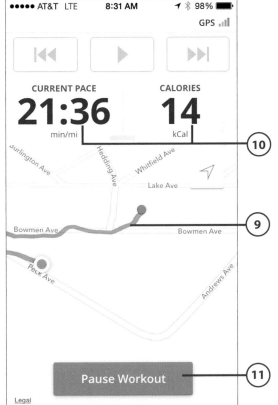

12 At the conclusion of my walk, the app summarized all elements of the workout.

13 Swipe left to see the elements of your walk, such as elevation gain and average minutes per mile.

Map My Walk is a great app to maintain a log of your workouts, even if it seems like all you are doing is walking your dog. This is definitely worth checking out.

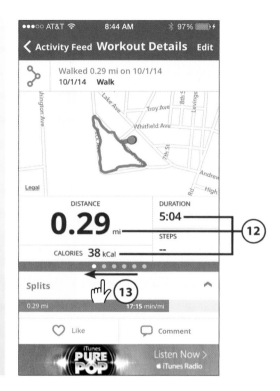

Staying on Track with Medication Reminder Apps

MedCoach Medication Reminder is one app that helps you keep track of your medications, and acts as a storage device for prescriptions, your doctor's contact info, and reminders for when you need to reorder your medications. MedCoach provides help you might need to be sure you follow your doctor's orders and stay on track with your medication. Other apps available include Pill Alert and Pill Reminder.

1 Open the App Store and type **MedCoach Medication Reminder** in the Search field. Tap Get, and then tap Install to download the app. Tap Open.

2 Med Coach opens with a screen asking to send you notifications. Tap OK.

3 If you have not already registered, tap Register. Enter your email address. Create and confirm a password. Tap Register. On the next screen, tap Accept & Get Started.

4 The app is actually an iPhone app. Tap the 2x button in the bottom-right corner to make the image full screen on the iPad.

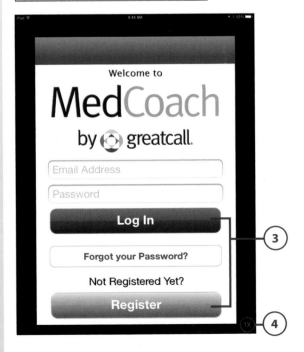

5 Tap Start Here, and the primary MedCoach page opens. You are urged to start with the medications sections. Tap Medications.

6 I have asthma and use an inhaler daily. I decided to add that medication by tapping Lookup Medication.

Other Medication Reminder Apps

There are several other apps in the App Store similar to MedCoach that are iPad-only. Pill Alert and Pill Reminder are both free apps, but do have in-app purchases in order to access more features. The best thing to do is to read the reviews of these apps by others who have already tried them.

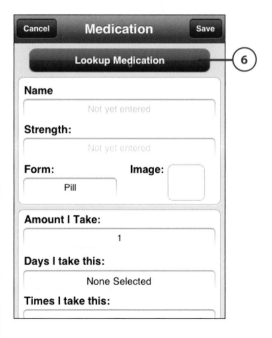

7 To begin, start typing the name of your medication. I typed **Advair**. I no sooner typed adv, and Advair came up as an option in the results list. Tap your medication name in the results list.

8 I tapped Advair Diskus, and a dosage chart appeared. I tapped my dosage, 250-50.

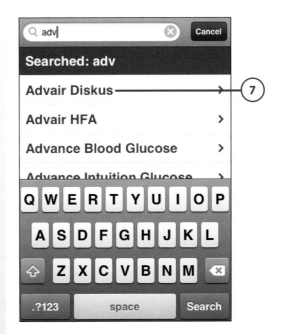

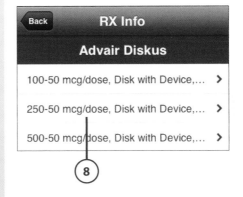

9 The next screen shows the added medication and the dosage.

10 Several other items of information are now clearly displayed that need to be tapped and completed. I entered the amount, days, and times I take this medication. An image of the medication is shown to help ensure I chose the right one. Tap Save after you've finished entering your information.

Adding a Photo

Tap the box next to Image to add a photo of your medication. This can help you keep track of what you are taking. You can either take a photo, or use a photo you've taken previously. Tap OK when asked if the app can have access to your Photos app. See step 11 for more on this.

(11) After completing all the fields, I also took a photo of my Advair Diskus with my iPad and posted it so I would be sure to know which med I was referring to.

Take Your iPad Along

It is handy to have all your medication and physician information in one place. Whether you are talking to a doctor, specialist, or pharmacist, you won't have to worry that you've forgotten to mention one of your medications. I will be bringing my iPad to the office the next time I see a doctor!

(12) Tap Reminders. As you can see, I missed my 8 a.m. dose, and MedCoach noted that for me. Reminders are handy if you have trouble remembering to take your medication, or if you have multiple medications to take throughout the day at different times.

(13) While sipping a beverage that evening on my back porch, my iPad made a strange noise. I picked it up to see a message from MedCoach that I had missed my evening dose of medicine. This is obviously the kind of help I need.

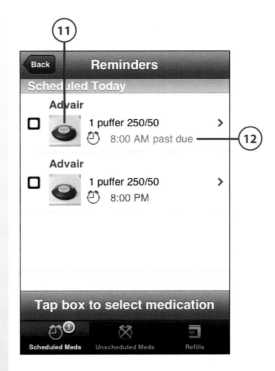

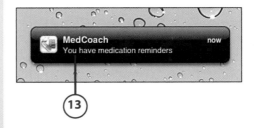

Using a Pharmacy App to Refill Prescriptions

The App Store contains many apps specific to businesses you might deal with, such as pharmacies. As the choice of app depends on the pharmacy you work with, your app may differ somewhat from the one shown in this task, but most of the concepts should be similar. I've chosen to take a look at the CVS Pharmacy app.

① Open the App Store and type **CVS Pharmacy** in the Search field. Tap Get, and then tap Install to download the app. Tap Open.

② The opening page asks you to share with Facebook and other social media sites. To skip this, tap the X in the upper-left corner.

3 To continue, you must accept the end user license agreements. Tap I Agree.

4 To access the CVS prescription option, you first need an account. If you don't already have a CVS online account, tap Create Account. Fill in the requested information, including an email address, and create a password.

5 You can now sign in by simply typing the email address and password you entered when you created your account.

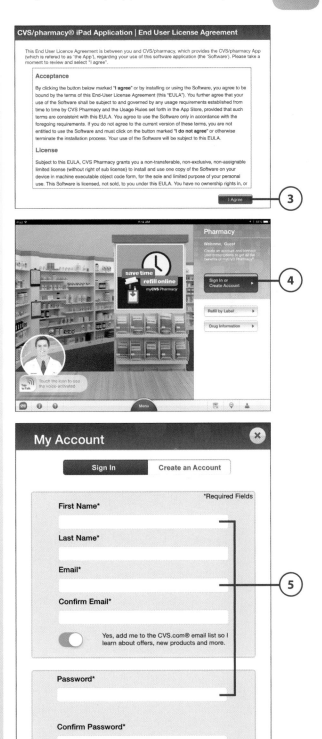

(6) You can refill your prescriptions using a number of different approaches. You can tap Prescription Center to see the prescriptions you currently have with CVS, Refill by Label to enter information off your prescription bottle label, or Refill by Scan to use your iPad's camera to scan the label's barcode.

(7) CVS communicates the status of your prescriptions in the Ready for Refill, Ready for Pickup, or Requires Renewal areas.

(8) Tap Menu to go to another section of the app, or tap Sign Out to prevent anyone else who uses your iPad from accessing your information.

(9) Tap the Ad button to see the CVS weekly ad.

Many major pharmacies offer the convenience of ordering prescriptions and maintaining information on prescriptions via their iPad app. It sure beats standing in line at the pharmacy, handing off the prescription, and then waiting to get your medication.

Getting Medical Information from WebMD for iPad

There are thousands of medical related apps that you can access via your iPad. For this task, I chose to take a look at WebMD for iPad. At the time of this writing, there were more than 1,700 users who rated it 4/5 stars. (I always check the feedback from other users before installing an app, and certainly prior to buying one.) This app has a great deal of information—and it's free!

1. Open the App Store and type **WebMD for iPad** in the Search field. Tap Get, and then tap Install to download the app. Tap Open.

2. The first time you open the app, you see a reminder to review the policies and terms of use. Tap OK to continue.

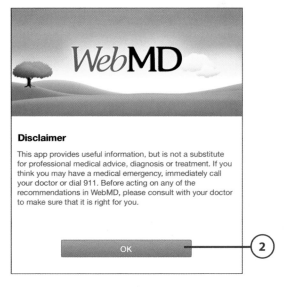

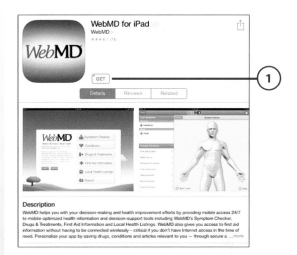

(3) There are many areas to explore, from Symptom Checker, to Local Health Listings, to items you choose to save after you sign up and create a profile. You can individualize WebMD to meet your needs.

(4) Tap Symptom Checker.

(5) The first time you use the app, you see a How to Get Started screen. Review the instructions, and then click OK.

WebMD®
Better information. Better health.

Search WebMD.com

Check your symptoms, access drug & treatment information, get first aid essentials, and check local health listings from the most trusted brand in health information. Personalize your app by saving drugs, conditions and articles relevant to you — through secure access and easy sign-in.

About
Sign Up

Symptom Checker

Conditions

Drugs & Treatments

First Aid Information

Local Health Listings

Saved

How to Get Started

1. **Profile:** Click Profile to set or edit your personal information.

2. **Symptoms:** Click the Body where you have symptoms. Pinch/spread to zoom in & out.

3. **Conditions:** Possible conditions automatically appear to the left. Click one to learn more.

4. **List View:** Click List View to quickly access general & skin related symptoms.

OK

6 The next screen is a drawing of the front view of a body. You can tap anywhere you might have a medical issue you want to explore.

7 Tap a body part. I tapped the head. A long list of issues with the head popped up. You can swipe up and down in the list to see more of the list. You can also be more specific by tapping the cheek, the jaw, and other specific parts of the head to narrow the results.

8 Tap Back View to find issues related to that part of the body.

9 Tap List View to search the lists for your ailment. Each general category leads to a more specific place, such as nose or sternum. After you pin down the specific area, a list of potential symptoms appears. You can tap the symptom to further narrow your search until you receive a potential diagnosis.

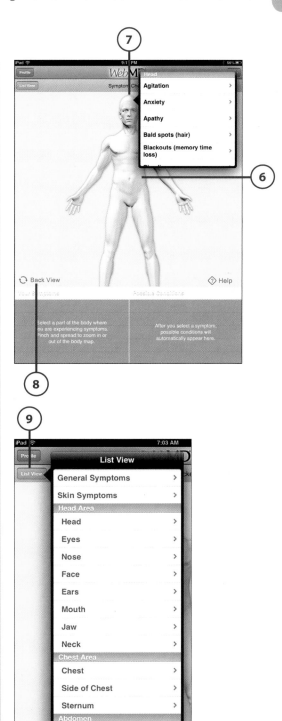

10 You can take the same approach for Conditions, Drugs & Treatments, First Aid Information, and Local Health Listings. Tap the home icon in the upper-right corner (image of a house), and then tap First Aid. A notice to call 911 if you are having an emergency is shown along with another How to Get Started List. Tap First Aid List in the upper-left corner. A long, scrollable list containing the top searches in First Aid opens.

11 Tap View All to see all of the First Aid topics. Clearly this is an extensive list.

12 Tap the home icon again, and then tap Local Health Listings. If you have not allowed the WebMD app to use your location (by typing your ZIP code into your Profile), you are asked to allow it now. Tap OK to allow.

13 The Local Health Listings page enables you to search for a doctor, hospital, or pharmacy in your area. Tap Hospital to see stick pins indicating hospitals within a 25-mile area of where you are. Pinch the map to zoom into a location and narrow your search.

14 Tap Physician or Pharmacy for similar results.

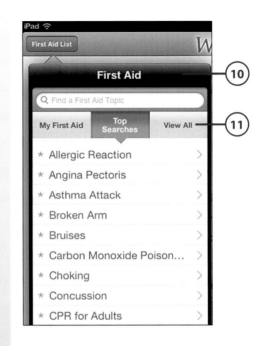

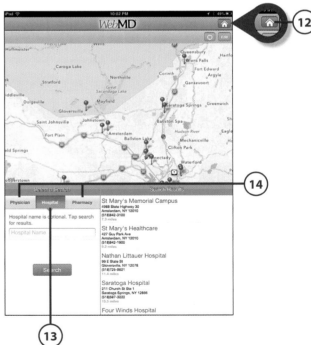

15 You can tap Conditions, or Drugs and Treatment, to search some fairly in-depth information in those areas. First, you see the Get Started screen with directions on how to proceed.

16 In the upper-left corner, tap the Conditions List to see a scrollable list of conditions that can be researched. The same process can be followed for Drugs and Treatments.

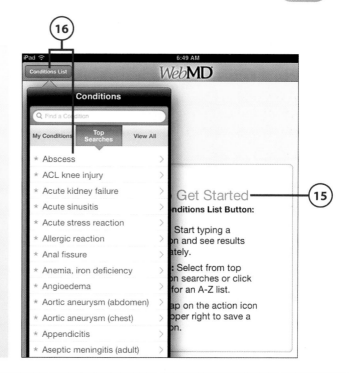

>>>Go Further

MORE USEFUL APPS FOR LIFE

Here's a brief list of apps that can also help you improve your life in one way or another. Whether your goal is to relieve stress, find new ways to improve your health, or just get a little help, these apps are worth checking out.

- **AARP**—The AARP app contains a number of helpful health tips, brain health exercises, as well as great tips to improve your life. This app is continually being updated and revised to enhance your life experience.

- **Magnifying Glass with Light**—This is a handy app to help enhance any image that might be difficult to see. After you have loaded the app, point your iPad's camera at whatever you want to magnify, and you are able to see the enlarged image on your screen. There is also an option to further enlarge the image.

Make purchases
using the
Amazon app.

Find the best gas
prices using Gas
Buddy.

Learn about all
things traffic-
related using WAZE.

Find and save
creative ideas
using Pinterest.

Use eBay and
Craigslist to find
that unique item.

Discover your heritage
using Ancestry.

In this chapter, you look at apps that can enhance your daily living experiences. These apps include

→ Explore Ancestry.com to learn about your roots.
→ Use Amazon, Craigslist, and eBay to enhance online purchasing opportunities.
→ Use an app to find the best prices on gasoline within your area.
→ Use gadgets, such as iDevices® Kitchen Thermometer, with your iPad to make your life easier, fun, or more efficient.
→ Use Pinterest to save and organize ideas, products, and other things you find on websites.
→ Check traffic before getting in your car.

Using Apps to Enhance Your Daily Life and Save Money

There are hundreds of thousands of apps in the App Store. It seems that there are apps for almost everything. When I was considering buying my iPad, I went to my local Apple store early one morning to look around, ask questions, and try out this amazing device. Standing next to me was a 70ish man in overalls with large, calloused hands. He was holding an iPad, looking it over carefully and obviously pondering something.

I asked him how he planned to use his iPad. He looked at me and said, "I've been a farmer for 50 years. My neighbor feeds his chickens using one of these. I'm going to get one and feed my chickens from my living room!" Well, needless to say, a whole new world of uses for the iPad came to mind that day. Although I've never found the chicken-feeding app, I'm sure that there are apps that can make all of our lives a bit easier.

Finding Your Roots with Ancestry

Most of us are interested to know our roots—curious to know if our ancestors arrived on the Mayflower or were horse thieves. I know that my grandparents were Carnies, a fact that I hold near and dear to my heart. The Ancestry app from Ancestry.com has accumulated a huge amount of data to help us pin down our ancestors. This is a must when searching for those who came before us.

Scratching the Surface

This task shows you how to get started with Ancestry. The more information you are able to provide, the greater the ability for Ancestry to add to and fill in the gaps of your family tree. Initially, Ancestry is a free app. After you have started, there is a limited amount of information you can access before Ancestry requires you to pay to gain additional information. If you are serious about tracing your family tree, this will be money well spent.

1. Tap the App Store icon on your Home screen. Type **ancestry** in the Search field at the top right of the App Store. When you find it, tap Get to download and install it. The Get button becomes Open. Tap it to access the app.

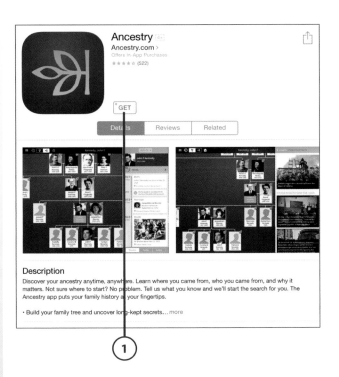

(2) The Ancestry app starts with a
screen telling you to swipe to
see more. There is also a Sign
In button at the bottom. (If you
already have an Ancestry.com
account, tap Sign In and enter
your login information.)

(3) Swipe left to continue through
the opening screens.

(4) The next screen indicates that
14 billion records are being
searched.

(5) Swipe left to see the next
screen.

Other Genealogy Apps to Try

There are several other apps you can
use for family history research. You
can also check out FamilySearch - Tree,
MyHeritage, and RootsMagic, to name
just a few.

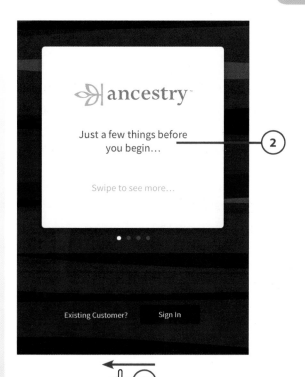

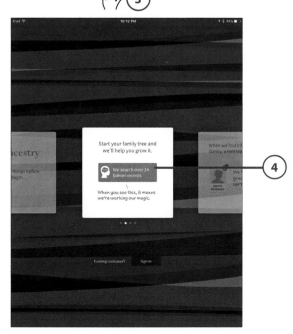

(6) This screen explains that a leaf sign is a hint that Ancestry has found some information about your family.

(7) Swipe left again to move on.

(8) Tap Get Started to begin.

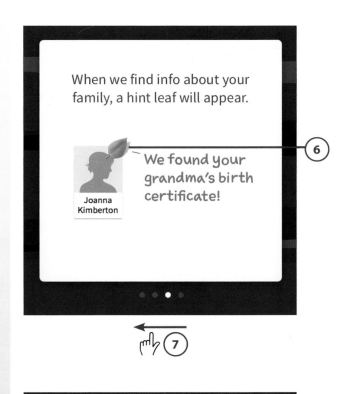

9 Begin by providing information about yourself. Tap Add Yourself.

10 The Ancestry app provides prompts for the information it requires. After you have completed that information, it is summarized and your family tree has begun.

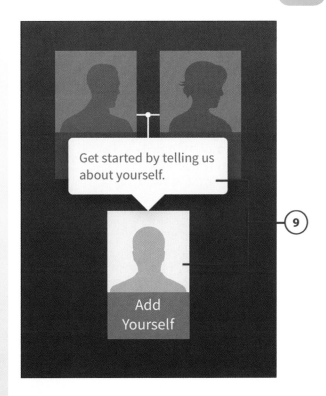

(11) Tap Add Mother or Add Father to add information about your parents.

(12) After you begin to fill in your family information, Ancestry automatically searches its records to see what is available. In my example, it immediately found a hint about my mother. I tapped to view the hint.

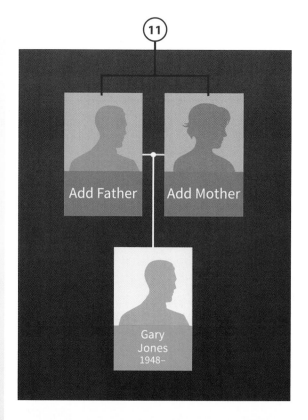

13 Ancestry found a photograph of the 1930 census when my mother Constance was 4 years old. It was fascinating to read this record of my mother and grandparents.

14 As I continued to fill in information on my mother's side of the family, Ancestry continued to find additional information.

The more detailed information you can provide Ancestry, the more it will be able to help you fill in your family tree. This is a remarkable resource for anyone interested in finding their roots.

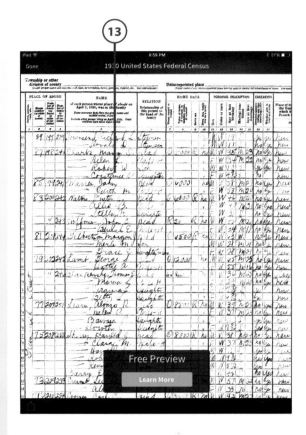

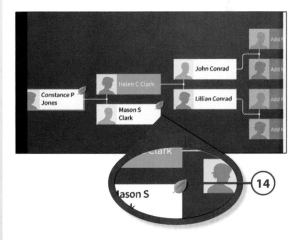

Shopping on the iPad Using Amazon

Although I am definitely an advocate of supporting local merchants, there is also something beneficial about the concept of smart shopping. The Internet has changed the face of shopping forever. You can now buy almost anything from the comfort of your living room and, in most cases, have it shipped, often for free. So, before you run out to make that big purchase, it makes sense to take a look at an online shopping app. It's also nice to have whatever you purchase delivered to your door. This can also be a huge help to those who don't have time or find it difficult to leave their homes to shop. This task takes a look at the Amazon app.

1. Open the App Store, and type **Amazon App** in the Search field. Tap Get, and then tap Install to download the app. Tap Open.

2 The ever-changing Amazon home page comes up with items that might pique your interest. It does a good job suggesting products, based on your recent searches.

3 Tap Sign in.

4 Enter your Amazon login info, or tap Create Account if you do not have an account already.

5 Tap in the Search field and type the name or description of the item you are searching for.

6 Tap the Search button on the keyboard.

7 The Search Amazon list enables you to refine your search, if you choose.

8 Along the left side of the screen, you see a long, scrollable list of items that match your search criteria. Tap an item you are interested in.

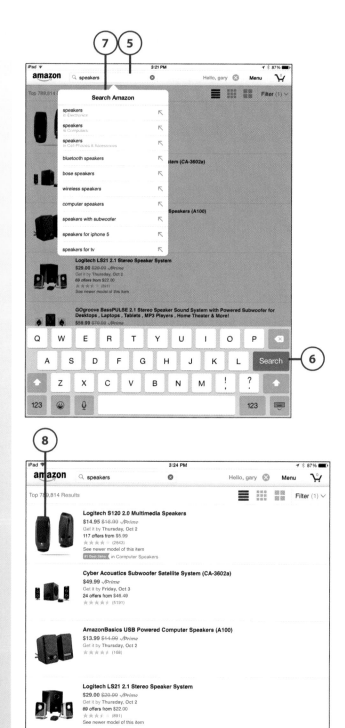

9 The details of that item are shown, including the reviews, rating, price, and whether it is currently in stock. There are other options that you can use, if you are logged in to your Amazon.com account, including Add to Wish List and Share Item.

10 Making purchases on Amazon is almost too easy. Simply tap Add to Cart, and immediately the item is added to your shopping cart. You can proceed to check out or continue shopping.

11 Tap Deals to see Amazon's Deals of the Day.

12 You can swipe the Lightning Deals and Best Deals sections to see more, or tap See All to expand those sections.

13 Tap Your Account.

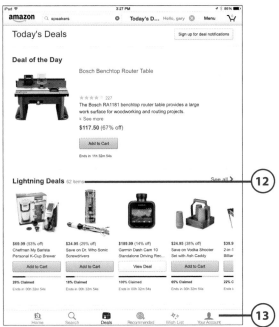

14 The Your Account button brings up a page that enables you to track your orders or personalize a number of account settings.

15 Recommended is determined by searching/buying patterns, and Wish List shows anything you've saved to a Wish List on your account (whether on a mobile or browser version).

16 Tap Cart.

17 You can now alter your purchase by saving it for later or deleting it.

18 You can also choose to make the purchase by tapping Proceed to Checkout.

19 You can log out by tapping the x next to your name.

The Amazon app is easy to use—not many bells and whistles, just thousands of products for you to search, learn about, and in many cases, buy.

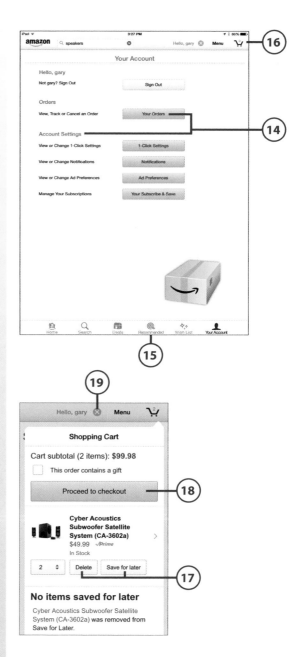

Finding Deals Using the Craigslist App

A guy named Craig Newmark created Craigslist in 1995 as an email distribution list among friends in the San Francisco Bay area. Since then, it has expanded to cover 50 countries worldwide. Craigslist is a forum where you can buy, sell, trade, find a job, find a relationship, have a discussion, post a personal message—just about anything you can find in a traditional classified ad, only far more. For anyone looking for almost anything, Craigslist is the place to go, and it's free!

(1) Open the App Store and type **Craigslist for iPad** in the Search field. Tap Get and then tap Install to download the app. Tap Open. You are asked permission for Craigslist to use your present location; tap OK to see the Craigslist offerings in your area. Additionally, you need to accept the terms of use to access the Craigslist app.

Choosing Locations Manually

If you prefer not to let this app know your location automatically, tap Don't Allow when you are asked about your location. After you open the app, tap Choose Locations, and you can set some specific locations for which you want to see listings. That way, the app doesn't "follow" your location wherever you roam.

(**2**) When the app opens, you see the listings for your current location (or nearby). You can add other locations by tapping the arrow next to the location name, and then tapping the plus sign. As you can see, you can use Craigslist worldwide.

(**3**) Listings are broken into categories that you can tap to yield advertisements within those categories. Swipe up and down the list to see additional categories. For this task, I swiped down the list and decided to tap farm+garden.

More Classifieds

You can also find other apps that show classified ads in the App Store. Check out Auto Trader for vehicles and Classifieds for another app similar to Craigslist.

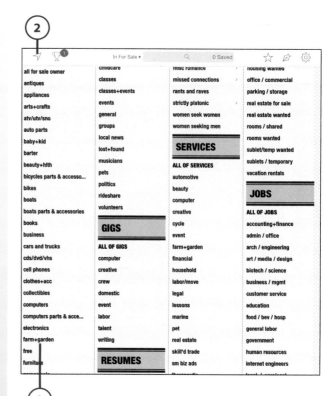

4 In an effort to test the Craigslist diversity, I typed **Kubota** into the search field to search for Kubota tractors.

5 Tap Search.

6 Scan the ads for the item you are seeking. I spotted an interesting Kubota tractor and tapped on the ad to take a closer look.

7. The ad opens showing several photos.

8. A full description of the item and contact information is provided. If you see an ad that has very little information, it might not be legitimate, and isn't one you want to respond to.

9. Tap the image of a printer along the right side to print the ad.

10. Tap Map on the previous page to see the locations of all items on this page.

Printing from an iPad

You can print from your iPad without connecting any cables. Apple calls this function AirPrint. You can print a web page or document directly from your iPad over your wireless network. The one catch? It works only with printers that support AirPrint. Fortunately, the list is growing fast and now includes printers by many companies. You can find an updated list of AirPrint printers at http://support.apple.com/kb/HT4356.

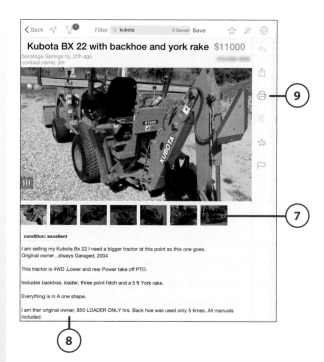

It's Not All Good

Play It Safe

Over the years scammers have learned how to use Craigslist to take advantage of people. For example, if you find an apartment or house to rent that appears just too good to be true, it probably is. Scammers typically ask for a deposit upfront from several people to be considered as a potential renter and then take their money and run. Others have bought cars with bogus certified checks; the seller goes to cash the check, and it bounces, but the car is gone! It's clearly a buyer-beware situation, though the vast majority of Craigslist users are honest and simply use this service as they would a classified ad.

Bidding on eBay for iPad

In 1995, a software engineer created an auction website and listed a broken laser pointer for sale. Much to his surprise, the laser pointer sold for $14.83. He told the prospective buyer that it was a BROKEN laser pointer and was told, "I collect broken laser pointers." That was the beginning of eBay, the Internet auction site where you can buy and sell almost anything.

1 Open the App Store and type **Ebay for iPad** into the search field. Tap Get, and then tap Install to download. When the app finishes downloading, tap Open.

(2) On the next page, tap Enter Manually to sign in to eBay. You are required to add your email address and create a password.

(3) The Opening eBay shopping page enables you to search by category.

(4) You can also search by typing your search terms in the Search box.

(5) You can further refine your search by tapping Condition, Auction & Buy It Now, or Best Match buttons at the top. For this task, I chose to tap Auction & Buy It Now.

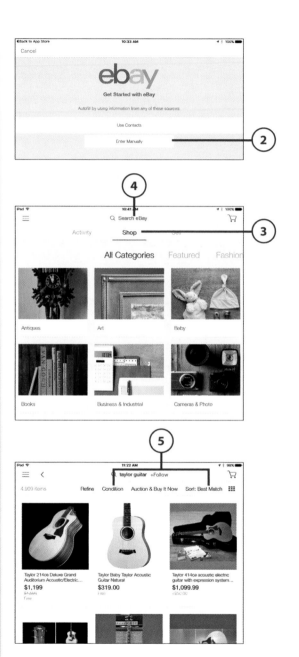

(6) All the Taylor guitars for sale via an auction or the Buy It Now option of eBay are now shown. Buy It Now allows the seller to set a price that, if accepted, will end the auction immediately. I tapped the Taylor Baby BT1 Acoustic Guitar to take a closer look.

(7) A full description of the guitar is included at the bottom. If you scroll down, you also see the time left, the cost of shipping, payment options, and information about the seller.

(8) You have two options here: place a bid, or watch the auction. If it's early in the auction, you might want to watch it for a while to see just how high the bids go. Often in an eBay auction, a flurry of bidding occurs in the final minute or two of the auction.

(9) I tapped Place Bid; the next page shows a keyboard where I can place a maximum bid. Note that once you place a bid, you are committed to pay that amount should you end up being the high bidder. At the conclusion of the auction, the buyer and seller communicate to arrange payment and shipping of the eBay item.

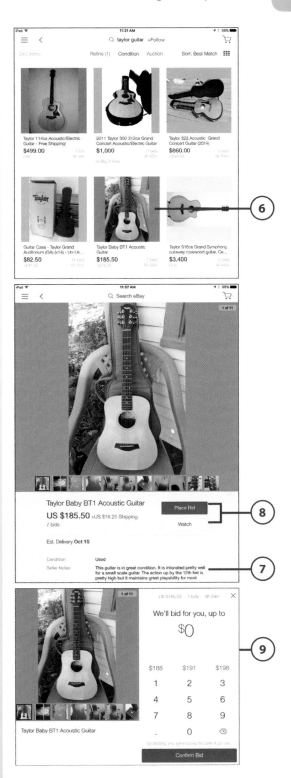

Paying Less at the Pump

Several apps in the App Store can help you check gas prices. Gas Buddy is another iPhone app that works just fine on your iPad. The sole purpose of this app is to make sure that you pay no more than absolutely necessary to put fuel in your car. Relying on members' input, Gas Buddy tracks gas prices and enables you to make an intelligent decision when filling up your car. Other gas price-monitoring apps you can find in the App Store include Fuelzee and Gas Guru, among others. These are also iPhone apps, so be sure to change the option at the top-left of the App Store to iPhone Only, as noted in step 1 of this task.

1 To find this app, tap App Store on your Home screen and type **gas** in the search field in the upper-right corner. Make sure that you are searching iPhone apps by selecting it from the drop-down list.

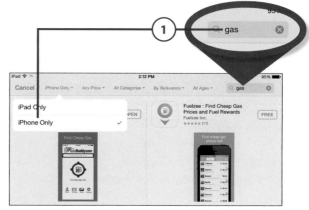

2 Tap Get to download and install the app. When the app is installed, the button changes to Open. Tap it to open the app.

3 Gas Buddy asks how you would like to sign up. Three choices are available: Sign Up with Email, Log in with Facebook, or Log in with Google.

4 I chose the No thanks, maybe later option instead so that I could take a look at the app before signing up.

5 Along the bottom of the next screen are several options to enhance your Gas Buddy experience.

6 The primary purpose for downloading this app is to search gas prices in your area. I typed my zip code into the box near the top, and then tapped the gas pump in the center to see local gas prices.

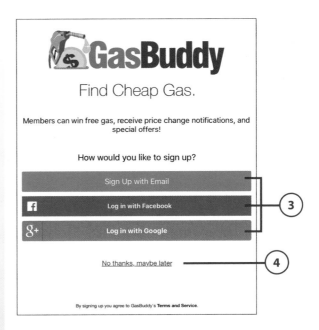

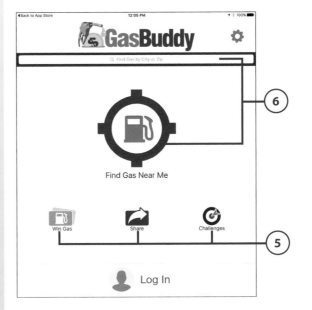

(7) Next, I get a list of gas stations in my immediate area, the distance from my home, and the price of gas at each place.

(8) The right side of the page also includes a map showing the exact location of each gas station.

Now, thanks to Gas Buddy, I have all the information I need to fill up at the best price possible.

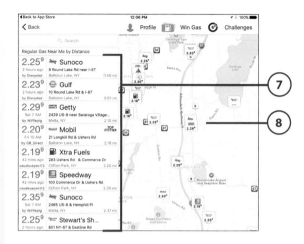

Using Gadgets with iPad

The iPad has literally thousands of compatible gadgets to make our lives easier, more fun, or more efficient. You can find everything from drones to blood pressure readers to kitchen gadgets. In this example, we take a look at the iDevices® Kitchen Thermometer, an amazing device that allows you to monitor with your iPad the temperature of whatever you may be roasting in an oven. The setup of just about any kind of iPad gadget is similar to the process used in this task. You connect the gadget to your iPad with a cord (if it has one) or by using Bluetooth. Then, if the gadget has its own app, you configure its settings using the app you download from the App Store. The iDevices® Kitchen Thermometer, as well as many other gadgets for your iPad, are available from places like Amazon.com, the Apple Store, Target, and Walmart.

1. In the App Store, search for the iDevices Connected app. Tap Get, and then tap Install to load the app. After the app downloads, tap Open to begin using the app.

2. Follow the directions to set up the Bluetooth connection of the app. This allows your iPad to "talk" with the iDevices® Kitchen Thermometer.

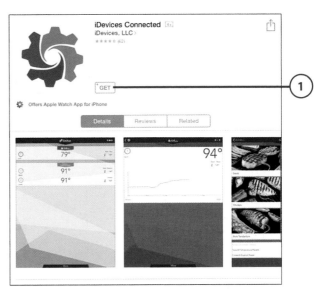

Activate Bluetooth ®

You can activate Bluetooth without leaving this app by accessing Control Center. Swipe up from the bottom of your screen to expose Control Center. Tap on the Bluetooth icon to activate it and swipe down on Control Center to tuck it away. That's it!

Activate Bluetooth ®

You can activate Bluetooth without leaving this app by accessing Control Center. Swipe up from the bottom of your screen to expose Control Center. Tap on the Bluetooth icon to activate it and swipe down on Control Center to tuck it away. That's it!

③ Plug the end of the probe into the monitor.

④ Press the button to turn on your thermometer.

⑤ Going back to the app on your iPad, and at the top of the screen tap Connect my Product.

⑥ On the next screen, you can see that your thermometer is reading the ambient temperature.

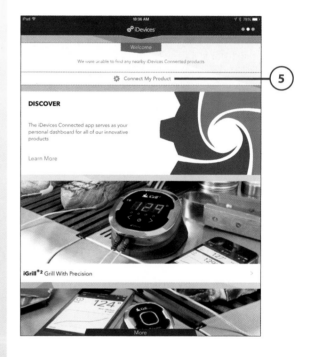

(7) You are now ready to begin cooking. Insert the probe into the piece of meat.

(8) After the temperature probe is placed in the meat, check your iPad to see the temperature. In this example, the meat had recently come out of the refrigerator and the iDevice app is now reading 45 degrees.

(9) Next, tap More to set up the temperature parameters.

(10) There are several options you can explore, but for this task just tap Settings.

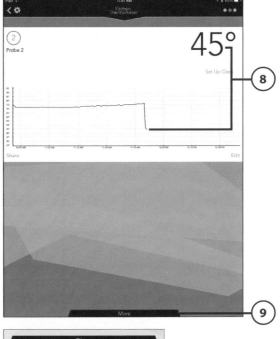

(11) You should now see a number of preset temperatures that ensure the doneness of the product you are cooking.

(12) In the example for this task, the Pork-Medium option is selected.

(13) Over the course of the cooking time, iThermometer provides you with a graphic representation of the iDevices® Kitchen Thermometer changes as the meat cooks.

(14) You hear a beep and receive a message when you are 10 degrees away from the desired temperature.

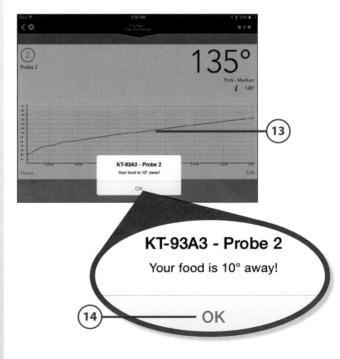

KT-93A3 - Probe 2

Your food is 10° away!

OK

(15) Another beep alert occurs on your iPad after the desired temperature is reached.

Using Pinterest to Save and Organize Website Links

Pinterest is an app with what seems to be an endless supply of interesting ideas to explore. You can find links to everything from travel to recipes, as well as great do-it-yourself tips. Additionally, when you find something of interest on a website, you can "pin" that link to one of your Pinterest "boards" for later use. No matter what your areas of interest, Pinterest provides a great way to save ideas for later reference or search for ideas from other users' pins.

(1) In the App Store, search for the Pinterest for iPad app. Tap Get, and then tap Install to load the app. After the app loads, tap Open to begin working with Pinterest.

Cloud Instead of Get or Buy

If you see a cloud icon with a downward-facing arrow instead a button with the word Get or a price, this indicates that you have previously downloaded this app under the Apple ID that is logged into the App Store. Tap that icon to download the app again, or to download it to another iPad that uses your Apple ID for the App Store.

(2) After you open Pinterest the first time, you are asked to sign up using either Facebook or your email address.

(3) Complete the sign-up information for either the Facebook option or the Email option. This task shows the Email option. Fill in the required information.

(4) Tap Create Account.

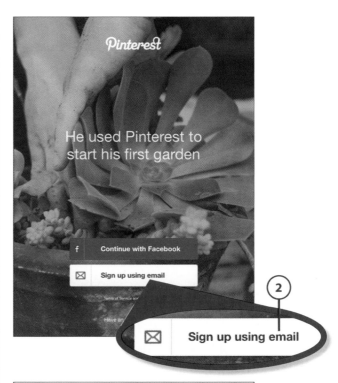

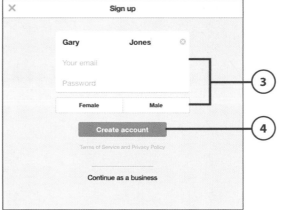

5 Pinterest asks to send you push notifications. This can include reminders or notifications of new content in topic areas in which you have shown interest. It is your choice whether you want to participate. Tap Don't Allow or OK to proceed.

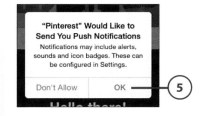

Creating Boards

When you create your account, Pinterest creates default "boards" for your "pins" based on the areas of interest that you choose (see step 7). As you start to explore topics on Pinterest, you can create more boards based on the topic for which you want to save pins. For example, you might create boards for travel, recipes, home improvements, arts and crafts, and anything else you find interesting. Then, when you find a related pin as you are exploring Pinterest (or a website that you find on the Internet), you can "pin" that link to your own board for later reference.

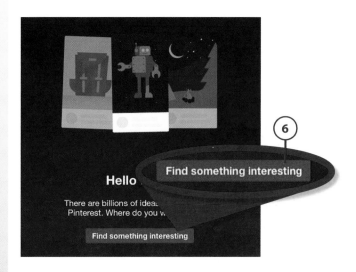

6 Tap the Find something interesting button to continue.

7 On the next page, you are asked to choose five areas of interest to assist Pinterest in narrowing the topics that you might enjoy exploring.

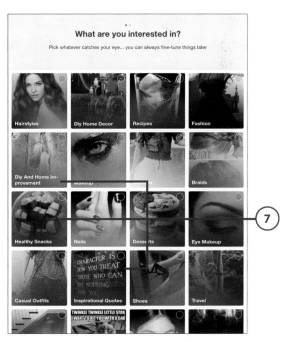

(8) Pinterest creates a page that summarizes your interests. Tap any of the suggested topics to explore them in greater detail.

(9) Tap the search icon at the bottom to look for other areas of interest.

(10) Pinterest returns to the general categories. Type a search criteria into the Search field at the top of the screen, and then tap a result to explore.

(11) Another option is to tap any of the other general categories to continue exploring the pinned sites.

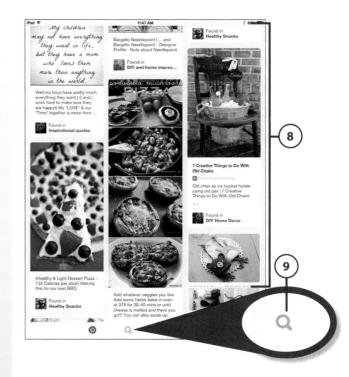

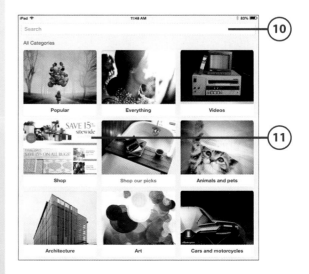

Avoiding Traffic Jams

Waze is a "community based traffic and navigation app." What this means is that via Waze, drivers communicate information about traffic and related issues within the area that you choose to search. It's a great way to anticipate just what you might encounter when enroute to work or to the store. Waze has been successful in getting a community of drivers to communicate accurate information on what they see as they travel from place to place.

Check Before You Leave

Waze will only work on your iPad while in your car if you have purchased the model with cellular connectivity. If you have the WiFi-only iPad as I do, you need to check your route while still in a WiFi network. Checking before heading off to your destination also helps you to make a more informed choice of routes.

(1) Tap the App Store icon on your Home screen. Type **Waze** in the Search field in the App Store. When you locate the app, tap Get to download and install it. When the Get button changes to Open, tap it to access the app.

(2) Your first task is to allow Waze to use your current location. This enables you to see Waze traffic reports in your local area.

More Traffic Apps

Other apps similar to Waze that provide traffic updates include Scout GPS and MapQuest.

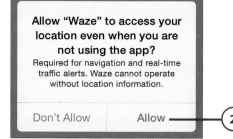

Location Services Settings

Locations Services is turned on using the Settings app. Tap the Settings app icon on your Home screen. Tap Privacy on the left side. Tap Location Services on the right side. If Location Services is turned off, slide the switch to on (green). Look in the list below Location Services and locate the app for which you want to add or remove permission to know your location. Turn Location Services on or off for any apps listed.

3 Tap Accept on the Waze License agreement on the next page.

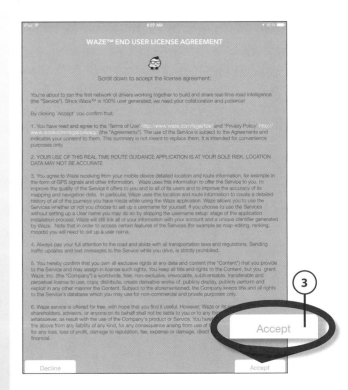

(4) If you want WAZE to send you a text message with your verification code, add your phone number and tap Next. If you do not have texting capability on your phone, tap Skip in the lower-right corner.

(5) When you receive your verification code, enter it and tap Next.

(6) Create your Profile by entering your name, and then tap Next. (Tap Import from Facebook to import your profile from your Facebook account.)

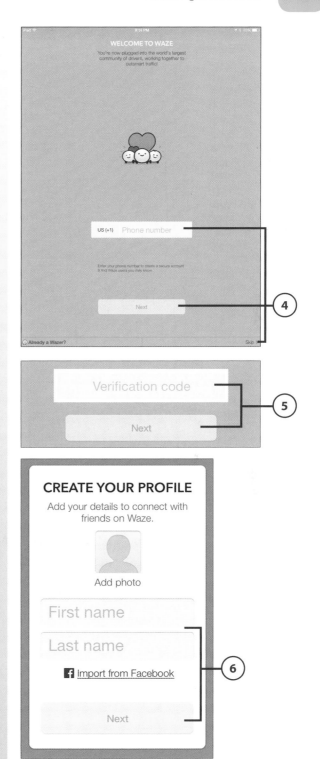

(7) Waze assigns you a username, which you can change to something else.

(8) Tap Next.

Don't iPad and Drive

Never operate WAZE while you are actually driving a car. You will be able to assess driving conditions from your living room prior to departing.

(9) Tap the symbol in the bottom-right corner to learn how to read the map and the Waze symbols.

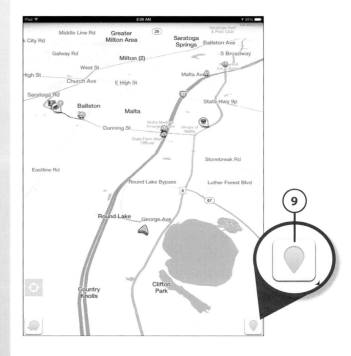

(10) The next page shows what each symbol stands for, such as police, traffic, accidents, map chats, and hazards.

(11) If you tap All, you leave the map and see each item described by place, time, and distance away from you.

(12) Tap the back arrow at the top to go back to the map of your area.

(13) Tap the symbol in the bottom-left corner to report a problem. Again, this should not be attempted while driving.

(14) A list of symbols representing possible problems appears. Tap the appropriate symbol for the problem you want to report.

(15) The next screen allows you to add specific information about the problem you have reported. The accuracy and effectiveness of Waze is related to this final step.

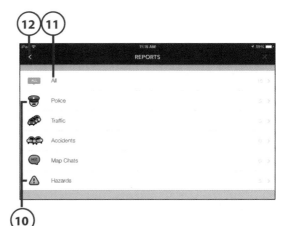

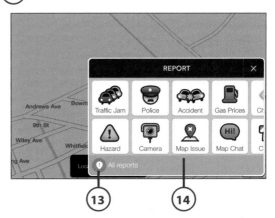

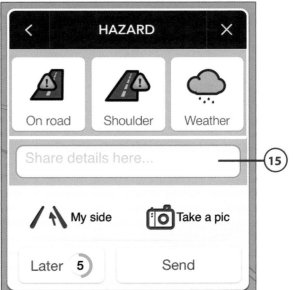

>>>*Go Further*

FIND MORE USEFUL APPS

Given the huge number of apps, and the fact that new ones are added daily, it is impossible to stay current with all of them. The goal in this chapter is to give you a peek at how to use apps to enhance your life. The following list suggests a few you might enjoy:

- **Catalog Spree**—An app that enables you to view your favorite catalog, find what you want, and order it all without cluttering up your mailbox or having to recycle all that paper.

- **Groupon**—A free app that offers you deals on goods and services in your area.

- **Jumbo Calculator**—Your iPad does not arrive with a built-in calculator. This free app solves that problem.

- **Maglight**—A free app that enables you to use your iPad camera as a magnifying glass.

- **Wikipedia Mobile**—An encyclopedia app where you can find information on almost any question you have.

- **Trulia and Zillow**—Real estate apps you should consider if you are moving to another location. These apps show houses for sale, homes recently sold, and estimates of property values.

Index

Symbols

24-Hour Time switch, 51

8500+ Drink and Cocktail Recipes app, 336

(pound sign), 345

A

AARP app, 272-274, 465

AARP travel website, 274

About settings, 60

accessibility, 58-59

Access Within Apps, 61

accommodations
    finding
        Airbnb app, 275-281
        Kayak app, 289-292
    home exchanges, 285-288

accounts, creating
    Amazon accounts, 475
    email accounts, 186-188
    ESPN accounts, 424
    Netflix accounts, 387
    Shutterfly accounts, 356
    Skype accounts, 353
    YouTube accounts, 364

Add Account option (Mail Settings), 186-188

Add a Fingerprint command, 49

Add Bookmark command (Safari), 168

Add Calendar command (Calendars), 146

Add List option (Reminders), 154

Add Songs button (Music), 93

Add to Existing Contact command (Mail), 190

Add to Home Screen option (Safari), 173

Add to Reading List option (Safari), 174

AE/AF Lock, 211

Afterlight, 216

AIM, 367

Airbnb app, 275-281

AirDrop, 37, 80-81
    enabling, 80
    sharing photos with, 226

AirPlay, 37
  accessing, 109-110
  viewing photos on Apple TV, 226
Airports by Travel Nerd, 312
air travel, booking
  Kayak app, 289-292
  SeatGuru app, 295-298
Alarm button (Clock), 155
alarms
  deleting, 156
  editing, 156
  setting, 155-157
albums
  creating, 232-233, 357-358
  overview, 230
  Recently Added album, 233
  Recently Deleted album, 233
  viewing, 230-231
alerts, 267
  alert sounds, 43-45
  setting, 140
Allow Photo Access option (Shutterfly), 356
All Recipes app, 335
Always Bcc Myself option (Mail), 201
Amazon app, 474-478
Amazon Instant Video app, 106
Ancestry app, 468-473
app folders, creating, 245-247
Apple IDs, 68-69, 426
Apple iPad Smart Cover, 7
Apple Music, 76
  cancelling, 101
  overview, 100
  playing music via, 102-104
  signing up for, 101
Apple password, resetting, 68
Apple TV, 226

apps, 239. *See also specific apps* (for example, Mail)
  app folders, 245-247
  arranging on Home screen, 244-245
  contacting developers of, 259
  deleting, 244, 250
  downloading, 241, 410
  finding in App Store, 255-256
  free versus paid, 243, 449
  fremium apps, 243
  grouping in folders, 245-247
  help, 257-258
  in-app purchases, 243
  iPhone/iPod touch apps, 256-257
  monitoring
    app storage information, 260-262
    battery usage, 262-263
    information sharing permissions, 265
    location usage, 263-264
    notification settings, 266-268
  opening, 392
  paid apps, 243
  purchasing, 239-243
  quitting, 249-250
  recommended apps, 256
  redownloading, 243
  reviewing, 259
  searching Google for, 256
  sharing with family, 259
  switching between, 248
  syncing, 67-71, 79
  viewing currently running apps, 248
  viewing multiple apps
    Picture-in-Picture, 254-255
    Slide Over, 250-252
    Split View, 252-253
app screens, 14
App Store, 239
  finding apps in, 255-256
  purchasing apps from, 239-243
App Support button, 258

articles, viewing with Safari Reader, 167

Ask Before Deleting option (Mail), 200

asking Siri questions, 30-31

Ask to Join Networks option, 61

auctions, eBay, 483-485

audio. *See* sound

Auto-Capitalization, 52

Auto-Correction, 52

AutoFill, 178-183
    filling out web forms with, 181-182
    security, 180-181
    setting up, 179-181
    troubleshooting, 183

Auto-Lock setting, 46

automatic downloads, 59-60, 241

Auto-Night Theme switch (iBooks), 122

Auto Trader, 480

Auto Upload (Shutterfly), 357

B

backing up data, 74. *See also* syncing

Back Up Now button, 74

Badge App Icon, 267

bandwidth usage with iTunes Radio, 114

Banners, 267

Battery Usage settings, 262-263

bidding on eBay, 483-485

Blackjack, 406

blip.tv, 106

Blocked option (Messages), 203

blocking users in Messages, 203-204

Block this Caller option (Messages), 204

boards (Pinterest), 495

booking
    accommodations
        Airbnb app, 275-281
        Kayak, 289-292
    flights
        Kayak app, 289-292
        SeatGuru app, 295-298

bookmarks
    iBooks, 125
    Safari, 168-170
        creating, 168-170
        deleting, 172
        Home screen bookmarks, 173
        syncing, 172

Bookmarks button (iBooks), 125

books
    buying
        from iBooks, 117-119
        from other sellers, 118
    deleting, 128
    finding, 120
    free, 131
    in iCloud, 126
    organizing in iBooks, 125-128
    reading in iBooks, 381
        bookmarks, 125
        highlights, 123-124
        notes, 123-124
        reading aids, 121-122
        viewing books, 120-121
    reading in Kindle app, 129-130
    reading with Google Play Books app, 131
    reading with Nook app, 131
    syncing, 79-80

Brain Training Calibration (Fit Brains Trainer), 437

brain training with Fit Brains Trainer, 435-439

brightness settings, 58-59, 121

browser. *See* Safari

browsing
   photos, 221-224
   to URLs, 160-163
Buy App button (App Store), 242
buying. *See* purchasing
Buy It Now (eBay for iPad), 485

C

calculator apps, Jumbo Calculator, 502
Calendar app
   calendars
      creating, 145-147
      default calendar, 147
      deleting, 147
      sharing, 147
   Day view, 141-142
   default calendar, 147
   events
      creating, 139-140
      deleting, 140
   Month view, 144-145
   Week view, 143
   syncing with iCloud, 67-71
   Year view, 142
calls
   muting, 351
   video calls, 347
      FaceTime, 348-354
      Skype, 352-354
Camera, 209
   AE/AF Lock, 211
   Camera Roll, 211
   editing photos, 212-216
   focus and exposure area, 211
   modes, 210
   panoramic photos, 216-218
   photos
      editing, 212-219
      panoramic photos, 216-219
      sharing, 226-230
      taking, 209-212
      viewing, 225-226
Camera+, 216
Camera Roll, 211
Cancel button (Mail), 195
canceling Apple Music, 101
capitalizing words, 19
capturing screen, 235
cars (Uber), requesting, 306-311
Catalog Spree, 502
Cellular Data, turning on, 65-67
checking
   storage space, 60, 71
   traffic with Waze, 497-501
   version of iOS, 60
checklists, creating in notes, 150
Choose a New Wallpaper option, 40
City Papers app, 409-413
Classifieds, 480
classifieds apps
   Auto Trader, 480
   Classifieds, 480
   Craigslist for iPad, 479-483
Clock app, 155-157, 325
closing
   apps, 249
   Control Center, 37
CNBC Real-Time for iPad app, 414-417
CNN App for iPad, 417-419
Collections button (iBooks), 120
Collections level (Photos), 222
collections of books, creating, 126-128
color themes (iBooks), 122
commercials (iTunes Radio), 114

communication. *See also* photo
  management apps
  AIM, 367
  calls
    FaceTime, 348-354
    muting, 351
    Skype, 352-354
  Dragon Dictation, 367
  email, 185, 339-340
    composing, 192-194
    configuring how email is received,
      197-198
    deleting, 194-196
    email accounts, 186-188
    folders, 192
    handing off, 193-194
    images, 193
    moving, 194-196
    multiple inboxes, 191
    previewing, 200
    providers, 188
    reading, 189-192
    recovering deleted email, 195
    searching, 196
    sending, 192
    settings, 200-202
    signatures, 199-200
    spam filters, 196
    syncing with iCloud, 67-71
    undeleting, 195
    VIPs, 192
  Facebook, 340-343
  FaceTime, 347-354
  Instagram, 344-347
  Skype, 347, 352-354
  Twitter, 368
  YouTube, 363-367
Compose button
  Mail, 192
  Notes, 148

composing
  email, 192-194
  text messages, 204-207
connections. *See* networks
contacting app developers, 259
Contacts
  adding, 133-136
  composing email to, 138
  copying, 137
  editing, 138
  in iCloud, 133
  nicknames, 136
  searching for, 136-137
  sharing, 80-81, 138
  syncing with iCloud, 67
  VIPs, 192
Control Center, 9, 36-37
  accessing, 61
  Access Within Apps, 61
  closing, 37
  opening, 36-37
Copy command, 28
copying
  contacts, 137
  copy and paste, 28-29
  text, 28-29
copy protection (video), 108
Craigslist for iPad, 479-483
Create a New Apple ID option, 68
Create New Contact command (Mail), 190
credit cards, scanning, 176
Crop button (Camera), 213
cropping photos, 214
culinary resources, 315
  8500+ Drink and Cocktail Recipes, 336
  All Recipes, 335
  Epicurious, 316-321
  Escoffier Cook's Companion, 321-325

Fooducate, 445-448

Foodgawker, 336

Harvest to Hand, 336

HealthyOut, 446

My Diet Diary, 446

Nutrition Menu, 446

Open Table, 328-331

Urban Spoon, 336

Yelp, 332-335

Zest, 336

currency converter app, 312

currently running apps, viewing, 248

customization, 39

alert sounds, 43-45

date/time, 51

display and brightness, 58-59

Do Not Disturb settings, 54-55

iBooks display, 121-122

keyboard settings, 52-54

parental restrictions, 56-57

password protection, 45-48

side switch functionality, 50

Touch ID, 49-50

wallpaper, 40-43

custom ringtones, 45

CVS Pharmacy app, 458-460

D

Data Roaming, 67

Date & Time settings, 51

Day view (Calendar), 141-142

Deals of the Day (Amazon), 477

Default Account option (Mail), 201

default calendar, 147

Define button (iBooks), 123

deleting

apps, 244, 250

bookmarks (Safari), 172

books, 128

calendars, 147

clock alarms, 156

email, 194-196

events, 140

photos, 213

reminders, 154

dictation, 25-27, 367

diet apps. See fitness apps

dining reservations, making with Open Table, 328-331

directions, getting with Maps app, 292-294

dismissing notifications, 35

Display & Brightness settings, 58-59

display settings, 58-59

Dock command, 22

documents

sharing with AirDrop, 80-81

syncing with iCloud, 67-71

Done button

Contacts, 135

Reminders, 154

Do Not Disturb mode, 37, 54-55

downloads

apps, 241, 410

automatic downloads, 59-60, 241

movies from iTunes, 381-383

dragging, 11

Dragon Dictation, 367

Drippler app, 419-423

DVDs, importing, 107

Dvorak keyboard, 52

Dynamic wallpapers, 41

E

eBay for iPad, 483-485

Edit button
    Camera, 213
    Clock, 155

email, 185, 339-340
    composing, 192-194
    configuring how email is received, 197-198
    deleting, 194-196
    email accounts, 186-188
    folders, 192
    handing off, 193-194
    images, 193
    moving, 194-196
    multiple inboxes, 191
    previewing, 200
    providers, 188
    reading, 189-192
    recovering deleted email, 195
    searching, 196
    sending, 192
    settings, 200-202
    signatures, 199-200
    spam filters, 196
    syncing with iCloud, 67-71
    undeleting, 195
    VIPs, 192

Enable LTE option, 65

Enable Restrictions option, 56

enabling. *See* customization; setting up

encyclopedia apps, Wikipedia Mobile, 502

Ends field (Calendar), 139

Enhance button (Camera), 213

enhancing photos, 213

enlarging text, 58

entertainment apps, 371
    Blackjack, 406
    Fandango, 372-375

iBooks, 381
IMDb, 406
iTunes
    playing music, 384
    renting movies, 381-383
Netflix, 386-390
NPR (National Public Radio) for iPad, 384-386
Pandora Radio, 390-394
Pinterest, 406
Podcasts, 394-401
Seat Geek, 401-405
Solitaire, 376-378
Stitcher, 406
TED, 398-401
Words with Friends, 379-380
Yesterday USA, 406

Entire Music Library option (iTunes), 74

Epicurious, 316-321

Erase Data feature, 47

Escoffier Cook's Companion, 321-325

ESPN ScoreCenter app, 423-425

events (Calendar)
    creating, 139-140
    deleting, 140

event tickets, purchasing with Seat Geek, 401-405

exchanging homes, 285-288

exercise apps. *See* fitness apps

extensions (Safari), 183

F

Facebook, 226, 340-343

FaceTime, 347-352

family, communicating with.
  See communication; social media apps

FamilySearch - Tree, 469

Family Sharing, 97-100, 259

family tree, tracing with Ancestry app, 468-473

Fandango app, 372-375

farmer's markets, finding with Harvest to Hand, 336

Favorites
  Camera, 213
  Safari, 168-170

Featured podcasts (Podcasts), 104

fetch delivery, 197-198

Fetch New Data setting (Mail), 197-198

files
  iCloud Drive files
    accessing, 83-85
    opening, 85
  PDFs, adding to iBook library, 118

filling in web forms
  AutoFill, 178-183
    filling out web forms with, 181-182
    security, 180-181
    setting up, 179-181
    troubleshooting, 183
  manually, 177-178

filters (photo), 215, 218-219

financial news, CNBC Real-Time for iPad, 414-417

finding. *See* searches

Find My iPad, 71

fingerprints, adding to Touch ID, 49-50

Fit Brains Trainer, 435-439

fitness apps
  AARP, 465
  CVS Pharmacy, 458-460
  Fit Brains Trainer, 435-439
  FitStar, 439-445
  Fooducate, 445-448
  HealthyOut, 446

Map My Walk, 449-452

MedCoach Medication Reminder, 452-457

My Diet Diary, 446

Nutrition Menu, 446

Pill Alert, 454

Pill Reminder, 454

Walkmeter GPS Pedometer, 450

WebMD for iPad, 461-465

FitStar, 439-445

flicking, 11

Flickr, 354, 359-362

flights, booking
  Kayak app, 289-292
  SeatGuru app, 295-298

focus and exposure area (Camera), 211

folders
  app folders, 245-247
  email folders, 192

fonts
  iBooks, 122
  Kindle, 130

Foodgawker, 336

food-related resources, 315
  8500+ Drink and Cocktail Recipes, 336
  All Recipes, 335
  Epicurious, 316-321
  Escoffier Cook's Companion, 321-325
  Fooducate, 445-448
  Foodgawker, 336
  Harvest to Hand, 336
  HealthyOut, 446
  My Diet Diary, 446
  Nutrition Menu, 446
  Open Table, 328-331
  Urban Spoon, 336
  Yelp, 332-335
  Zest, 336

Fooducate app, 445-448

force closing apps, 249

foreign languages, translating, 298-302

Forgot Apple ID or Password option, 68

forgotten passcodes, 48

four-finger gestures, 12

Foursquare app, 282-285

Fragment Prismatic Effects, 216

free apps, 243, 449

fremium apps, 243

friends, communicating with.
  See communication; social media apps

Fuelzee, 486

G

gadgets, iDevices® Kitchen Thermometer, 488-493

games, 375
    Blackjack, 406
    Solitaire, 376-378
    Words with Friends, 379-380

Gas Buddy, 486-488

genealogy apps
    Ancestry, 468-473
    FamilySearch - Tree, 469
    MyHeritage, 469
    RootsMagic, 469

General Settings
    About settings, 60
    Auto-Lock, 46
    Date & Time, 51
    Handoff, 193
    Keyboard, 52-54
    Language & Region, 26
    Lock Rotation, 50
    Lock/Unlock, 61
    Mute, 50
    Reset, 61
    Restrictions, 56-57, 410

Siri, 29
Spotlight Search, 61
Storage & iCloud Usage
    Battery Usage, 262-263
    Manage Storage option, 260-262

generations of iPads, 3
    identifying your iPad, 4
    iOS 9, 5

Geofence, 264

gestures
    dragging, 11
    flicking, 11
    four-finger gestures, 12
    pinching, 10
    pulling down and releasing, 11
    shaking, 10
    switching between apps, 248
    tapping, 10
    touching, 10

Get Sample button (iBooks), 119

Google searches, 256

Google Play Books app, 131

GPS pedometers
    Map My Walk app, 449-452
    Walkmeter GPS Pedometer, 450

grouping apps in folders, 245-247

Groupon, 502

H

Handbrake, 107

Handoff, 82, 193-194

Hangouts, 368

Harvest to Hand app, 336

hashtags, 345

HD (high definition), 108

HDR button (Camera), 211

HDR (High Dynamic Range Imaging), 211

health apps
  AARP, 465
  CVS Pharmacy, 458-460
  Fit Brains Trainer, 435-439
  FitStar, 439-445
  Fooducate, 445-448
  HealthyOut, 446
  Magnifying Glass with Light, 465
  Map My Walk, 449-452
  MedCoach Medication Reminder,
   452-457
  My Diet Diary, 446
  Nutrition Menu, 446
  Pill Alert, 454
  Pill Reminder, 454
  Walkmeter GPS Pedometer, 450
  WebMD for iPad, 461-465

HealthyOut app, 446

help
  app help, 257-258
  AutoFill, 183

Hey Siri feature, 32

high definition (HD), 108

High Dynamic Range Imaging (HDR), 211

Highlight button (iBooks), 123

highlighting books, 123-124

History (Safari), 170-171

Home button, 6

home exchanges, 285-288

Home screen
  arranging apps on, 244-245
  bookmarks, 173
  overview, 13-14
  searching from, 14-16

Home Sharing, 110-111

home videos, 107

horizontal orientation, 212

iBooks, 381
  bookmarks, 125
  buying books, 117-119
  customizing display, 121
  deleting books, 128
  opening PDFs in, 118
  organizing books, 125-128
  reading books
   bookmarks, 125
   highlights, 123-124
   notes, 123-124
   reading aids, 121-122
   viewing and turning pages, 120-121

iCloud, 71
  backing up to, 74
  contacts, 133
  iCloud Drive app, 86
  iCloud Drive files
   accessing, 83-85
   opening, 85
  Family Sharing, 97-100
  notes, 149
  Photo Library, 220
  Photo Sharing, 221, 226
  purchased books, 126
  reminders, 155
  signing in, 68
  syncing with, 67-71

ID (Apple), 426

identifying iPad versions, 4

iDevices® Connected app, 489-493

iDevices® Kitchen Thermometer, 488-493

images
  adding
   to email messages, 193
   to email signatures, 199
   to text messages, 205

photos. *See* photos
    setting as wallpaper, 40-43

IMDb app, 406

iMessage, turning on, 202

importing DVDs, 107

in-app purchases, 243

inboxes, multiple, 191

information sharing permissions, viewing, 265

Instagram, 344-347

installing Safari extensions, 183

instant messaging
    AIM, 367
    Messages app
        blocking users, 203-204
        sending/receiving text messages, 204-207
        setting up, 202

interface elements. *See also* Siri
    Control Center, 36-*37*
    copy and paste, 28
    dictating text, 25
    editing text, 27
    menus, 18
    notifications
        dismissing, 35
        Notifications Center, 32-35
    on-screen keyboard, 19
        keyboard as trackpad, 29
        keyboard modes, 19-24
        keyboard shortcut bar, 22-24
        splitting, 21
        undocking, 21
    tab bars, 18
    toolbars, 17

Internet connections
    Cellular Data, 65-67
    Data Roaming, 67
    Wi-Fi network connections, 63-65

Intervac Home Exchange app, 286-288

iOS 9, 5

iPad Pro Smart Keyboard, 7

iPhone apps, 256-257, 275, 307

iPod touch apps, 256-257

iThermometer, 488-493

iTunes. *See also* Apple Music
    Apple Music, 76
    Family Sharing, 97-100
    Home Sharing, 110-111
    iTunes Match, 76, *92*
    iTunes Radio, 384
        bandwidth, 114
        commercials, 114
        listening to, 111-113
    playing music, 384
    purchasing media from, 94-97
    Radio, 384
    renting movies, 381-383
    syncing with, 72-76, 96
        Apple Music, 76
        capabilities, 78-80
        iTunes Match, 76
        manual syncing, 76
        music syncing, 74-75
        photo syncing, 76-78
        syncing options, 73-74
        types of data that can be synced, 78-80

J

jogging with Map My Walk app, 449-452

Join Apple Music setting, 101

Jumbo Calculator, 502

K

Kayak app, 289-292
keyboard
　dictation, 25-27
　Dvorak keyboard, 52
　keyboard as trackpad, 29
　keyboard modes, 19-20
　keyboard shortcut bar, 22-24
　predictive text, 24-25
　QWERTY keyboard, 52
　third-party keyboards, 54
　settings, 52-54
　splitting, 21
　undocking, 21
Keyboard Clicks setting, 44
Keyboards button, 52
keyboard shortcut bar, 22-24
Kindle app, 129-130
Kitchen Thermometer, 488-493

L

Label option (Clock), 156
Language & Region settings, 26
languages, translating, 298-302
libraries
　iBooks library, 118, 121
　iCloud Photo Library, 220
Library button (iBooks), 121
listening
　to music
　　AirPlay, 109-110
　　Apple Music, 102-104
　　Home Sharing, 110-111
　　iTunes, 384
　　iTunes Radio, 111-113
　　Music app, 89-92
　　NPR (National Public Radio) for IPad,
　　　384-386
　　Pandora Radio, 390-394
　　playlists, 92-94
　　Siri, 92
　　third-party apps, 92
　to podcasts, 104-105, 394-397
　to TED Talks, 398-401
lists, Recents list, 248
Load Remote Images option (Mail), 201
location information in photos, 224
locations, finding, 292-294
Location Services, 264, 283, 292, 309, 498
location usage, viewing, 263-264
locking orientation, 37
Lock Rotation, 50
Lock screen, 13
Lock Sounds setting, 44
Lock/Unlock settings, 61
LTE, enabling, 65-67
Lyft, finding rides, 312

M

Maglight app, 502
magnifying glass app, 502
Magnifying Glass with Light app, 465
Mail app, 185
　composing email, 192-194
　configuring how email is received,
　　197-198
　creating folders, 192
　creating signatures, 199-200
　deleting email, 194-196
　email settings, 200-202
　handing off email, 193-194
　keyboard shortcut bar, 23
　moving email, 194-196
　multiple inboxes, 191
　reading email, 189-192

recovering deleted email, 195
searching email, 196
setting up email accounts, 186-188
spam filters, 196
VIPs, 192

Manage Storage setting, 260-262

Manually Manage Music and Videos option, 73, 76

Manual setting (Mail), 197-198

Map My Walk, 449

MapQuest, 497

Maps app, 292-294

MedCoach Medication Reminder, 452-457

medical apps. *See* health apps

Medication Reminder app, 452-457

medications
    medication-reminder apps
        MedCoach Medication Reminder, 452-457
        Pill Alert, 454
        Pill Reminder, 454
    refilling with pharmacy apps, 458-460

menus, 18

Merge command, 21

messages. *See* email; text messages

Messages app
    blocking users, 203-204
    sending/receiving text messages, 204-207
    setting up, 202

microphone button, 25

Minube, 312

mirroring iPad screen, 110

model number, finding, 61

models of iPad, 4

modes
    Camera, 210
    keyboard modes, 19-20

Moments (Camera), 224, 225

monitoring apps
    app storage information, 260-262
    battery usage, 262-263
    information sharing permissions, 265
    location usage, 263-264
    notification settings, 266-268

Month view (Calendar), 144-145

More button (Messages), 206

The Moth, 396

Move button
    iBooks, 119
    Mail, 194

movement detection, 9

movies
    buying versus renting, 108
    Family Sharing, *97-100*
    finding movie information with IMDb, 406
    HD Versus SD, 108
    movie tickets, buying, 372-375
    movie times, finding, 372-375
    playing
        AirPlay, 109-110
        iTunes movie rental, 381-383
        Netflix app, 386-390
        third-party apps, 106
        Videos app, 106-108
    purchasing
        from iTunes, 94-97
        from other online stores, 94
    renting on iTunes, 381-383
    sharing
        Family Sharing, 97-100
        Home Sharing, 110-111
    syncing, 79

moving
    between apps, 248
    email, 194-196

Multi-Pass, 108

multiple apps, viewing
Picture-in-Picture, 254-255
Slide Over, 250-252
Split View, 252-253

multiple email inboxes, 191

multitasking
Picture-in-Picture, 254-255
Slide Over, 250-252
Split View, 252-253

music
Apple Music, 76
cancelling, 101
overview, 100
playing music via, 102-104
signing up for, 101
buying
from iTunes, 94-97
from other online stores, 94
playback controls, 36-37
playing
AirPlay, 109-110
Apple Music, 102-104
Control Center music playback controls, 36-37
Home Sharing, 110-111
iTunes, 384
iTunes Match, 92
iTunes Radio, 111-113
Music app, 89-92
NPR (National Public Radio) for IPad, 384-386
Pandora Radio, 390-394
playlists, 92-94
Siri, 92
third-party apps, 92
playlists, 92-94
sharing
Family Sharing, 97-100
Home Sharing, 110-111
syncing with iTunes, 74-75

Music app. *See also* Apple Music
creating playlists, 92-94
playing music, 89-92

mute switch, 9, 37, 50, 351

My Books (iBooks), 126

My Diet Diary, 446

MyHeritage, 469

My Info (AutoFill), 179

My Music (Music), 90

My Podcasts (Podcasts), 104

My Radar, 425-428

N

Names and Passwords switch (AutoFill), 179

National Public Radio (NPR) for iPad, 384-386

Netflix app, 106, 386-390

networks
Cellular Data, 65-67
Data Roaming, 67
syncing manually, 76
syncing with iCloud, 67-71
syncing with iTunes, 73
capabilities, 78-80
iTunes Match, 76
music, 74
photos, 76-78
Wi-Fi network connections
Ask to Join Networks option, 61
security, 65
setting up, 63-65

New Collection button (iBooks), 126

New Contact form, 134

Newmark, Craig, 479

New Message button (Messages), 204

news, reading
City Papers, 409-413
CNBC Real-Time for iPad, 414-417
CNN App for iPad, 417-419
Drippler app, 419-423
ESPN SportsCenter, 423-425
Yahoo! Tech, 431-432

News Feed (Facebook), 342

nicknames, adding to contacts, 136

None alert style, 267

Nook app, 131

Note button (iBooks), 124

notes
adding photos/sketches to, 151-152
adding to books, 123-124
checklists in, 150
compared to reminders, 150
creating, 147-152
syncing through iCloud, 149
taking, 148-149

Notes app, 147-152
adding photos/sketches to notes, 151-152
creating checklists in notes, 150
creating notes, 148-149
limitations of, 149
notes versus reminders, 150
syncing through iCloud, 149

notifications
dismissing, 35
modifying, 266-268
Notifications Center, 32-35
Push Notifications, 436

Notifications Center, 32-35

NPR (National Public Radio) for iPad, 384-386

nutrition apps. See food-related apps; health apps

Nutrition Menu, 446

O

On/Off (Wake/Sleep) button, 7

on-screen keyboard, 19
dictation, 25
keyboard as trackpad, 29
keyboard modes, 19-20
keyboard shortcut bar, 22-24
predictive text, 24-25
splitting, 21
undocking, 21

opening
apps, 392
Control Center, 36-37
iCloud Drive files, 85
Notifications Center, 33-35
PDFs in iBooks, 118

Opening eBay shopping page (eBay for iPad), 484

Open in iBooks option, 118

Open in New Tab option (Safari), 165

Open iTunes When This iPad Is Connected option, 73

Open Table app, 328-331

organizing
apps
arranging apps on Home screen, 244-245
creating app folders, 245-247
books in iBooks, 125-128

orientation, 107
detection, 9
in iBooks, 122
orientation lock, 9, 37

P

PackPoint Packing List Travel Companion, 312

paid apps, 243

Pandora Radio, 92, 390-394

Pano mode (Camera), 210, 216-219

panoramic photos, 216-218

parental guidance (Family Sharing), 100

parental restrictions, 56-57

passcodes
  forgotten passcodes, 48
  setting, 45-48, 180

password protection, 45-48
  passcodes, 45-48, 180
  Apple passwords, 68, 426

pasting text, 28-29

PDFs, opening in iBooks, 118

pedometer apps
  Map My Walk app, 449-452
  Walkmeter GPS Pedometer, 450

permissions, information sharing permissions, *265*

Perspective Zoom, 42

pharmacy apps, 458-460

Photo Booth, 218-219

Photo button (Notes), 151

Photo Library, 220

photo management apps, 354
  Flickr, 359-362
  Instagram, 344-347
  Shutterfly, 355-358

Photo mode (Camera), 210

photos
  adding
    to contacts, 135
    to notes, 151-152

albums
  creating, 232-233
  overview, 230
  Recently Added album, 233
  Recently Deleted album, 233
  viewing, 230-231
browsing, 221-224
cropping, 214
deleting, 213
editing
  Camera app, 212-216
  Instagram, 346
  Photo Booth, 218-219
enhancing, 213
filtering, 215, 218-219
High Dynamic Range Imaging, 211
location information, 224
marking as favorite, 213
panoramic photos, 216-218
photo sources, 220-221
rotating, 214, 226
screen captures, 235
setting as wallpaper, 40-43
sharing, 213, 226-230
  Facebook, 340-343
  Flickr, 354, 359-362
  Instagram, 344-347
  Shutterfly, 354-358
sharing with AirDrop, 80-81
slideshows, 234
  creating, 233-234
  sharing, 236
  stopping, 234
syncing, 76-80, 220
taking
  Camera app, 209-212
  Photo Booth app, 218-219
viewing, 225-226
zooming, 214, 226

Photos app
  albums
    creating, 232-233
    overview, 230
    viewing, 230-231
  photos, 226
    browsing, 221-224
    photo sources, 220-221
  screen captures, 235
  slideshows
    creating, 233-234
    sharing, 236
    stopping, 234

Photo Sharing, 221

Photo Stream, 220

Picture-in-Picture, 254-255

Pill Alert app, 454

Pill Reminder app, 454

pinching, 10

Pinterest, 406, 493-496

Place Bid option (eBay for iPad), 485

placing calls
  FaceTime calls, 348-354
  Skype calls, 352-354

Play button (Podcasts), 105

playing
  games
    Solitaire, 376-378
    Words with Friends, 379-380
  music
    AirPlay, 109-110
    Apple Music, 102-104
    Control Center music playback controls,
      36-37
    Home Sharing, 110-111
    iTunes, 384
    iTunes Match, 92
    iTunes Radio, 111-113
    Music app, 89-92

NPR (National Public Radio) for iPad,
  384-386
    Pandora Radio, 390-394
    playlists, 92-94
    Siri, 92
    third-party apps, 92
  podcasts, 104-105
    Podcasts app, 394-397
    Stitcher app, 406
  TED Talks, 398-401
  video
    AirPlay, 109-110
    iTunes movie rental, 381-383
    Netflix app, 386-390
    Picture-in-Picture, 254-255
    third-party apps, 106
    Videos app, 106-108
    YouTube videos, 363-367

playlists, 92-94

Playlists button (Music), 93

podcasts
  listening to, 104-105
    Podcast app, 394-397
    Stitcher, 406
  The Moth, 396
  subscribing to, 104-105
  syncing, 79
  TED app, 398-401
  This American Life, 396

Podcasts app, 104-105, 394-397

posting to Facebook, 340-343

pound sign (#), 345

predictive text, 24-25, 53

prescriptions
  medication-reminder apps
    MedCoach Medication Reminder,
      452-457
    Pill Alert, 454
    Pill Reminder, 454
  refilling with pharmacy apps, 458-460

previewing email, 200

Preview settings (Mail), 200

printing, 355-358, 482

privacy
Flickr, 360
information sharing permissions, 265
Location Services, 264
Safari, 166
Vine, 347

private browsing (Safari), 166

processors, 5

public domain movies and videos, 106

Public Website option (Photos), 229

pulling down and releasing, 11

purchasing
airline tickets, *289-292*
apps, 239-243
books
from iBooks, 117-119
from other sellers, 118
event tickets, 401-404
in-app purchases, 243
movies/TV shows
from iTunes, 94-97, 381-383
from other online stores, 94
movie tickets, 372-375
music
from iTunes, 94-97
from other online stores, 94

push delivery, 197-198

Push Notifications, 436

Q

questioning Siri, 30-31

quitting apps, 6, 249

QWERTY keyboard, 52

R

radio apps
iTunes Radio, 111-114, 384
NPR (National Public Radio) for iPad, 384-386
Pandora Radio, 390-394
Yesterday USA, 406

Reader button (Safari), 167

reading
books
in iBooks, 120-125, 381
with Google Play Books app, 131
with Kindle app, 129-130
with Nook app, 131
email, 189-192
news
City Papers, 409-413
CNBC Real-Time for iPad, 414-417
CNN App for iPad, 417-419
Drippler app, 419-423
ESPN SportsCenter, 423-425
Yahoo! Tech, 431-432

reading lists (Safari), 174-175

real estate apps
Trulia, 502
Zillow, 502

receiving
email, 197-202
text messages, 204-207

Recently Added album, 233

Recently Deleted album, 233

Recents list, 248

recipes, finding
8500+ Drink and Cocktail Recipes, 336
All Recipes, 335
Big Oven, 335
Epicurious, 316-321
Escoffier Cook's Companion, 321-325
Foodgawker, 336

Food Network, 336
Internet searches, 326-328
Zest, 336

recommended apps, 256

recovering deleted email, 195

Redeem button (Apple Store), 241

redeeming codes in App Store, 241

redownloading apps, 243

refilling prescriptions with pharmacy apps, 458-460

registering for Netflix accounts, 388

remembering medications
MedCoach Medication Reminder, 452-457
Pill Alert app, 454
Pill Reminder app, 454

Reminders
compared to notes, 150
setting, 152-155
syncing with iCloud, 155

renaming app folders, 246

renting movies, 108, 381-383

re-ordering Reminders, 154

Repeat Alerts, 268

Repeat button (Music), 90

Request Desktop Site option (Safari), 162

Require Passcode button, 47

reservations (restaurant), making with Open Table, 328-331

Reset settings, 61

resetting
Apple password, 68
your iPad, 61

restaurants
choosing
Urban Spoon, 336
Yelp, 332-335

making reservations with Open Table, 328-331

Restrictions settings, 56-57, 410

Resume button (iBooks), 121

reviewing apps, 259

reviews
Airbnb, 280-281
Urban Spoon, 336
Yelp, 332-335

Reviews (Podcasts), 105

rides, finding with
Lyft, 312
Uber app, 306-311

ringtones
custom ringtones, 45
syncing, 79

RootsMagic, 469

Rotate button (Camera), 214

rotating photos, 214, 226

running apps, viewing, 248

S

Safari
bookmarks, 168-170
creating, 168-170
deleting, 172
Home screen bookmarks, 173
syncing, 172
browsing to URLs, 160-163
extensions, 183
favorites, 168-170
History, 170-171
opening multiple pages, 165-166
overview, 159
private browsing, 166
reading lists, *174-175*
Safari Reader, 167
searching, 160-163

viewing articles with Safari Reader, 167

viewing web pages, 163-164

web forms

    AutoFill, 178-183

    filling in manually, 177-178

zooming in/out, 164

Sample button (iBooks), 119

Save button (Clock), 156

Saved Credit Cards (AutoFill), 180

Save Password option (AutoFill), 181

scams on Craigslist, 483

Scan Credit Card button, 176

scanning credit cards, 176

ScoreCenter app (ESPN), 423-425

Scrabble. *See* Words with Friends

screen captures, 235

screens, 13-16

Scrolling View (iBooks), 122

SD (standard definition), 108

searches

    accommodations

        Airbnb app, 275-281

        Kayak app, 289-292

    Ancestry app, 468-473

    apps, 255-256

    books, 120-121, 130

    contacts, 136-137

    eBay, 484

    email, 196

    farmer's markets with Harvest to Hand, 336

    from Home screen, 14-16

    locations, 292-294

    Mail, 196

    model number, 61

    Music, 91

    Netflix, 389

    Pinterest, 496

    podcasts, 394-401, 406

    recipes

        8500+ Drink and Cocktail Recipes, 336

        All Recipes, 335

        Epicurious, 316-321

        Escoffier Cook's Companion, 321-325

        Foodgawker, 336

        Internet searches, 326-328

        Zest, 336

    rides, 306-311

    search suggestions, 15

    Spotlight Search, 14-16, 61

    web, 160-163

    YouTube, 367

season passes (TV shows), 108

Seat Geek, 401-404

SeatGuru, 295-298

security

    AutoFill, 180-181

    Auto-Lock setting, 46

    parental restrictions, 56-57

    password protection, 45-48

    Touch ID, 49-50

    Wi-Fi network connections, 65

    wireless networks, 65

Send button (Mail), 192

sending

    email, 192-194

    text messages, 204-207

Set Both option (wallpaper), 42

Set Home Screen, 42

Set Lock Screen, 42

Settings app

    AutoFill, 179-181

    automatic downloads, 59-60

    Cellular Data, 65-67

    Display & Brightness, 58-59

    Do Not Disturb, 54-55

FaceTime, 348
General Settings
 About settings, 60
 Auto-Lock, 46
 Battery Usage, 262-263
 Data/Time, 51
 Date & Time, 51
 Handoff, 193
 Keyboard, 52-54
 Language & Region, 26
 Lock Rotation, 50
 Lock/Unlock, 61
 Manage Storage, 260-262
 Mute, 50
 Reset, 61
 Restrictions, 56-57, 410
 Siri, 29
 Spotlight Search, 61
iCloud, 68-71
 Family Sharing, 97-100
 iCloud Drive, 83-85
Location Services, 292, 309, 498
Mail, 200-202
 Add Account, 186-188
 Fetch New Data, 197-198
 Signature, 199-200
Messages, 202-204
miscellaneous settings, 60-61
Music
 Home Sharing, 110-111
 Join Apple Music, 101
Notifications, 266-268
Privacy
 information sharing permissions, 265
 Location Services, 264
Sounds, 43-45
Touch ID & Passcode
 password protection, 45-48
 Touch ID, 49-50
Wallpaper, 40-43
Wi-Fi, 64

setting up iPad. *See also* customization
 3G/4G connections, 65
 AirDrop, 80
 AutoFill, 179-181
 email
  email accounts, 186-188
  how email is received, 197
  signatures, 199-200
 Family Sharing, 97-100
 Handoff feature, 193
 iMessage, 202
 Location Services, 283, 292, 309
 LTE, 65-67
 Messages app, 202
 parental restrictions, 56-57
 Push Notifications, 436
 Siri, 29
 Touch ID, 49-50
 Wi-Fi network connections, 63-65
Set Up Family Sharing setting, 97
shaking, 10
Share button
 iBooks, 123
 Notes, 149
shared links (Safari), 175
sharing
 AirDrop, 80-81
 apps with family, 259
 calendars, 147
 contacts, 138
 Family Sharing, 259
 from iBooks, 123
 information sharing permissions, *265*
 media
  Family Sharing, 97-100
  Home Sharing, 110-111
 photos, 213, 221, 226-230
 photos/videos
  Facebook, 340-343
  Flickr, 359-362

Instagram, 344-347
Shutterfly, 354, 355-358
YouTube, 363-367
slideshows, 236

shooting photos. *See* taking photos

shopping apps
Amazon, 474-478
Auto Trader, 480
Catalog Spree, 502
Classifieds, 480
Craigslist for iPad, 479-483
Ebay for iPad, 483-485
Gas Buddy, 486-488
Groupon, 502

shortcut bar (keyboard), 22-24

Short Message Service (SMS), 206

Show Completed option (Reminders), 154

Show in Notifications Center option, 267

Show on Home Screen option, 83

Show on Lock Screen option, 267

Show Preview option, 267

Show To/Cc Label option (Mail), 200

Shuffle button (Music), 91

Shutterfly, 354-358

side switch, 9, 50

signatures (email), 199-200

signing into iCloud, 68

signing up for Apple Music, 101

silencing clock alarms, 157

Siri, 29-32
calendar events, creating, 140
clock alarms, creating, 157
contacts, finding, 136
email
checking, 198
sending, 193
Hey Siri feature, 32

music, playing, 92
nicknames, adding, 136
reminders, creating, 153
schedule, checking, 145
text messages, sending, 207
tips, 31
turning on, 29
web searches, 162

size of text, 58

sketches, adding to notes, 151-152

Skype, 347, 352-354

Sleep/Wake button, 7

Slide Over feature, 250-252

Slideshow button (Photos), 233

slideshows
creating, 233-234
sharing, 236
stopping, 234

Smart Case, 7

Smart Cover, 7

Smart Keyboard, 7

SMS Relay, 206

SMS (Short Message Service), 206

Snapfish, 354

Snooze (Clock), 156-157

social media apps. *See also* photo
management apps
Facebook, 340-343
Instagram, 344-347
Pinterest, 406, 493-496
Twitter, 368

Solitaire, 376-378

songs. *See* music

sound. *See also* music
alert sounds, 43-61
clock alarms, 155-157
Mute option, 50

muting, 37
podcasts
    listening to, 104-105, 394-397, 406
    The Moth, 396
    subscribing to, 104-105
    syncing, 79
    TED app, 398-401
    This American Life, 396
  Settings, 43-45
  volume control, 8
Sound Sleeper, 312
spam filters, 196
Split command, 21
Split View, 252-253
splitting keyboards, 21
sports, following with ESPN SportsCenter
  app, 423-425
Spotify, 92
Spotlight Search, 14-16, 61
Square mode (Camera), 210
standard definition (SD), 108
Starts field (Calendar), 139
stations (iTunes Radio), 112-113
Sticky Notes, 43
Stills, 41
Stitcher, 406
stopping slideshows, 234
Storage & iCloud Usage settings, 260-262
storage information
  checking, 60, 71
  viewing for apps, 260-262
styles in email signatures, 199
Subscribe button (Podcasts), 105
subscribing
  to Apple Music, 101
  to podcasts, 104-105

surfing the web. *See* web surfing
switches, 17
switching between apps, 248
Swype, 54
Symptom Checker (WebMD), 462-465
syncing, 78, 96
  bookmarks (Safari), 172
  with iCloud, 67-71
  with iTunes, 72-74
    Apple Music, 76
    capabilities, 78-80
    iTunes Match, 76
    manual syncing, 76
    music syncing, 74-75
    photo syncing, 76-78
    syncing options, 73-74
    types of data that can be synced, 78-80
  photos, 220
  Reading List, 175
  reminders, 155
Sync Music command (iTunes), 75

T

tab bars, 18
Table of Contents button (iBooks), 120
tabs (Safari), 165-166
taking
  notes, *148-149*
  photos
    Camera app, 209, 210-212
    panoramic photos, 216-219
    Photo Booth app, 218-219
Talking Translator, 298-302
TapFactory Sticky Notes, 43
tapping, 10
technology news
  Drippler app, 419-423
  Yahoo! Tech website, 431-433

TED app, 398-401

TED Talks, viewing, 398-401

text
  capitalizing, 19
  copying and pasting, 28-29
  dictating, 25-27
  editing, 27
  entering, 18
    copy and paste, 28-29
    dictation, 25-27
    predictive text, 24-25
    with keyboard. See keyboard
  making text easier to read, 58-59
  predictive text, 24-25
  Predictive text option, 53
  size of, 58, 122

TextExpander 3, 54

text messages
  blocking, 204
  composing, 204-207
  sending/receiving, 204-207
  setting up, 202
  SMS (Short Message Service), 206

thermometers, iDevices® Kitchen
  Thermometer, 488-493

third-party keyboards, 54

This American Life, 396

tickets, purchasing
  airline tickets, 289-292
  event tickets, 401-404

time settings, 51

time delay (Camera), 211

time-delayed rentals, 108

Time-Lapse mode (Camera), 210

timer (Clock), 325

Time Zone button, 51

toolbars, 17

Top Charts
  App Store, 240
  iBooks, 119

Touch ID
  making purchases via, 50
  setting up, 49-50

touching, 10

TouchPal, 54

trackpads, keyboards as, 29

traffic, checking with Waze, 497-501

Transfer Service From Another iPad option,
  66

translating foreign languages, 298-302

transportation
  flights, booking
    Kayak app, 289-292
    SeatGuru app, 295-298
  rides, finding with Uber app, 306-311

Trash button (Notes), 149

Trash (Mail), 190, 194-195

travel apps, 271
  AARP, 272-274
  Airbnb, 275-281
  Airports by Travel Nerd, 312
  Foursquare, 282-285
  Intervac, 286-288
  Kayak, 289-292
  Lyft, 312
  Maps, 292-294
  Minube, 312
  PackPoint Packing List Travel Companion,
    312
  SeatGuru, 295-298
  Sound Sleeper, 312
  Talking Translator, 298-302
  TripAdvisor, 302-306
  Uber, 306-311
  XE Currency Converter, 312

TripAdvisor, 302-306

troubleshooting
    apps, 257-258
    AutoFill, 183
Trulia, 502
turning book pages
    in iBooks, 120-121
    in Kindle app, 130
turning off iPad, 8
turning on/off
    Auto-Capitalization, 52
    Auto-Correction, 52
    Cellular Data, 65
    iMessage, 202
    iTunes Match, 76
    parental restrictions, 56-57
    Push Notifications, 436
    Siri, 29
Turn Passcode On option, 46
TV shows
    buying versus renting, 108
    HD Versus SD, 108
    Multi-Pass, 108
    playing
        AirPlay, 109-110
        iTunes, 381-383
        Netflix app, 386-390
        third-party apps, 106
        Videos app, 106-108
    purchasing
        from iTunes, 94-97
        from other online stores, 94
    season passes, 108
    sharing
        Family Sharing, 97-100
        Home Sharing, 110-111
    syncing, 79
Twitter, 368
typing URLs, 160

U

Uber app, 306-311
undeleting email, 195
Undock command, 21
undocking keyboards, 21
Universal Resource Locators. *See* URLs
Unlock setting, 61
uploading photos. *See* sharing photos
Urban Spoon, 336
URLs
    browsing to, 160-163
    typing, 160
Usage settings
    Battery Usage, 262-263
    Manage Storage, 260-262
Use Contact Info switch (AutoFill), 179
users, blocking in Messages, 203

V

version of iOS, checking, 60
video
    HD Versus SD, 108
    playing
        AirPlay, 109-110
        iTunes movie rental, 381-383
        Netflix app, 386-390
        Picture-in-Picture, 254-255
        third-party apps, 106
        Videos app, 106-108
    purchasing
        buying versus renting, 108
        from iTunes, 94-97
        from other online stores, 94
    sharing
        Facebook, 340-343
        Family Sharing, 97-100
        Home Sharing, 110-111

Instagram, 344-347
YouTube, 363-367
video calls, 347
FaceTime, 348-354
Skype, 352-354
video chat with Hangouts, 368
Video mode (Camera), 210

Videos app, 106-108

views
Calendar
Day view, 141-142
Month view, 144-145
Week view, 143
Year view, 142
Split View, 252-253

Vine app, 347

VIPs (email), 192

voice recognition
dictation, 25-27
Siri. *See* Siri

volume control, 8

W

Wake/Sleep button, 7, 48

walking with Map My Walk app, 449-452

Walkmeter GPS Pedometer, 450

wallpaper, changing, 40-43

watching. *See* playing

Waze, 497-501

weather apps
My Radar, 425-428
The Weather Channel for iPad, 428-431

The Weather Channel for iPad app, 428-431

web forms
AutoFill, 178-183
filling out web forms with, 181-182
security, 180-181

setting up, 179-181
troubleshooting, 183
filling in manually, 177-178
overview, 176

WebMD for iPad, 461-465

websites
AARP travel website, 274
Yahoo! Tech, 431-432

web surfing
articles, reading with Safari Reader, 167
bookmarks, 168-170
creating, 168-170
deleting, 172
Home screen bookmarks, 173
syncing, 172
overview, 159
private browsing, 166
reading lists, 174-175
Safari extensions, 183
web forms
AutoFill, 178-183
filling in manually, 177-178
overview, 176
web pages
bookmarks, 168-173
browsing to URLs, 160-163
favorites, 168-170
History, 170-171
opening multiple, 165-166
searching, 160-163
viewing, 163-164
zooming in/out, 164

Week view (Calendar), 143

weight loss apps. *See* fitness apps

Wi-Fi network connections
Ask to Join Networks option, 61
Data Roaming, 67
security, 65
setting up, 63-65

Wikipedia Mobile, 502

wireless network connections. *See* Wi-Fi
  network connections

Words with Friends, 379-380

workout apps. *See* fitness apps

X-Y

XE Currency Converter, 312

Yahoo! ID, 359

Yahoo! Tech website, 431-432

Years level (Photos), 222

Year view (Calendar), 142

Yelp, 332-335

Yesterday USA, 406

YouTube, 363-367

Z

Zest app, 336

Zillow, 502

zooming in/out
    Perspective Zoom, 42
    photos, 214, 226
    web pages, 164

REGISTER THIS PRODUCT
SAVE 35%*
ON YOUR NEXT PURCHASE!

How to Register Your Product

- Go to quepublishing.com/register
- Sign in or create an account
- Enter the 10- or 13-digit ISBN that appears on the back cover of your product

Benefits of Registering

- Ability to download product updates
- Access to bonus chapters and workshop files
- A 35% coupon to be used on your next purchase – valid for 30 days
  To obtain your coupon, click on "Manage Codes" in the right column of your Account page
- Receive special offers on new editions and related Que products

Please note that the benefits for registering may vary by product. Benefits will be listed on your Account page under Registered Products.

We value and respect your privacy. Your email address will not be sold to any third party company.

* 35% discount code presented after product registration is valid on most print books, eBooks, and full-course videos sold on QuePublishing.com. Discount may not be combined with any other offer and is not redeemable for cash. Discount code expires after 30 days from the time of product registration. Offer subject to change.

quepublishing.com